Inkscape 0.48 Illustrator's Cookbook

109 recipes to create scalable vector graphics with Inkscape

Mihaela Jurković

Rigel Di Scala

[PACKT] open source✳
PUBLISHING   community experience distilled

BIRMINGHAM - MUMBAI

Inkscape 0.48 Illustrator's Cookbook

First published: April 2011

Production Reference: 1180411

Published by Packt Publishing Ltd.
32 Lincoln Road
Olton
Birmingham, B27 6PA, UK.

ISBN 978-1-849512-66-4

www.packtpub.com

Cover Image by Asher Wishkerman (a.wishkerman@mpic.de)

Credits

Authors
Mihaela Jurković

Rigel Di Scala

Reviewer
Issa Mahasneh

Acquisition Editor
Dilip Venkatesh

Development Editor
Hyacintha D'Souza

Technical Editors
Vanjeet D'souza

Conrad Sardinha

Copy Editor
Neha Shetty

Indexer
Hemangini Bari

Editorial Team Leader
Akshara Aware

Project Team Leader
Priya Mukherji

Project Coordinator
Jovita Pinto

Proofreader
Aaron Nash

Production Coordinator
Kruthika Bangera

Cover Work
Kruthika Bangera

About the Authors

Mihaela Jurković is the owner of a small Croatian web development shop. Drupal, Inkscape, and Linux are the most common words in her open source dictionary. In addition to being a friendly ghost on the Inkscape forum she also enjoys photography, hiking, TED talks, and lolcats.

Rigel Di Scala discovered computer graphics on a Commodore VIC-20 as a young child. Before going insane trying to render artistic landscapes using only the limited character set of his primitive 8-bit computer, he upgraded to a CBM Amiga 500 and started creating his first bitmaps with Dan Silva's Deluxe Paint II.

During his college years he started working part-time as a Web developer and consultant for several institutions and companies, and later as a system administrator, journalist, and editor in the computer games industry.

Today he works as a web application developer for an IT company based in Milan. He promotes and uses open-source technology exclusively in his projects. Inkscape is his tool of choice for developing vector graphics.

In his free time, he likes to freeclimb, skydive, and read Reddit.

I would like to thank my family for their constant support in everything I do.

About the Reviewer

Issa Mahasneh is an independent open source consultant with relevant experience in web development and design using open source technologies.

Issa got a B.Sc. in Computer Science from the Jordan University of Science and Technology (JUST) and worked as a supervisor of the open source department in a software company located in Amman. For years, he has been involved in several projects including Drupal, Songbird, and Mozilla.

Since 2009, he is the president of the Jordan Open Source Association (`http://jordanopensource.org`), a non-profit organization that promotes Free Software and Free Culture in Jordan and the Arab World. A frequent speaker in open source conferences and events, Issa also organizes local BarCamps, Drupal Meetups, and Linux installation fests.

I would like to thank my parents, my brother, and my sister. A special thanks to my one-year old nephew, Muhammad, who made the review of this book more challenging by randomly pressing keys on my keyboard and by constantly trying to turn off my PC!

www.PacktPub.com

Support files, eBooks, discount offers and more

You might want to visit www.PacktPub.com for support files and downloads related to your book.

Did you know that Packt offers eBook versions of every book published, with PDF and ePub files available? You can upgrade to the eBook version at www.PacktPub.com and as a print book customer, you are entitled to a discount on the eBook copy. Get in touch with us at service@packtpub.com for more details.

At www.PacktPub.com, you can also read a collection of free technical articles, sign up for a range of free newsletters and receive exclusive discounts and offers on Packt books and eBooks.

http://PacktLib.PacktPub.com

Do you need instant solutions to your IT questions? PacktLib is Packt's online digital book library. Here, you can access, read and search across Packt's entire library of books.

Why Subscribe?

- ▶ Fully searchable across every book published by Packt
- ▶ Copy and paste, print and bookmark content
- ▶ On demand and accessible via web browser

Free Access for Packt account holders

If you have an account with Packt at www.PacktPub.com, you can use this to access PacktLib today and view nine entirely free books. Simply use your login credentials for immediate access.

Table of Contents

Preface

Inkscape is frequently mentioned, and lauded, as one of the best examples of open-source software available today. It is a mature, feature-full and flexible product, thanks to a very dedicated developer community. The latest version, 0.48, adds new tools, such as the Airbrush (which many have longed for), and advanced path editing, among many other additions and improvements.

Vector graphics are becoming increasingly important at the turn of this decade, now that the World Wide Web has begun its transition towards HTML5 technologies. All the major Web browsers are striving to conform to the SVG specification, as the attractiveness of scalable, high definition, three-dimensional, and *Flash*-free Web sites and games is irresistible. The future is bright, but the true outcome will ultimately depend on one decisive factor: *user and developer adoption*.

This is why a *non-proprietary* authoring tool such as Inkscape is important: it is a professional package for creating quality vector graphics which is freely available for everybody to use. Whether you wish to create Web site mockups, wallpapers to share with an Internet community, high-quality advertisements for the newspaper industry, digital art for a gallery exposition, or simply a Happy Birthday for your grandmother, Inkscape is available *now and without limitations,* to help you achieve your goal.

What this book covers

Chapter 1, Creating and Editing Objects – Familiarize yourself with the user-interface and start drawing simple vector shapes.

Chapter 2, Editing Colors – Learn the basics of coloring and use gradients to their full effect, by replicating an iconic image of a famous movie.

Chapter 3, Speeding Up Your Workflow – Streamline and accelerate development with a set of commonly used techniques, tips and tricks.

Chapter 4, Creating and Editing Clones – Use shape cloning to rapidly create interesting complexity in your drawing.

Chapter 5, *Live Path Effects* – Create, assemble, and replicate objects programmatically in a variety of scenarios.

Chapter 6, *Extensions* – Take full advantage of the many extensions available in Inkscape, to inspire and enhance your work.

Chapter 7, *SVG Filters* – Experiment with SVG filter effects, taking vector graphics to a new level of sophistication, and create your own!

Chapter 8, *Putting it All Together* – Use your knowledge, skills, and intuition to solve graphical problems in a variety of scenarios.

Chapter 9, *Raster and Almost Raster* – Befriend bitmaps and use them in your vector drawings, by importing, converting (tracing), and exporting.

Chapter 10, *Web Graphics Preparation* – Learn to design and prepare graphics for the modern web, from small but detailed widgets to the complete layout of webpage mockup.

Chapter 11, *SVG in Websites* – Use vector graphics in your websites, games, and presentations, with the help of new extensions available in version 0.48.

Chapter 12, *Draw Freely* – Complete your knowledge on SVG and Inkscape, by learning about document metadata, compiling the software from source, and programming your own extensions using Python!

What you need for this book

You will, of course, need a working installation of Inkscape 0.48, or a more recent version if available. You can download an installer for your operating system from the official website:

```
http://inkscape.org/download
```

You will also need a programmers text-editor, perhaps a little more advanced than a vanilla notepad. Consider using TextEdit (Mac), GEdit (GNOME), KWrite (KDE), or Notepad++ (Windows). This last editor can be downloaded for free at:

```
http://notepad-plus-plus.org
```

Finally, if you are interested in developing extensions for Inkscape, you will need to install the Python programming library and tools in order to complete the relative recipes in this book. You can download the necessary software from the official Python web portal:

```
http://www.python.org
```

Who this book is for

The first chapters of this book are aimed at the beginner with no previous experience of vector graphics design software packages. We will provide the fundamental concepts, an overview of the user interface, and start drawing straight away. No artistic talent is needed, just a bit of curiosity. The intermediate user will find these initial recipes useful in improving his or her competence in the use of the basic tools and workflows. The goal is to bring the reader to a level of expertise adequate for tackling the rest of the material in the book.

The more expert users will appreciate the later chapters, where we will illustrate advanced topics and demonstrate techniques for producing professional quality art, for use in web design, game development, and many other realms.

Whether you are a beginner or a battle-hardened veteran, a casual doodler or an academic artist, we hope you will enjoy the recipes in this book and find inspiration for your future works of art.

Conventions

In this book, you will find a number of styles of text that distinguish between different kinds of information. Here are some examples of these styles, and an explanation of their meaning.

Code words in text are shown as follows: " License information is also inserted under `svg:metadata` element."

A block of code is set as follows:

```
r=int(round(max(r*FACTOR,0)))
g=int(round(max(g*FACTOR,0)))
b=int(round(max(b*FACTOR,0)))
return '%02x%02x%02x' % (r,g,b)
```

When we wish to draw your attention to a particular part of a code block, the relevant lines or items are set in bold:

```
r=int(round(max(r*FACTOR,0)))
g=int(round(max(g*FACTOR,0)))
b=int(round(max(b*FACTOR,0)))
return '%02x%02x%02x' % (r,g,b)
```

Any command-line input or output is written as follows:

```
$ inkscape --usage
Usage: inkscape [-VzgDCjtTXYWHSx?] [-V|--version] [-z|--without-gui]
        [-g|--with-gui] [-f|--file=FILENAME] [-p|--print=FILENAME]
        [-e|--export-png=FILENAME] [-d|--export-dpi=DPI]
```

New terms and important words are shown in bold. Words that you see on the screen, in menus or dialog boxes for example, appear in the text like this: " The information we entered into the Document Metadata dialog is inserted into SVG code."

Warnings or important notes appear in a box like this.

Tips and tricks appear like this.

Reader feedback

Feedback from our readers is always welcome. Let us know what you think about this book—what you liked or may have disliked. Reader feedback is important for us to develop titles that you really get the most out of.

To send us general feedback, simply send an e-mail to feedback@packtpub.com, and mention the book title via the subject of your message.

If there is a book that you need and would like to see us publish, please send us a note in the SUGGEST A TITLE form on www.packtpub.com or e-mail suggest@packtpub.com.

If there is a topic that you have expertise in and you are interested in either writing or contributing to a book, see our author guide on www.packtpub.com/authors.

Customer support

Now that you are the proud owner of a Packt book, we have a number of things to help you to get the most from your purchase.

Downloading the example code

You can download the example code files for all Packt books you have purchased from your account at http://www.PacktPub.com. If you purchased this book elsewhere, you can visit http://www.PacktPub.com/support and register to have the files e-mailed directly to you.

Errata

Although we have taken every care to ensure the accuracy of our content, mistakes do happen. If you find a mistake in one of our books—maybe a mistake in the text or the code—we would be grateful if you would report this to us. By doing so, you can save other readers from frustration and help us improve subsequent versions of this book. If you find any errata, please report them by visiting `http://www.packtpub.com/support`, selecting your book, clicking on the errata submission form link, and entering the details of your errata. Once your errata are verified, your submission will be accepted and the errata will be uploaded on our website, or added to any list of existing errata, under the Errata section of that title. Any existing errata can be viewed by selecting your title from `http://www.packtpub.com/support`.

Piracy

Piracy of copyright material on the Internet is an ongoing problem across all media. At Packt, we take the protection of our copyright and licenses very seriously. If you come across any illegal copies of our works, in any form, on the Internet, please provide us with the location address or website name immediately so that we can pursue a remedy.

Please contact us at `copyright@packtpub.com` with a link to the suspected pirated material.

We appreciate your help in protecting our authors, and our ability to bring you valuable content.

Questions

You can contact us at `questions@packtpub.com` if you are having a problem with any aspect of the book, and we will do our best to address it.

1
Creating and Editing Objects

In this chapter, we will cover:

- ▸ Creating and editing 2D geometric shapes
- ▸ Creating freehand and straight lines
- ▸ Editing paths with the Node tool
- ▸ Creating paths using the Pen (Bezier) tool
- ▸ Creating smooth paths with Spiro Spline
- ▸ Creating calligraphic shapes
- ▸ Using the Eraser tool
- ▸ Creating and editing 3D boxes
- ▸ Creating and editing text
- ▸ Clipping
- ▸ Masking
- ▸ Path operations

Introduction

In this first chapter we will start with the basics of vector graphics design, by creating and manipulating simple geometric objects. Several important techniques used daily by graphics artists, such as shape editing, clipping, and masking, will help us greatly when building more complex objects later on.

Creating and editing 2D geometric shapes

Inkscape is a full-featured software package that provides us with a powerful and flexible set of tools. These tools can build beautiful drawings out of fundamental geometric objects (primitives), such as straight or curved lines, simple or complex polygons, or curved shapes.

Getting ready

Before we start drawing, let's take a quick look at the user interface and the facilities it provides:

- **The Commands bar**: Normally displayed under the Menu, it contains buttons of common application commands, such as file opening and saving, history browsing (undo and redo), zooming, and some common operations related to objects and groups.

- **The Snapping bar**: Snapping facilitates the placement of objects in the Canvas and is often a valuable timesaver, although in some cases it might get in the way, such as when you need the freedom to position an object in a particular spot. Using this tool bar, you can enable or disable snapping to the page border, grids, and other objects, in order to get the exact behaviour you need.

- **The Canvas**: This is the large central area where all the drawing is done. You will find rulers on the top and on the left of the Canvas, which provide information on scaling, dimensioning, and positioning.

- **The Toolbox**: Normally found on the left of the Canvas, it contains all the buttons related to drawing tools used to create primitives.

- **The Tools Controls bar**: The content of this bar changes according to the tool you have selected in the Toolbox, exposing its specific functionality. In the following picture we can see what the Tool Controls bar would show us if we were using the **Selector** tool.

- **The Palette**: This tool contains a swatch line with all the colors associated with the currently chosen palette.

- **The Status bar**: This bar is normally located beneath the Canvas and provides a wealth of miscellaneous information, such as the style of the currently selected object, the name of the layer we are editing, some help messages on the function of the selected tool, and the current mouse pointer coordinates.

How to do it...

We will begin with a couple of four sided polygons that we are all very familiar with:

- **Rectangles and squares**

1. Select the **Rectangle** tool ▢ (*F4* or *R*).

2. Click and drag on the Canvas holding the *Ctrl* key to create a **golden ratio rectangle**. While dragging with the mouse, you will see more information on the shape you are creating in the help message area of the Status bar.

3. Let go of the mouse button when you are happy with the dimensions of your rectangle. You will now notice two little white square handles and one circle handle at the corners. The Status bar will provide some useful tips if you hover the mouse pointer over them.

4. Click on the circle handle while holding the *Ctrl* key and drag downwards to make the corners evenly rounded.

5. Move one of the square handles to resize the rectangle without changing the corner's radii, keeping the horizontal and vertical radii the same. Notice that if you reduce the width or height more than the corner radius, it will change to accommodate the lack of space.

6. Switch to the **Selector** tool ▶ (*Space* or *F1* or *S*). Several arrow shaped handles will now be visible on the sides of the rectangle.

7. Grab the right-hand middle arrow handle and make the rectangle narrower. Notice how the horizontal corner radius now scales proportionally, adapting to change in width, so the horizontal and vertical radii are no longer the same.

8. Select the **Rectangle** tool (*Space* or *F4* or *R*) again and click the **Make corners sharp** button on the rectangle toolbar or click on one of the circular handles while holding *Shift*. This option cancels all the changes made to round the corners. You can also specify precisely the values of the horizontal (**Rx**) and vertical (**Ry**) radii in the **rectangle toolbar**.

▶ **Ellipses, circles, and arcs**

1. Select the **Ellipse** tool ⬤ (*F5* or *E*).

2. Click and drag on the canvas to create an **ellipse**. Notice two little white square handles and one circle handle. As we did before, hover over the handles with your mouse pointer and read the tips that appear in the Status bar.

3. Move one of the square handles to resize the ellipse.

4. Click on the circle handle and drag to the right and down to delimit a **circular segment**. Notice there are now two circle handles that control the span of the arc.

5. Continue dragging one of the circle handles around the ellipse always keeping it outside of the ellipse area to create a "pacman" like shape.

6. Click on one of the circle handles and drag inside the ellipse area to change the segment into a **circular arc**. Drag the cursor inside and outside the ellipse area to see how the shape changes.

7. Click on the **Make the shape a whole ellipse, not arc or segment** ⬤ button on the ellipse toolbar to get the full ellipse shape back.

8. Create a circle by holding *Ctrl* while dragging with the selected **Ellipse** tool.

9. Create another ellipse by holding the *Shift* key while dragging. This time the mouse click determines the position of the ellipse center, instead of the top-left corner of the bounding box as before.

10. Create another ellipse by holding the *Alt* key while dragging. This time the first click and the release point will be on the ellipse edge and not the object bounding box.

11. Create a circle by determining its center with the first click and its radius upon release by holding *Shift* + *Ctrl* + *Alt* while dragging.

 In Linux and Mac OS X, the *Alt* key may not be immediately usable in Inkscape because it might be already assigned to a system shortcut. Refer to the Inkscape FAQ for a solution:

`http://wiki.inkscape.org/wiki/index.php/FAQ`

▶ **Polygons and stars**:

1. Select the **Star** tool ⬤ (*Shift* + *F9* or ***).

2. Click and drag towards the top while holding *Ctrl* to create an "upright" **star**.

3. Hover over the star handles and read the Status bar tips to see which one is the **tip radius** and which one is the **base radius**. Drag the base radius outwards evenly by holding *Ctrl* so it's longer than the tip radius.

4. Increase the number of corners to 8 by editing the **Corners:** option on the Star toolbar.

5. Drag the tip radius while holding *Shift* to round it. The **Rounded:** number on the toolbar will be negative.

6. Drag the base radius while holding *Shift* to round it in the other direction. The **Rounded:** number on the toolbar will be positive.

7. Turn the star into a **polygon** by clicking on the **Regular polygon** ⬠ button on the toolbar. Notice how the corners are still rounded.

8. Hover over the polygon tip radius handle and notice what the Status bar has to say about it. Then, drag the handle while holding the *Alt* key to apply randomization to the position of the corners and create an irregular shape.

▶ **Spirals**:

1. Select the **Spiral** tool 🌀 (*F9* or *I*).

2. Click and drag on the canvas to create an Archimedean **spiral**.

3. Hover over the spiral's inside and outside handles and read the Status bar tips.

4. Drag the inside handle to unwind it one turn, then drag the outside handle to create one more turn.

5. Drag the inside handle upwards while holding *Alt* to decrease the divergence and then downwards to increase it.

Here's what some of the preceding steps look like:

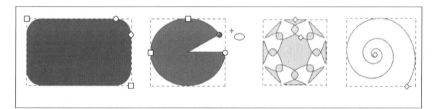

How it works...

As we have seen, Inkscape's 2D shape tools create special kinds of objects because they have additional editing parameters for their geometric qualities. By converting them to regular path objects by using the **Object to Path** 🔧 (*Shift* + *Ctrl* + *C*) option, these special parameters will be lost in the process. This is a tradeoff we will sometimes need to make in order to make use of some extensions and effects that can only be applied to regular paths.

There's more...

Now that we know how to create simple shapes, we can advance to more interesting objects.

Creating complex shapes in seconds with Star tool

Moving the base radius handle away from its usual position can create wildly different shapes because tips and star inner corners form different relations, especially when combined with rounded corners. Try to recreate the following examples (you can find them in the `StarsComplex.svg` file):

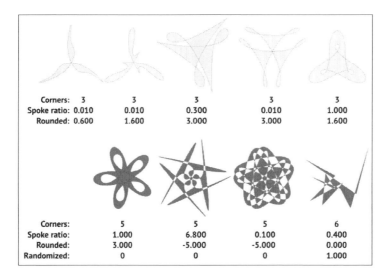

Corners:	3	3	3	3	3
Spoke ratio:	0.010	0.010	0.300	0.010	1.000
Rounded:	0.600	1.600	3.000	3.000	1.600

Corners:	5	5	5	6
Spoke ratio:	1.000	6.800	0.100	0.400
Rounded:	3.000	-5.000	-5.000	0.000
Randomized:	0	0	0	1.000

Dotted spirals

You can also change the spiral stroke style to different kinds of dashes. Some very pretty effects can be achieved. (`SpiralsDashed.svg`):

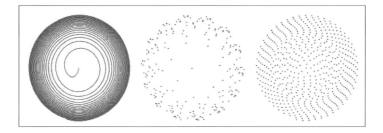

Creating freehand and straight lines

Users trying Inkscape for the first time are sometimes confused when they don't find a special tool that creates lines. Such a tool isn't necessary because *every object in Inkscape can be made to look like a line*: remove the fill, adjust the stroke to your desired look and you've got a line. This means that all tools in Inkscape can be used to create lines, although some of them are more straightforward and better suited for what most users expect in that area.

In this recipe we will explore how to create freehand and straight lines.

How to do it...

Follow these steps to draw freehand and straight lines:

1. Select the **Pencil** tool  (*F6* or *P*) and draw the letter "O", dragging with your mouse on the Canvas as if you were using a pencil on a sheet of paper.

2. Switch to the **Selector** tool (*Space, F1* or *S*).The information in the Status bar notification area will tell you how many nodes are present in the object.

3. Switch back to the **Pencil** tool (*Space, F6* or *P*), set **Smoothing:** slider on the Pencil toolbar to 50 and create another "O".

4. Switch to the **Selector tool** (*Space, F1* or *S*) again and read the information in the Status bar notification area. Notice that there are fewer nodes this time and the line is smoother.

5. Select the **Pen (Bezier)** tool (*Shift + F6* or *B*) and change its mode on the toolbar to **Create a sequence of straight line segments** so we can create a shape similar to the musical instrument, the triangle.

6. Click on the Canvas to draw the starting point of a line. Move the mouse to the right and you will see a red helper line. Hold *Ctrl* to keep the angle 0° and look at the Status bar to adjust the line width. Click when the distance is roughly 500 px.

7. Move the mouse to the top-left holding *Ctrl* to set the angle to 120° and, when you reach approximately a distance of 500 px, click to create the top triangle corner.

8. Release the *Ctrl* key and move your mouse downwards and to the left. Click to create a point when you reach roughly -123° and a distance of 480 px. The Status bar will report the current values as you move your mouse pointer.

9. Right-click anywhere or press *Enter* to finish the object.

How it works...

With the **Pencil** tool it is important to adjust the **Smoothing:** slider in order to obtain the desired smoothness in our curved lines, as it determines how sensitive the line is to our mouse movements.

The easiest way to create straight lines is to use one of the modes of the **Pen (Bezier)** tool (named after the French mathematician Pierre Étienne Bézier) that disables the feature to draw curved segments and **creates a sequence of straight line segments**.

There's more...

The objects we created have default styles applied to make them look like lines, but they can also take fill color.

Stroke styles can affect the look of our "lines," and can be set in the **Fill and Stroke** dialogue (*Shift + Ctrl + F*) under the **Stroke style** tab. Joins can be **Miter**, **Round**, and **Bevel**, and Caps can be **Butt**, **Round**, and **Square**. Individual nodes (control points) of the path can be styled with a custom marker. The marker can be different for start, end, and middle nodes:

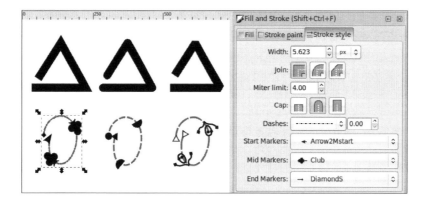

Tapered lines using shapes in Pencil and Pen tools

Both **Pencil** and **Pen** tools come with the option to automatically draw tapered lines. This can make creating lines more interesting, especially when using a graphics tablet. Before drawing a line we simply select a shape from the toolbar and the shape gets applied to the line when we finish drawing. Readymade shapes are **Triangle in**, **Triangle out**, **Ellipse**, and a custom shape that can be used by copying it and using the **From clipboard** option.

The following are some examples (they can be found in the `Lines.svg` file accompanying this chapter) where we used the Pencil with **Smoothing:** set to 50 and drew the letter "O":

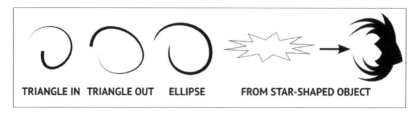

TRIANGLE IN   TRIANGLE OUT   ELLIPSE   FROM STAR-SHAPED OBJECT

Creating "lines" using the Calligraphy tool

In Inkscape, lines created by the **Calligraphy** tool  are actually objects with a fill and no stroke. Although we can't bend them easily like we would with lines, they still are quite valuable in a lot of situations, especially when created with a graphics tablet—a highly recommended purchase for any artist interested in creating freehand computer graphics.

Sketch mode—fixing the path while drawing

Sketch mode is a special mode provided by the Pencil tool when holding the *Alt* key. This will treat all strokes as an attempt to draw one line, by computing the average and rendering the final result. Our various attempts are displayed in green as we keep drawing and a red line displays the current average, so we can keep tweaking the path until we are satisfied. The following example has been exaggerated to clarify the process; usually strokes are drawn closer together:

Creating dots using Pencil and Pen tools

You might have guessed that the **Pencil** and modes of the **Pen** tool we used in this recipe can't create dots by simply clicking on canvas. However, there is a shortcut that simulates dots by drawing circles of a certain size, by holding *Ctrl* and clicking with **Pencil** and straight line modes of the **Pen** tool. Dot size can be adjusted in **Inkscape Preferences** (*Shift + Ctrl + P*). Using *Shift + Ctrl* will double the dot size and *Ctrl + Alt* will make it random.

See also

For more information, refer to the recipes *Creating calligraphic shapes* and *Creating smooth paths with Spiro Spline* in this chapter, also refer to *Chapter 5, Live Path Effects*.

Editing paths using the Node tool

Nodes are control points that control the path shape. Nodes can also have tangent control handles that also contribute to the overall result. In this recipe we will use some of the most common node editing facilities.

How to do it...

The following steps will show you how to edit paths:

1. Create an ellipse and convert it to a path (*Shift + Ctrl + C*) so we can edit it using **Node tool**. Remove the fill and make the stroke thick (16 worked in my case).

2. Select **Node tool** 🔍 (*F2* or *N*), and you will see that our ellipse now has four nodes.

3. Select the top and right node by using a rubber band selection box around them or by clicking on them while holding *Shift*.

4. Make the path open by deleting the segment. Use the **Delete segment between two non-endpoint nodes** ⬚ button, from the toolbar.

5. Select the bottom node by clicking on it and convert it to a **cusp (corner) node** by clicking on the **Make selected nodes corner** ⬚ button (*Shift + C*).

6. Hover over the right node handle and read the tip in the Status bar. Hold *Ctrl + Alt* to constrain angles to certain values and to lock handle length while moving, then drag upwards until you reach 90°.

7. Do the same for the left handle, but this time move upwards until it reaches the same point as the right handle.

8. Click and drag the bottom node downwards while holding *Ctrl* to constrain movement to the vertical Y axis.

9. Select the left and top nodes using a rubber band box.

10. On the toolbar select the **Show transformation handles for selected nodes** ⬚ button. The transformation handles will now appear around the selected nodes.

11. Click on one of the nodes to change handles to skew/rotate, and position the rotation center over the left node by dragging it there.

12. Drag the top right rotate handle counter-clockwise and release when you reach an angle of roughly 200°.

13. Add another node between the two selected ones by pressing *Insert* key or by using the **Insert new nodes into selected segments** ⬚ toolbar button.

14. Select the inserted and the two left-most nodes and convert the segment between them into a straight line by using the **Make selected segments lines** ⬚ toolbar button (*Shift + L*).

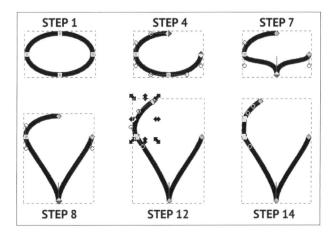

There's more...

There are many shortcuts available for editing nodes and this recipe only uses some of them, so you are encouraged to go through the complete list. You can find them under **Help | Keys and Mouse Reference** (it will open a page in your default Web browser).

Once you learn the most common keyboard shortcuts for each editing mode, you will create graphics in a faster, more productive, and enjoyable way.

Symmetric and auto-smooth nodes

Pencil and Pen tools only create **cusp nodes** and **smooth nodes**, but **symmetric nodes** and **auto-smooth nodes** are also available. As we would expect, symmetric nodes have both handles of equal length and are collinear. To convert a node to symmetric, use *Shift + Y* or the **Make selected nodes symmetric** button on the toolbar. Auto-smooth nodes make sure that the segments they touch always remain smooth. If we move a handle of an auto-smooth node it will automatically become a smooth node. Use the **Make selected nodes auto-smooth** button (*Shift + A*) to convert any node into an auto-smooth node.

Deleting nodes

When we use the *Delete* key to delete selected nodes Inkscape will try to preserve the path shape as much as possible by changing the adjacent node types and handles angles and lengths. There are some cases where this kind of behavior is undesirable; for example, in an object that consists only of straight segments, we expect to get a straight line when we delete a node, and to get that kind of behavior we can use *Ctrl + Del*. There is an option to toggle this behavior in Inkscape preferences (*Shift + Ctrl + P*) under **Tools | Node | Editing preferences**.

Using Simplify to smooth paths after creation

In the previous recipe we saw that the **Smoothing** option in Pencil tool can affect the overall number of nodes created while drawing the path. If we need to smoothen or reduce the number of nodes in an existing path we can use the **Simplify** option 〰 *(Ctrl + L)*. **Inkscape preferences** *(Shift + Ctrl + P)* under **Misc** hold an option where we can set the strength of the **Simplify** command; the larger the number, the more nodes are removed and the more distorted the path will be. It might be better to just start with the default value and, if needed, quickly use the **Simplify** option several times in succession for a better effect.

Node sculpting

By holding the *Alt* key while moving nodes, we will move them in a non-uniform way. The nodes closer to the one that is actually clicked on to move the selection will move with an incremented step. Some fine examples of node sculpting can be viewed in the screenshots gallery of the Inkscape website:

```
http://inkscape.org/screenshots/gallery/
```

Path direction

Path direction is important when putting text on paths or when using markers on strokes. It also affects the order in which nodes are selected using the *Tab* key. Visual indicators for path direction can be enabled in **Inkscape preferences** *(Shift + Ctrl + P)* under **Tools | Node | Path outline**. They only appear when path outline is enabled which can be done by toggling the **Show path outline (without path effects)** button 〰 on the **Node** toolbar:

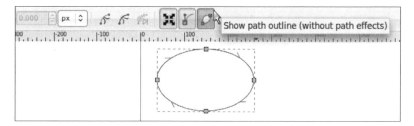

See also

For more information, refer to *Creating freehand and straight lines* and *Creating paths using the Pen (Brazier) tool* in this chapter.

Creating paths using the Pen (Bezier) tool

The **Pen (Bezier)** tool is generally considered somewhat difficult to master but after some practice it can become a valuable tool when we need precision while drawing or tracing something along the edges. In this recipe we will write out the word "Mud" using the Pen tool. Our object will be composed of 2 sub-paths, one for the letters "Mu" and the other for the letter "d".

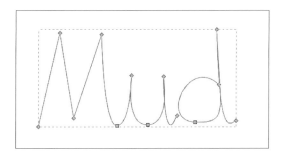

How to do it...

The following steps will show how to write words using the **Pen** tool:

1. Select the **Pen (Bezier)** tool (*Shift + F6* or *B*) and make sure the selected mode on the toolbar is **Create regular Bezier path**.

2. Clicking without dragging creates a **cusp (corner) node**, so click four times to create the first four points of the letter "M" (at this point it will look like an "N").

3. The fifth and final point of the letter "M" will be a smooth transition into the letter "u". Choose a place where we want the "M" to finish, click, and slightly drag the pointer horizontally without releasing the mouse button to create a **smooth node**.

4. Click where you want the first point of the letter "u" to be.

5. Click and drag horizontally, where you want the bottom of the letter "u" to be, to create a smooth node. If you're not satisfied with the result, press *Del* to delete the last node and try again.

6. Click to create the third, top right "u" node.

7. Create the last "u" node by moving to the bottom right, clicking and dragging slightly towards top right until the red helper line partially fits over the previous segment.

8. Right-click or press *Enter* to finish the first path.

9. Hold *Shift* while creating the first node of "d", to add the path we are about to create to the first one. Click and drag upwards and to the left.

10. Click and drag downwards and to the right to create the second node of "d" (consult with the screenshot that follows).

11. Click where you want the highest point of "d" to be and drag upwards to adjust the ascenders as you see fit. Don't release the mouse yet.

12. Press *Shift* while still holding down the mouse button. Move the pointer downwards until you almost reach the baseline of the text; release both the *Shift* key and the mouse button to create the handle.

13. Click where you want the "d" terminal to end and drag upwards and to the right to adjust the last segment.

14. Right-click or press *Enter* to complete the path.

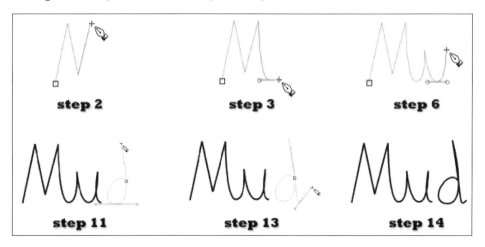

How it works...

A simple click on the canvas will create a cusp (corner) node, while clicking and dragging will create handles of smooth nodes that control the path curvature. When we are creating a cusp node that comes after a curved segment that needs adjusting, we need to use *Shift* so we can reposition the second handle to create a cusp node. This procedure isn't very intuitive so some users don't think cusp nodes can even be created in such a case, as we have seen, the "d" ascender example proved differently.

There's more...

We only used some of the keyboard shortcuts and options available for the **Pen (Bezier)** tool. Look for more under **Help | Keys and Mouse Reference**. For example, if you want to fine-tune the position of the last node you've drawn, you can move it using the arrow keys. If you don't like the last node you've created, you can quickly delete it using the *Backspace* or *Del* keys. *Esc* or *Ctrl + Z* will undo the entire path we are drawing, and holding down *Ctrl* will conveniently snap the rotation handles.

Finally, use the **Node tool** to make any extra adjustments to the path you've just created.

See also

For more information, refer to the recipes on *Creating freehand and straight lines* and *Editing paths with the Node tool* in this chapter.

Creating smooth paths with Spiro Spline

Spiro Spline is implemented in Inkscape as a live path effect (**LPE**), but it is conveniently added to the **Pencil** and **Pen** tools. Although **Spiro Spline** was developed for creating fonts, we can use it to quickly and easily create smooth paths.

We will see what the Spiro modes in those tools have to offer in this recipe.

How to do it...

The following steps show how to create a smooth path using **Spiro Spline**:

1. Select the Pencil tool (*F6* or *P*). On the toolbar, select the **Create Spiro path** button and set **Smoothing:** to 50.

2. Create a curved shape by writing out the letter "S" as if we were drawing on a sheet of paper.

3. Switch to **Node tool** (*F2* or *N*) and turn on the path outline by clicking on the **Show path outline (without path effects)** toolbar button. You will now see both the **Spiro** shape and the red outline (also called skeleton) of the regular path. The outline shows what the shape would look like without Spiro effect applied.

4. Make the handles visible by using the **Show Bezier handles of selected nodes** button and selecting all the nodes (*Ctrl + A*).

5. Try moving one of the handles. Notice how the red outline changes but the end result (the Spiro path) remains intact.

6. Move the nodes around and observe how the movements that affect the Spiro path shape always remain smooth.

7. Create a new node at the bottom of the shape by double-clicking on the outline. Notice that you can't do this by clicking on the Spiro path. The more nodes you add to the path the more the outline and Spiro shape look alike.

8. Select the node we just created and convert it to a cusp (corner) node by using the **Make selected nodes corner** (*Shift + C*) on the toolbar.

9. Move one of the handles so they aren't collinear any more. If the Spiro path doesn't change, also move the node so the Spiro path has a clear corner point at that node.

10. Create two more nodes that are adjacent to each other by double-clicking on the outline.

11. Select both nodes and convert the segment into a line by using the **Make selected segments lines** button 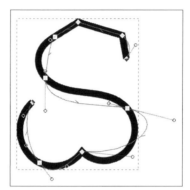 (*Shift + L*). Notice how this segment is also a straight line in Spiro shape but it smoothly transitions into adjacent segments.

12. Select one of the nodes from the straight line and add its adjacent smooth node to the selection.

13. Convert them to cusp (corner) nodes by using the toolbar button or *Shift + C*, then use the same option to retract the handles. Since the handles were changed they were no longer collinear so the segment became a straight line even in the Spiro path.

14. Convert the Spiro path to a regular path using the **Object to Path** option (*Shift + Ctrl + C*). We now have the shape we desired but without the Spiro editing ability.

How it works...

As we can see from this example, Spiro paths are affected by the node handles only as far as determining the node type. Collinear handles determine smoothness of the nodes by the curve points in Spiro path. If the handles aren't collinear the Spiro point will be a corner point. The overall shape of a Spiro path is determined by the node types and its positions.

See also

For more information, refer to the recipes on *Creating freehand and straight lines*, *Editing paths with the Node tool*, and *Creating paths using the Pen (Bezier) tool* in this chapter, as well as *Chapter 5, Live Path Effects*.

Creating calligraphic shapes

The **Calligraphy** tool comes with a lot of options to change the resulting shape as if we are changing how we use the calligraphic pen or we are using a different brush to create our objects. This recipe will introduce us to those options.

How to do it...

The following steps will show how to use the **Calligraphy** tool:

1. Select the **Calligraphy** tool (*Ctrl + F6* or *C*) and create a wavy calligraphic object. Notice how the options from the toolbar affected the shape.

2. Increase the **Width:** to 70 and **Thinning:** to 85 and create another wavy object with a similar hand stroke like in step one.

3. Set **Width:** to 30 and **Thinning:** to 0 and create another similar shape but this time change the pen width by pressing the *Left Arrow* and *Right Arrow* in turns. Draw slowly to enhance the effect.

4. Create another wavy object but this time alternate between *Home* and *End* keys while drawing. This will abruptly change the pen width from minimum to maximum.

5. Set the **Width:** to 40 and alternate between the *Up Arrow* and *Down Arrow* keys while drawing. This will change the pen angle as we draw.

6. Set the **Angle:** back to 30, set **Fixation:** to 0, and **Caps:** to 3, and create another wavy object. Notice how the ends are capped.

7. Set the **Tremor:** to 40 and create another wavy object. Notice the irregular edges.

8. Set the **Tremor:** to 0 and **Wiggle:** to 80 and create another wavy object. Notice how the object shape doesn't strictly comply to our mouse movement.

9. Set **Wiggle:** to 0 and **Mass:** to 45 and create another object. Notice how drawing it feels slow. We have enough time to move the mouse in the desired direction creating smooth transitions.

There's more...

The **Calligraphy** tool can't be experienced fully without a hardware graphics tablet. If you have one, plug it in, configure it using the **Input Devices...** option under the **File** menu and have fun creating new and elaborate calligraphic shapes.

Erasing using Calligraphy tool

Holding *Alt* while creating calligraphic paths will work as an eraser on selected objects. This can be convenient when we need to quickly edit objects by trimming parts away because we can use all the calligraphy options or presets. Here is a very quick drawing of a star with the edges and insides treated with Wiggly preset while holding *Alt* to delete:

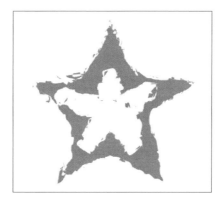

Calligraphy presets

Calligraphy tool comes with a set of presets we can use to achieve different calligraphy effects out of the box. Try them out and examine the toolbar settings to get an even better idea of how different settings can be combined.

Hatchings using Calligraphy tool

The **Calligraphy** tool can also be used to create **hatchings**; these are parallel, equidistant lines used to create patterns like those found in engravings. Select the path you want to track and hold the *Ctrl* key while tracking and moving to the next line to keep the path distances equal:

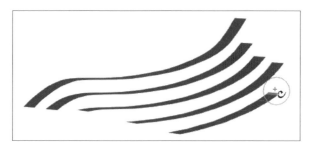

Changing calligraphy path colors

By default when a calligraphy object is created it remains selected, so if we want to change the color of the next object we first need to deselect the one we just created (*Esc*). If the workflow you like to use with the **Calligraphy** tool includes changing the object colors before the object is created, then deselect the option **Select new path** under **Tools | Calligraphy** in the **Inkscape Preferences** (*Shift + Ctrl + P*).

See also

For more information, refer to the following recipe.

Using the Eraser tool

Many users who come to Inkscape from other graphics applications look for an eraser tool when they want to remove something out from an object or do some other similar operations. Although the native way to operate on vector objects is with Boolean path operations. The **Eraser** tool can also come in handy.

How to do it...

The following steps will demonstrate how to properly use the **Eraser** tool:

1. Create a lot of objects by drawing a rectangle and repeatedly pressing *Space* while dragging the rectangle across the screen.
2. Select the **Eraser** tool (*Shift + E*) and make sure the **Delete objects touched by the eraser** button ▣ is selected.
3. Drag across the objects that you wish get deleted, they will be completely removed from the drawing.
4. Select the **Cut out from objects** button ▣ and increase the **Width:** to 30.
5. Drag over the objects, and the eraser trail will make holes in the objects. *Shapes will automatically be converted into paths*. If you want to restrict erasing to particular objects instead of using the whole drawing, select the objects before using the **Eraser tool**.

> When cutting out from objects, erasing using the **Calligraphy** tool (with *Alt*) might be more flexible than the **Eraser** tool because we can choose and adjust the pen shapes in order to create our custom "eraser brush."

See also

For more information, refer to *Creating calligraphic shapes* in this chapter.

Creating and editing 3D boxes

In Inkscape, 3D boxes are actually two-dimensional objects arranged according to a defined perspective, in order to provide the illusion of an additional dimension. This recipe shows us the basic options available to manipulate boxes in our fake but very convincing 3D space.

Getting ready

The default positions of the perspective vanishing points are the center of the vertical page edges. That is why it is recommended to start creating a box somewhere inside the page area. To prepare for this recipe open Inkscape and zoom to page size using the **Zoom to fit page in window** toolbar button (or the 5 key), **Zoom to fit page width in window** (*Ctrl* + *E* or *6*) on the **Zoom** (*F3* or *Z*) toolbar.

How to do it...

The following steps will show you how to create 3D boxes:

1. Select the **3D box** tool ![icon] (*Shift* + *F4* or *X*) and click and drag in the page center area to create the left-hand side of the box. Notice that the other box sides will be created automatically, some of them will be hidden from view. The vanishing points are located on vertical page edges.

2. There is a small cross at the box center that can be dragged to change the box position with respect to the current perspective. Move the box by dragging that cross in all directions and see how the box changes, then return it to the center.

3. Switch to the **Selector** tool (*Space*) and move the box object upwards.

4. Switch to the **3D box** tool (*Space*, *Shift* + *F4*, or *X*) again and notice how the vanishing points moved with the box preserving the box shape.

5. Grab the top box corner handle that is closest to the viewer and drag it downwards while holding *Ctrl* to make the movement vertical.

6. Grab the bottom box corner handle that is closest to the viewer and drag it upwards while holding *Ctrl* to make the movement vertical. The top and bottom sides of the box shouldn't be visible:

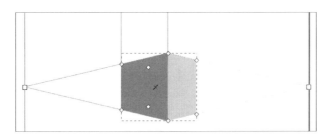

7. Grab the left corner handle of the left box side and drag it towards the right while holding *Ctrl* to constrain the movement along the converging line.

8. Grab the right corner handle of the right box side and drag it towards left while holding *Ctrl* to constrain the movement along the converging line. The box should become narrower.

9. Duplicate the box (*Ctrl + D*) and move it left while holding *Shift* to constrain the movement to the Z direction. Release when the two boxes stop overlapping.

10. Duplicate the box (*Ctrl + D*) and move it behind all the others by using *End* or *Page Down* keys, or the **Lower selection to bottom** button on the toolbar. Move it right by dragging the cross handle while holding *Shift* to constrain the movement to the Z direction. Release when it appears next to our original box.

11. Select the middle box by clicking on it.

12. Duplicate the box (*Ctrl + D*) and move it behind all the other ones by using *End* or *Page Down* keys. Move it towards the top while holding *Ctrl* to constrain the movement to the Y direction. Release when you can see its bottom side appear behind the middle box.

13. Duplicate the box (*Ctrl + D*) and move it behind all the others by using *End* or *Page Down* keys. Move it downwards while holding *Ctrl* to constrain the movement to the Y direction. Release when you can see its top side appear behind the middle box.

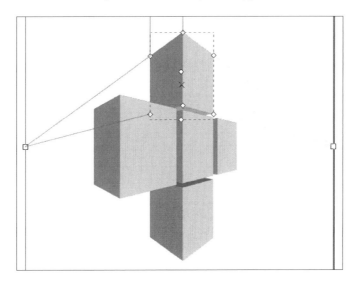

14. Move the left vanishing point towards the box, and move the right vanishing point away from the box (outside of the page area) to change the perspective. Notice how all the boxes change together because they all share the same perspective.

15. Move both of the vanishing points downwards and notice how the bottom box doesn't seem in the correct position with respect to the rest of them. Select that box and bring it to the front by using the *Home* or *Page Up* keys, or by clicking on the **Raise selection to front** button ▦ on the toolbar.

How it works...

3D boxes are actually groups of six quadrilaterals (shapes with four corners) assembled together for a three dimensional effect. The box sides can change some of its attributes independently while being parts of the box (color for example). However, if we need to perform some other functions on the box we need to convert it to a path (*Shift + Ctrl + C*). With that conversion we will lose the ability to edit it using the **3D Box** tool.

We can enter the 3D box so we can select the individual sides using the **Selector** tool by using the *Ctrl + Enter* shortcut. The **Node** tool can select individual sides even without entering the group.

There's more...

When there's more than one box sharing the perspective, holding *Shift* while clicking and dragging a vanishing point can change that box's perspective without affecting the other objects.

Isometric projection and 1, 2, and 3-point perspectives

The examples we used in this recipe all use 2-point perspective (two vanishing points), but 1-point and 3-point perspectives are also possible. To create a 1-point perspective we need to set X and Y vanishing points to infinity by using their respective parallel buttons on the **3D Box** toolbar. Set **Angle X:** to 180 and **Angle Y:** to 90. Make sure that the Z parallel button is off and drag the Z vanishing point to the drawing center. Toggling the parallel buttons can be done using the keyboard shortcuts: *Shift + X*, *Shift + Y*, and *Shift + Z*.

To create a 3-point perspective toggle off all three parallel buttons and drag the vanishing points where you like them (usually X and Z vanishing points are at the same level on opposite sides of the object).

An Isometric projection can also be achieved with the **3D box** tool. To create it all the parallel buttons must be on and the angles set to **X:** 150, **Y:** 90, **Z:** 30.

See also

For more information, refer to the recipe on *Assembling a modern chair using the 3D Box tool* in *Chapter 8*.

Creating and editing text

Inkscape is often used to produce leaflets, brochures, and User Interface themes, so a tool for creating text objects is obviously necessary. In this recipe we will explore what the **Text** tool has to offer.

How to do it...

The following steps will show you how to use the **Text** tool:

1. Select the **Text** tool **A** (*F8* or *T*) and create a text object by clicking on canvas (without dragging). Type "FUNstack" but place the "stack" on the next line.

2. Select your favorite font family from the drop-down list in the **Text** toolbar. The example in this book uses *'Doulos SIL'*.

3. Increase the text size to 144 by selecting it from the **Font size (px)** drop-down box.

4. Make the text bold by clicking on the **Bold** **A** button. This will work only if the bold variant of the font exists.

5. Center the text using the center toolbar button.

6. Reduce the spacing between lines (line-height or leading) by using the toolbar button or *Alt + Up Arrow* when the text cursor is positioned before the letter "s".

7. Select the letters "FUN" dragging with the **Text** tool across them and increase the spacing between letters by using *Alt + >* or the toolbar box.

8. Select the "t" letter and shift it upwards by using the vertical shift box or *Alt + Up Arrow*.

9. Rotate the "t" letter by using *Alt + [* or by using the toolbar button.

10. Select the letter "a" and move it to the left by using the *Alt + Left Arrow* or the toolbar button.

How it works...

Clicking on the Canvas with the **Text** tool creates a normal text object. The alternative is to click and drag to create a frame into which text will be written (a flowed text frame). Not all formatting options are available in flowed text frames (kerning for example) so we might use it to enter text into a predefined rectangle area and then convert it to a normal text object using the **Convert to text** option ![icon] from the **Text** menu.

There's more...

The **Text and Font** dialogue (*Shift + Ctrl + T*) can be used to preview any font changes before applying them, and it is also possible to choose the default settings for some of the text editing options.

Flow text into frame

A flowed text frame can be used when we need to have our text fit a rectangle shape, but if we need it to fill something more exotic we need to use the **Flow into Frame** option (*Alt + W*). Both the text object and the shape need to be selected before calling this option.

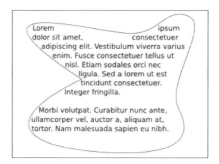

Text on a path

Putting text on paths is commonly used when we need to put text on a circle or some other shape. The direction of the path is important because it determines the text direction. *Shift + R* changes the path direction. You can visualize the path direction by enabling it in **Inkscape Preferences** ![icon] (*Shift + Ctrl + P*) under **Tools | Node** and turning on the path outline using the button on the **Node** toolbar. To place the text on the shape, select both objects and then choose **Text | Put on Path** ![icon] from the menu.

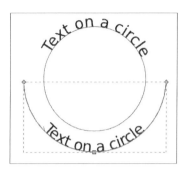

Clipping

In this recipe we will see how to completely hide parts of a drawing in a non-destructive manner.

How to do it...

The following steps will show you how to clip an object:

1. Select the **Star** tool (*Shift + F9* or ***) and create an upright star by dragging upwards while holding *Ctrl* key. This is the object we want to clip.

2. Select the **Ellipse** tool (*F5* or *E*) and create a circle by holding *Ctrl* while dragging. Make the circle a bit smaller than the star and position it above the star. The circle will be our clipping object.

3. Select both of our objects (*Ctrl + A*) and clip them by using the **Object | Clip | Set** command. Notice how the circle disappears from the drawing and parts of the star previously not covered by the circle are hidden. Check the Status bar notification area tips and you will see the star is labeled as **clipped**.

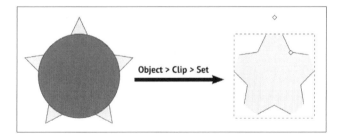

4. Select the **Star** tool (*Shift + F9* or ***) and move the star handles to change the shape of the object. Notice how the same circle area remains visible while the rest is hidden no matter how we edit the star.

5. Select the **Node** tool (*F2* or *N*) and enable the **Show clipping path(s) of selected object(s)** toolbar button ![icon]. You will now see the outline of the clipping object in green.

6. Edit the clipping circle by using the ellipse handles. Notice how this reveals or hides different parts of the star object.

How it works...

Although the clipped object looks like some of its parts have been cut off, they are actually only hidden and can be edited even while being clipped. To "unclip" an object use the **Object | Clip | Release** option.

Clipping object color

The clipping object color isn't relevant, as only the shape determines what is hidden or revealed, but it is helpful to color it differently from the rest of the drawing so it's easier for us to predict what the final result might look like.

Clipping is handy in many situations. For example, it can be used to rapidly produce galleries of banners or portraits using a common, irregularly shaped frame as the clipping object.

Editing shapes used as clipping objects

As of writing this book the option to edit clipping objects that are shapes (rectangle, ellipse, star) doesn't work, so if this is important to you convert the clipping object into a path (*Shift + Ctrl + C*) *before* clipping.

There's more...

We only used simple one object clippings in this recipe but clipping also works with groups, either as clipped or clipping objects. The following is an example where we clipped a group of stars with a group of circles:

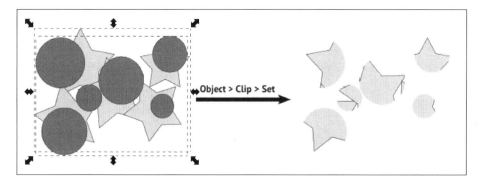

Clipping and automatic grouping

There is a very useful option in **Inkscape Preferences** (*Shift + Ctrl + P*) under **Clippaths and masks** to automatically group the object(s) we want to clip. If we set it to **Enclose every clipped/masked object in its own group** all objects will get their own independent clipping objects; if you edit one object's clipping path, the others will remain unchanged. If we choose **Put all clipped/ masked objects into one group**, editing the clipping path will affect the whole group of objects as if it was a single object.

Grouping a single object before clipping can be very useful when we need to position the object differently with respect to its clipping object, as we can enter the group and move the object around without moving the clipping object or unclipping.

See also

For more information, refer to the *Masking* and *Path operations* recipes in this chapter.

Masking

In this recipe we will see how to make certain areas of a drawing transparent without applying permanent changes to the elements of the drawing itself, thanks to the use of masking objects.

How to do it...

The following steps show you how to create an object masking:

1. Select the **Star** tool (*Shift + F9* or ***) and create an upright star by dragging upwards while holding *Ctrl* key. This is the object we want to mask.

2. Select the **Ellipse** tool (*F5* or *E*) and create a circle by holding *Ctrl* while dragging. Make the circle a bit smaller than the star and position it above the star. The circle will be our masking object.

3. Make the circle fill color **White** by clicking on the white colored chip in the color swatch under the canvas.

4. Create a radial gradient by selecting the **Gradient** tool , choosing the radial gradient, clicking in the center of our circle, and then dragging outwards. Increase the stroke width (10 worked in my case) and set its color to **White**.

5. Select both of our objects (*Ctrl + A*) and apply the masking by using the **Object | Mask | Set** command. The star will appear to be clipped, but if we read the Status bar notification area tip, we will see that the star is actually labeled as **masked**.

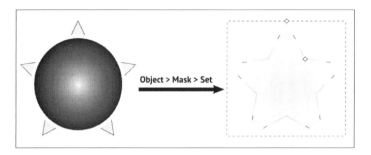

Object > Mask > Set

6. Select the **Star** tool (*Shift + F9* or ***) and move the star handles to change the star shape.

7. Select the **Node** tool (*F2* or *N*) and enable the **Show mask(s) of selected object(s)** toolbar button. You will now see the outline of the masking object in blue.

8. Edit the masking circle by using the ellipse handles.

How it works...

The masking object, in addition to acting as a clip path, will use its colors to make parts of an object opaque or transparent. In parts where the masking object is white, the masked object will be visible, and in parts where the masking object is black or transparent, the masked object will be transparent. Mask colors aren't limited to black and white though, any color can be used and the masking will be determined by the color lightness and opacity.

The masked object can be edited while being masked or it can be released from the mask by using the **Object | Mask | Release** option.

Editing shapes used as masking objects

As of writing this book the option to edit masking objects that are shapes (rectangle, ellipse, star) doesn't work, so if this is important to you convert the masking object into a path (*Shift + Ctrl + C*) before doing the masking.

There's more...

As with clipping, masking can also be performed on groups and by groups. The following are the two groups from the clipping recipe, only now we have used masking:

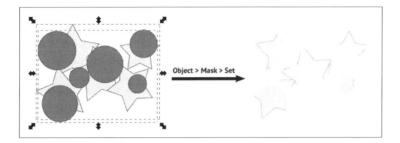

 Masking and automatic grouping

Masked objects can be automatically grouped before masking to make future editing easier. Read more about it in the *Clipping* recipe.

See also

For more information, refer to the *Making objects partially transparent* and *Creating linear gradients* in *Chapter 2*.

Path operations

Inkscape comes with several useful path operations that enable us to assemble complex objects from simpler ones, thus speeding up the process of creating elaborate drawings.

How to do it...

The following steps outline some useful path operations:

1. Create a rectangle using the **Rectangle** tool (*F4* or *R*) and a star using the **Star** tool (*Shift + F9* or ***). Position the star over the top rectangle edge so it partially overlaps the rectangle.

2. Select both objects (*Ctrl + A*) and perform a union on them using the **Path | Union** option or *Ctrl + +*. Notice how we now have only one object with the same outline as the previous objects combined:

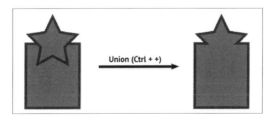

3. Create a circle with the **Ellipse** tool (*F5 or E*) and position it over the object we got in the previous step.

4. Select both objects (*Ctrl + A*) and perform a difference using the **Path | Difference** option  or *Ctrl + -* . Notice that we now have only one object that was made by subtracting the top from the bottom one:

Difference (Ctrl + -)

5. Create an ellipse using the **Ellipse** tool (*F5 or E*) that is a bit wider than the object from the previous step and position it over the upper half of that object (I also lowered the opacity a bit so it's easier to see what we're doing.)

6. Select both objects (*Ctrl + A*) and perform an intersection using the **Path | Intersection** option 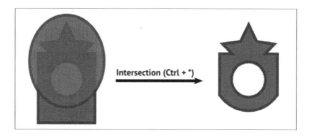 or *Ctrl + ***. This option is the same as **Clipping**, only destructive, since we can't get the original shape back:

Intersection (Ctrl + *)

7. Create a rectangle using the **Rectangle** tool (*F4 or R*) that is larger than the object from the previous step, and center it over that object (I also lowered the opacity a bit so it's easier to see what we're doing.)

8. Select both objects (*Ctrl + A*) and perform an exclusion using the **Path | Exclusion** option 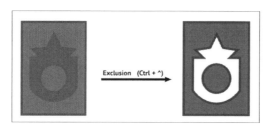 or *Ctrl + ^*. This operation is like a reverse **Difference**:

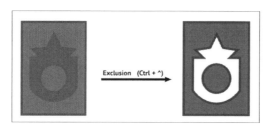

Exclusion (Ctrl + ^)

9. Create a rectangle using the **Rectangle** tool (*F4* or *R*) that is approximately half the size of the object from the previous step, and position it over the bottom area of that object (I also lowered the opacity a bit so it's easier to see what we're doing.)

10. Select both objects (*Ctrl + A*), duplicate them (*Ctrl + D*), and move away the selection (duplicated objects). We will use them in a later step.

11. Select the original two objects using a rubber band selection or by clicking on one and using *Shift* while clicking on the other to add it to the selection. Then perform a division using the **Path | Division** 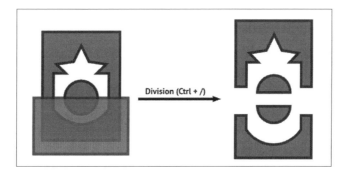 option or *Ctrl + /*.

12. Deselect using the *Esc* key and then select each of the resulting objects and move them away so that each subpath of the original object is divided separately.

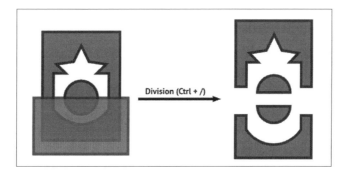

Division (Ctrl + /)

13. Select the objects we had previously duplicated and set aside, and cut the paths using the **Path | Cut Path** option 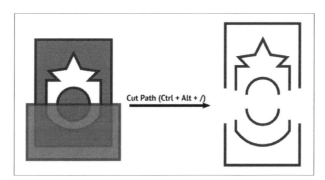 or *Ctrl + Alt + /*.

14. Deselect using the *Esc* key and then select each of the resulting objects and move them away to see how all the sub-paths of the original object were cut independently. Paths that are generated with the **Cut Path** operation are open so their fill is removed to make it more clear.

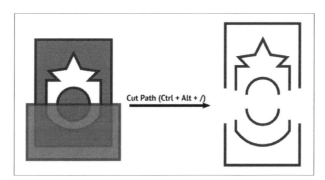

Cut Path (Ctrl + Alt + /)

There's more...

We only used two objects at a time to demonstrate different path operations but more than two paths can be used to perform **Union**, **Intersection**, and **Exclusion**.

If we use **Open Paths** with path operations they will be closed in the process by connecting its end points with a straight line. If we use shape objects (rectangle, ellipse, or stars) they will automatically be converted to paths.

Inset and Outset

Inset and **Outset** aren't path operations but what they do is similar enough to include them in this recipe. **Inset** (*Ctrl + ( )* and **Outset** (*Ctrl +)*) moves the path edge towards the center or away from the object center by an equal amount. Here are some examples:

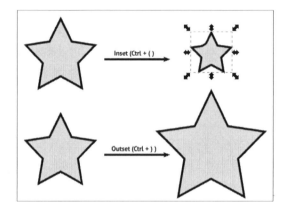

Dynamic Offset

Dynamic Offset moves the path edge towards or away from the object center using a square handle that appears when this option is selected. The end result is not an editable path, and if we want to edit it further we have to convert it to a path (*Shift + Ctrl + C*). This effect isn't destructive like the **Inset** and **Offset** options. Here are some examples:

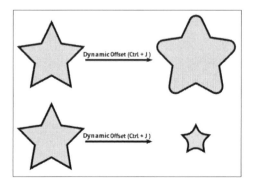

Linked Offset

Linked Offset duplicates the object before modifying it so we end up with two objects, the original one and the one with the offset. The offset is linked to the object and will be updated as we modify the original object. Here is an example:

See also

For more information, refer to the recipe on *Clipping* in this chapter.

2
Editing Colors

In this chapter, we will cover:

- ▶ Changing fill and stroke color using a palette
- ▶ Making objects partially transparent
- ▶ Creating linear gradients
- ▶ Recreating HAL 9000 using radial gradients
- ▶ Patterns
- ▶ Picking and assigning colors with the Dropper tool
- ▶ Adjusting Hue, Lightness, Saturation, and Stroke Width with Color Gestures
- ▶ Different color icon sets using the RGB Barrel

Introduction

In this chapter we will learn how to manipulate color in our drawings, while learning some time-saving tips in the process.

You'll be happy to know that Inkscape provides many facilities that manipulate color in a variety of ways, in the most commonly used color models, such as CMYK and RGB.

Gradients, when applied in a tasteful manner, can greatly enhance the overall effect of a drawing. Being so versatile, we will often use them in later chapters.

Changing fill and stroke color using a palette

In this recipe we will change the **Fill** and **Stroke** color of a rectangle using color chips from a **palette**.

Getting ready

Our currently selected palette is presented to us in a swatch panel, right under the Canvas.

Make sure that the Inkscape default color palette is chosen. You can select it by clicking the small, left pointing arrow button on the right-hand side of the swatch.

How to do it...

We shall see how to change the fill and stroke color of a rectangle in the following steps:

1. Select the **Rectangle** tool (*F4*).

2. Click and drag on the canvas to draw a rectangle. It will stay selected after you finish drawing.

3. Click on a light red color chip of your choice to change the **Fill** color of the rectangle.

4. Hold down the *Shift* key on your keyboard while clicking on a dark red color chip to change the **Stroke** color of the rectangle.

5. Increase the stroke width so the stroke color change is more obvious. You can do that by using the stroke width box in the bottom left corner of the window. The number shown is the width of the stroke of the currently selected object. Right-click on it and select a value of 16.

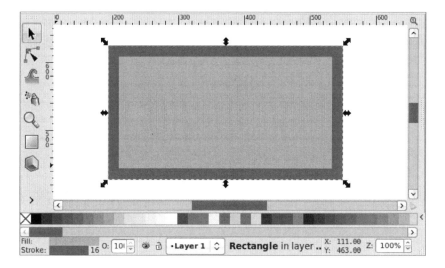

How it works...

In vector graphics, almost all objects have a fill and a stroke, and their colors can be changed independently. We used a rectangle in this recipe, but the same applies to all vector objects in Inkscape. The easiest and fastest way to change the colors of an object is to use the palette swatch on the bottom of the screen.

Inkscape's default installation comes with a convenient set of popular color palettes, that can help in creating icons for a specific theme (Windows OS icons, Tango icons for various free and open-source GUIs) or working with the gray scale color model (as in the case of black and white photos or logos).

There's more...

Right-clicking on a color chip will pop up a selection menu where we can choose that color for either the fill or the stroke of the currently selected object. We can also drag the color directly on the objects in the canvas to color them, without first selecting them.

There is a convenient style indicator at the bottom-left of the Inkscape window that shows the color information of the selected object. This can sometimes be helpful when dealing with objects that are covered by others, so you can easily figure out which one is actually selected.

If more than one object is selected, average values are calculated and displayed.

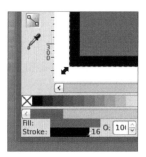

In the top-right corner of the window there is a new style indicator that appears when you click on a tool, such as the **Pen (Bezier)** or the **Rectangle** tool, and there are no objects selected. It shows what style would be applied to a new object if you started drawing with the currently selected tool. By clicking (or holding *Shift* and clicking) on the palette chips when no object is selected you can set the object colors before you start drawing it.

Clicking on it will open the **Inkscape Preferences** window, where we can choose the default style for the different objects we will create.

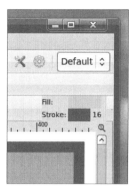

Changing color using the Fill and Stroke dialogue window

Using palettes isn't the only way to change object colors. You will find a full set of options in the **Fill and Stroke** dialogue window (*Shift + Ctrl + F*), **Menu | Object | Fill and Stroke** , or right-click and select **Fill and Stroke**), including several color pickers commonly found in graphics programs.

See also

For more information, refer to *Creating your own custom color swatches* and *Creating your own color palette* in *Chapter 3*, and also the rest of the material in this chapter.

Making objects partially transparent

Objects in Inkscape can be made partially transparent by manipulating their opacity level, so that the background and the objects below them show through.

The default Canvas background color in Inkscape is fully transparent (zero opacity), and therefore invisible. Although this isn't indicated by a checkerboard pattern like in some other graphics applications, when we export our drawing to the PNG format, the background (space around objects) will be transparent.

> **Exporting to PNG and transparency**
>
> Always use the **Export Bitmap** option when converting your drawing to the PNG format, and *not* **Save as... | Cairo PNG**. The latter may give unexpected results, including an opaque (white) background instead of a transparent one.

In this recipe we will create a number of objects with different levels of transparency applied to them. The final result should resemble the following screenshot:

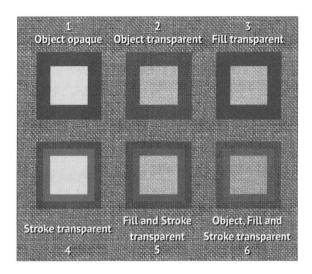

Getting ready

Start Inkscape and open the **Fill and Stroke** dialogue. Here we will find various options for manipulating the opacity of our objects. Changes in the opacity can be observed on a flat color background but are even more obvious if there is a pattern in the background.

Inkscape comes with several textured pattern fills; the most appropriate in this case are probably the **Camouflage**, **Cloth (bitmap)**, and **Old paint (bitmap)** options. Create a large rectangle the size of your page and click on the **Fill to Pattern** button to set its fill to one of the three previously mentioned patterns.

How to do it...

Carry out the following steps:

1. Select the **Rectangle** tool (*F4*).
2. Click and drag to create a small rectangle.
3. Change the stroke width to **32** using the **Stroke width** box in the bottom left of the Inkscape window (click with the right mouse button).
4. Change the rectangle **Fill** color to yellow and **Stroke** color to purple using color chips from the color palette.
5. Switch to the **Selector** tool (*F1* or *Space*).
6. Duplicate the rectangle five times so you have six in total. You can do this using the **Duplicate** button (*Ctrl + D*) or with stamping (click and hold the rectangle, don't release the mouse, and hit *Space* to drop a copy of the rectangle in that place while still not releasing the mouse).

7. Select the first rectangle and make sure that in the **Fill and Stroke** dialogue window the **Opacity, %** slider is set to 100, and the **A** (Alpha) opacity box of both fill and stroke is set to 255.

8. Select the second rectangle and set the **Opacity, %** slider to 60 while keeping the **A** opacity box of both fill and stroke at 255.

9. Select the third rectangle and set the fill **A** opacity box to 150 while keeping the **Opacity, %** slider at 100 and the stroke **A** opacity box at 255.

10. Select the fourth rectangle and set the stroke **A** opacity box to 150 while keeping the **Opacity, %** slider at 100 and the fill **A** opacity box at 255.

11. Select the fifth rectangle and set the **Opacity, %** slider to 100 and both the fill and stroke **A** opacity box to 150.

12. Select the sixth rectangle and set the **Opacity, %** slider to 80 and both the fill and stroke **A** opacity box to 150.

13. Optionally, add the text labels next to each of the rectangles to mark which transparency changes were made.

How it works...

Here's the table of opacity styles applied in this recipe:

	Rectangle 1	Rectangle 2	Rectangle 3	Rectangle 4	Rectangle 5	Rectangle 6
Object opacity	100,0%	60,0%	100,0%	100,0%	100,0%	80,0%
Fill A	255	255	150	255	150	150
Stroke A	255	255	255	150	150	150

As we can see from the earlier screenshot various effects can be achieved depending on where you apply the transparency. Making the whole object partially transparent or only setting the fill gives an expected result where you can see the background show through the whole object or only the fill area delimited by the fully opaque stroke.

In the second row, rectangles have their stroke only partially transparent; you'll have figured out by now that the stroke isn't actually positioned completely inside or outside the object, but it's actually centered on the object's edge, so that half of the stroke covers the fill and the other half is on the outside of the object.

When stroke is partially transparent and of a different color than fill, we can see that the colors mix in the area where stroke covers the fill producing a different hue. This effect gives the impression that we used more than one object to achieve this, and will come in handy in order to simplify your SVG document structure. It can also be used easily to add edge enhancement effects to your objects, such as buttons or information boxes.

There's more...

Just as you can make whole fill and stroke equally transparent across the entire surface of the object, you can also gradually apply varying transparency levels using gradients.

If you find yourself dealing with the haunting presence of a stubbornly invisible shape, revealing itelf only through its bounding box, don't panic: the poor object is probably having a bad case of "zero opacity" blues. To "cure" it and make it appear again, reset its Opacity value back to 100 (fully opaque).

Advanced effects, called **SVG filters**, can also produce partial transparency on objects and often much more complex effects than we have seen in this recipe. **SVG filters** deserve special attention so they are covered in detail in *Chapter 5* of this book.

The Cloth (bitmap) pattern used in this recipe was made by a Wikimedia user, SoylentGreen. The original bitmap can be accessed at:

`http://commons.wikimedia.org/wiki/Image:Jute_nahtlos.png`

See also

For more information, refer to the recipe on *Masking* in *Chapter 1*, and also *Creating linear gradients*, *Recreating HAL 9000 using radial gradients*, and *Picking and assigning colors with the Dropper tool* in this chapter.

Creating linear gradients

Using only flat colors on objects doesn't allow us much freedom in our artistic expressions; most often we want to use smooth blends of different colors, also known as gradients. Gradients have more uses than we can count, but are most often applied to make objects stand out in some way, by creating a realistic or appealing look. They can be applied to fills and strokes of objects.

By using the **Gradient** tool we can choose two end colors (Stops) and create a smooth transition between them.

Blending isn't limited to only two colors, and gradients can have many intermediate color stops in between the end stops. By default adding a stop to a gradient creates a linear blend between colors, but by moving the stops we can make it non-linear.

Inkscape comes with a **Gradient** tool that allows on-canvas editing of gradients, making the whole process quick and easy to master. It can also be accessed through the **Fill and Stroke** dialogue.

Getting ready

Start Inkscape, open the **Fill and Stroke** (*Shift + Ctrl + F*) dialogue window, and make sure that the **Inkscape default** color palette is the active one.

How to do it...

The following steps will show us how to create linear gradients:

1. Select **Ellipse** tool (*F5*).
2. Click and drag while holding *Ctrl* key to create a circle.
3. Make the fill and stroke **Maroon (#800000)** by clicking and *Shift*-clicking the color chip in the color palette.
4. Increase stroke width to 100 or 200 on the **Stroke style** tab on the **Fill and Stroke** dialogue window (the actual number depends on the size of the object).
5. Select **Gradient** tool 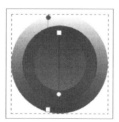 (*G*).
6. Click inside the ellipse near the top, drag towards the bottom holding the *Ctrl* key and release to create a vertical, transparent and maroon colored fill gradient.
7. Make the second color stop **Red (#FF0000)** by clicking on the color chip from the palette (the second color stop—marked with circle—is automatically selected after you stop dragging with the **Gradient** tool).
8. On the **Gradient** toolbar select the button **Create gradient in the stroke** instead of the **Create gradient in the fill**.
9. Click inside the ellipse near the bottom, drag towards the top holding the *Ctrl* key and release to create a vertical transparent maroon stroke gradient. If the handles snap together, simply press *Ctrl + Z* to start over, or temporarily disable the **Snap node or handles** button. Our object should now look like the following:

10. Make the second color stop **Red (#FF0000)** by clicking on the color chip from the palette (the second color stop—marked with circle—is automatically selected after you stop dragging with the **Gradient** tool).
11. This is the final circle with vertical gradients applied to both fill and stroke:

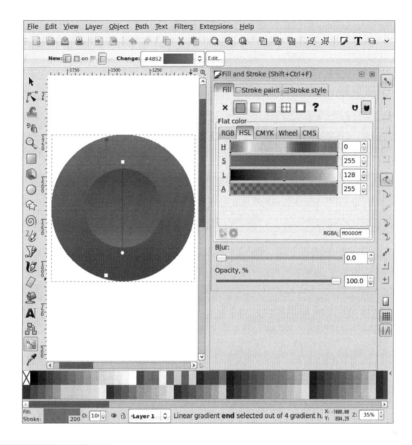

How it works...

Just like flat color, gradients can also be applied to an object's fill and stroke. Inkscape doesn't come with a set of ready-made gradients so we have to create our own.

To create a gradient you select an object (or objects) and simply drag on the Canvas using the **Gradient** tool (it doesn't have to be inside the selected object but it will affect the color of the stops), or select **Linear gradient** on the **Fill** or **Stroke** paint tab in **Fill and Stroke** dialogue window.

To be able to edit gradients easily they are represented by a gradient path, blue for fill and green for stroke. The gradient path doesn't have to be located inside the object it is applied to.

The first color stop is always marked with a square, the end one with a circle and all the intermediate ones with a diamond. The intermediate ones can be created by double-clicking on the gradient path where you want the new stop to appear. The new stop will be automatically colored in a way that doesn't change the current gradient look.

If the object we're trying to paint with a gradient has a flat color applied and we start dragging with the **Gradient** tool, inside the object, both start and end stops will inherit that color, only the start stop will be fully opaque and the end stop will be fully transparent.

We can also drag outside the object. In this case, the gradient will start with the color of the object under our mouse pointer, and finish with a fully transparent one. If the color of the object has not been set, the last used color will be selected and applied.

Color stops can be selected one by one by clicking on them with the **Gradient** tool, or many at once by holding *Shift* while making a rectangle selection around them. When selected their colors can be changed just like flat colors; using the **Fill** and **Stroke** boxes, **Fill and Stroke** dialogue, clicking the color palette color chips or dragging the color chips and dropping them on top of the gradient color stop.

Dragging a color chip from a palette and dropping it on a gradient path will automatically create a new color stop of the dragged color. This is depicted in the following image; the left screenshot shows how the mouse pointer changes as we drag an orange chip to the gradient path, and the right one shows the result you get after dropping the chip:

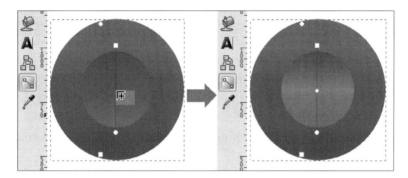

It is also possible to snap the end stops together so we can move both gradients at the same time. When we select the stop that is snapped to another one, the color boxes in the bottom left of the window and in the **Fill and Stroke** dialogue and the Style indicator will show the average of the two colors combined. To separate them again hold *Shift* while clicking and dragging either stop.

There's more...

Working with gradients doesn't *stop* there (pun intended). Several more options are available for us to make Inkscape gradients even more convenient and fun to use.

Gradient through multiple objects

Applying a gradient isn't restricted to just one object; it is possible to select more than one object and apply one gradient through all of them, with the same gradient path position. In the following image you can see a gradient with 10 color stops applied to the fills of three different objects at the same time:

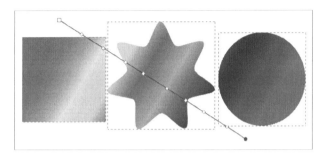

Gradient repeat

In the examples seen so far we have seen that the colors blend between color stops that are on the gradient path. If the gradient path is shorter than the object, the area beyond the end stops are filled with flat color of the end stops.

There is a way to repeat gradients beyond their paths, and there are two choices you can make: **reflected** or **direct**. You can find this option in the **Fill and Stroke** dialogue when an object with a gradient is selected. In the following image we can see three objects with the same gradient applied, but with different **Repeat** options chosen:

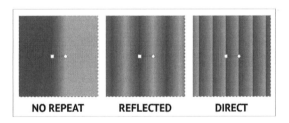

Moving gradients along with objects

In most cases when we move an object that has a gradient we want the overall look of the object to remain intact. Since the gradient path isn't attached to the object itself we have to make it move along with the object it is attached to. This is accomplished by enabling the **Move gradients (in fill or stroke) along with the objects** button 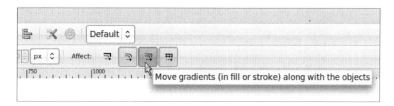 before moving the object. This button is located on the right-hand side of the **Selector** toolbar and is normally enabled by default.You have to switch to the **Selector** tool to use it, or you can set this option in **Inkscape Preferences** (*Shift + Ctrl + P*) | **Transforms** | **Transform gradients**.

Gradient sharing

There are many times when we need our objects to share colors. For example when creating a button set we want all our buttons to have the same look and feel. Perhaps the buttons need to fit into a website where blue palette dominates, so it makes sense to create bluish buttons. But what happens when we also want to use those buttons on a website where red is the primary color? Editing all the buttons one by one to adjust to a new base color is tedious and unnecessary.

Hopefully there is more than one way to solve our icon set problem, but here we'll describe only how sharing the same gradient between objects can help.

There is an option in Inkscape preferences under **Misc** that is on by default and prevents sharing of gradient definitions. So if you want to take advantage of sharing the same gradient between many objects you have to untick that box.

Once you do that, if you have objects styled with the same gradient and you modify that particular gradient by editing a stop, all the other objects "tagged" with that gradient will also be updated.

You can still share gradients between object even without selecting this option, by copying and pasting their style, but once you modify the gradient, it becomes a copy of the original and, therefore, independent.

The same applies to the gradient to the multiple objects case discussed earlier. If sharing gradients is prevented as soon as you change the gradient on one of those three objects a new gradient will be created for that object, and the other two will keep the old one.

Smoothing out abrupt color changes—simulating non-linear gradients

In gradients with more than two color stops we sometimes get transitions that don't seem smooth enough. The sudden unevenness can be seen at the intermediate color stops when differences in color between consecutive stops are too large. Here is an example:

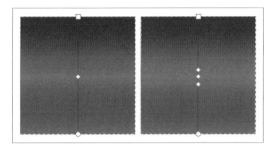

The left square seems to have a visible red line running through the middle. To make the area around the red stop smoother we create two additional stops very close to the red one. Create one a bit above the red stop, the other a bit below, and then move them away from the middle just a bit. The square on the right shows the final position of the stops.

The trick here is to guess where to create the additional stops and how much to move them away so you don't create more sharp changes. For best results, don't zoom in to add the stops, because that will put them too close to the middle one, and don't move them too far. Add more stops if the gradient is not smooth enough.

Moving intermediate stops along the gradient paths changes the blending dynamics so it's not linear any more looking at the whole gradient path between the end stops, although the blend is always linear between consecutive stops. This is how we simulate non-linear gradients using many smaller linear ones.

Reverse gradient orientation

Even though it is possible to simply drag the end stops of a gradient to change its orientation there is even a simpler way—using the *Shift + R* shortcut:

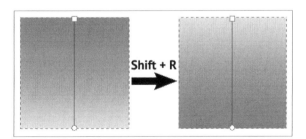

This shortcut doesn't exchange the end stops positions like in the case when dragging them by hand. The start (square) and end (circle) stops haven't moved, only their colors have changed. If there are intermediate stops their positions are adjusted to the change in the orientation.

This shortcut is especially useful when dealing with radial gradients because we can't reverse the radial gradient orientation by dragging handles.

Remove unnecessary stops from complex gradients

When creating complex and multi-color gradients, it's easy to get carried away by an artistic frenzy and end up with more stops than necessary. Maybe we created an intermediate stop but didn't change its color, or moved it and forgot about it. That kind of stop doesn't add any new information to the gradient and can freely be removed without any worries that the gradient will be changed.

To remove unnecessary gradient stops first select all the stops on the gradient path you suspect might be redundant ones. *Ctrl + A* will select them all, and click while holding *Shift* and drag around them to select only the ones in the area encompassed. Once we have the selection we want, **Simplify** (*Ctrl + L*, or **Menu | Path | Simplify**) will do the rest.

Editing gradients using other tools

Gradients, once created, can be edited using other tools, such as **Node**, **Tweak**, **Spray**, **Zoom**, all of the shapes, **Text**, and **Dropper**. New stops can also be created by dragging color chips from the palette onto the gradient path.

This saves us from a lot of tool switching when dealing with gradient tweaks.

See also

For more information, refer to *Recreating HAL 9000 using radial gradients*, the recipe that follows.

Recreating HAL 9000 using radial gradients

Along with linear gradients, Inkscape also comes with radial gradients. In radial gradients color stops define different circle radii and the color blends between them.

Everything we've learned about linear gradients can be applied to radial ones as well. Radial gradients also have some special features, we will take a look at them throughout this recipe.

In the following recipe, we will create a radial gradient by taking inspiration from an iconic image in sci-fi cinematography.

Getting ready

"Just what do you think you're doing, Dave?" – HAL 9000

If you haven't watched Stanley Kubrick's masterpiece *2001: A Space Odyssey*, you might not know what the iconic computer HAL 9000 looks like. Take a peek at the finished drawing on the following pages to see what we're about to create, or visit Wikipedia for a detailed description: `http://en.wikipedia.org/wiki/HAL_9000`.

Since the famous scene from the movie takes place in outer space, we will want to place HAL 9000 in a more appropriate visual context, such as a black background.

You can do this in **Document Properties** (*Shift + Ctrl + D*) on the **Page** tab. Don't forget to set the **A** (Alpha) box to 255 (fully opaque) because the default is set to 0 (fully transparent).

How to do it...

The following steps will show you how to create HAL 9000:

1. Select the **Ellipse** tool (*F5*).

2. Draw a large circle by holding the *Ctrl* key.

3. Fill the circle with **Yellow (#FFFF00)** color, set stroke width to 50 or 100, whichever makes more sense to serve as a rim, and color the stroke **30% Gray**.

4. Select **Gradient** tool (*G*).

5. Make sure that the button on the gradient toolbar **Create radial (elliptic or circular) gradient** ▢ and **Create gradient in the fill** ▢ are selected:

6. Hold *Ctrl* to constrain movement to vertical, click in the center of the bounding box, drag downwards to create a radial gradient fill and release when you reach object bounding box.

7. Click on the **Black** color chip to change the end stop to black.

8. Hold *Ctrl* while dragging the right end stop until you reach the object bounding box.

9. Hold *Ctrl + Shift* while clicking on the bottom end stop and move it towards the center, release after you've traveled approximately one third the distance towards the center. This is what you should end up with something closely similar to the following image:

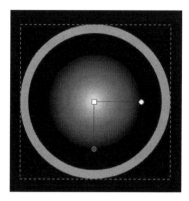

10. Create a new stop approximately at the center of the gradient path by double-clicking.

11. Select the new stop and color it **Red (#FF0000)**. Drag the red stop halfway towards the center and release it.

12. Create a new stop half way between the red and start (square) stop by double-clicking on the gradient path. Move the new stop half way towards the center. On the gradient toolbar select button **Create gradient in the stroke**:

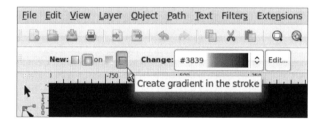

13. Increase the opacity of the end (circle) stop by replacing 0 with 100 in the **Opacity** box in the **Style** indicator.

14. Click and drag the start stop (square) towards the center until it snaps with the fill gradient start stop.

15. Hold *Ctrl* while dragging the top end stop until you reach the object bounding box. Hold *Ctrl* while dragging the left end stop until you reach the object bounding box. Hold *Ctrl + Shift* while clicking on the top end stop and move it a bit towards the center, release when you've traveled one third of the stroke width.

16. Create a new stop by double-clicking approximately at the center of the gradient path leg. Select the new stop and color it **80% Gray**. Drag the new gray stop outwards until it reaches the end stop over the stroke, you should end up with the final HAL 9000 staring eerily at us:

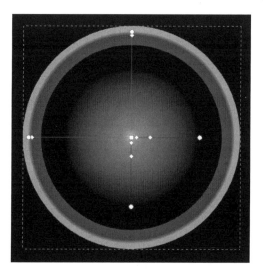

How it works...

Radial gradients are set by manipulating a gradient path that has two perpendicular legs. If the legs are the same length we get a circular gradient, if one is longer than the other we get an elliptical gradient.

We can also enhance the gradient by placing extra stops on of the legs; any additions will also be mirrored on the other legs. If the legs aren't of the same length the stops will be placed and moved proportionally.

Holding *Ctrl* while creating a new gradient can be of assistance when creating gradients constrained to specific angles. This is useful when creating circular gradients, and especially so when snapping is enabled. Start stops can be snapped to the object center and end stops can be snapped to object bounding box or object path.

To maintain the same leg-length ratio hold *Shift + Ctrl* while dragging one of the end stops.

It can be a bit challenging to edit gradients when both fill and stroke are set to circular gradients. Often we want their start stops to snap together at the object center, but after we do that we can't edit the start stops independently—whatever color you apply both stops will take it. The workaround is to edit one of the gradients off-center and snap it after you've achieved the desired look. Or simply detach one gradient from the other by holding *Shift* while dragging start stop away whenever a change is needed.

HAL 9000 can also be created without the stroke, by using a complex gradient on the fill. Look for the example without stroke in the SVG file `RadialGradients.svg` accompanying this chapter.

There's more...

HAL 9000 is a good example of what a few symmetric, circular gradients can accomplish. It is also possible to create asymmetric radial gradients by moving the gradient center away from the start stop. The gradient center isn't normally visible, but when dragged away from the start stop it is represented with a cross. Here's an example:

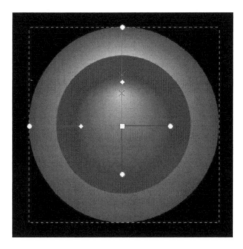

The fill radial gradient controls the little "orb" we see in the middle. Its gradient center is offset a bit towards the top creating a 3D effect. Stroke gradient center is also offset towards the top also providing a 3D effect on the stroke.

Can you guess how the following example was created? If not, peek inside `RadialGradients.svg` accompanying this chapter.

See also

For more information, refer to the recipe on *Creating linear gradients* in this chapter.

Patterns

Inkscape comes with several patterns ready to be applied to either fill or stroke of an object. Most of them are vector based but there are also three bitmap patterns available.

It is often necessary to create your own pattern which can be quite easy with the **Object to Pattern** option.

This recipe will provide an overview of the basics of pattern editing in Inkscape.

Getting ready

Assigning patterns can only be done from the **Fill and Stroke** dialogue window (*Shift + Ctrl + F*) so it's useful to keep it open when dealing with patterns.

How to do it...

The following steps will outline how to create patterns:

1. Select the **Ellipse** tool (*F5*) and draw a large ellipse to almost fill the page area.
2. Under the **Fill** tab of the **Fill and Stroke** dialogue window choose the **Pattern** button:

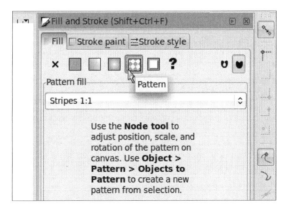

3. Choose **Ermine** from the **Pattern fill** drop-down list. Notice that three handles have now appeared on the top left of the page.
4. Click and drag the square handle while holding *Ctrl* to scale the pattern without changing its aspect ratio. Drag it downwards and to the right to make it larger.
5. Click and drag the round handle located on the top page border to rotate the pattern.

6. Click and drag the cross handle located at the top-left corner of the page to adjust the pattern offset, this is what you end up with:

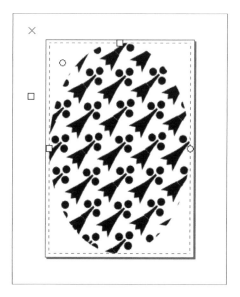

How it works...

All the patterns available for use on objects can be seen listed in the **Fill and Stroke** dialogue. User generated patterns will also appear on this list and will take precedence appearing at the top.

A pattern can be edited using the **Node** tool, all of the shapes, and the **Paint Bucket** tool. This is convenient because we don't have to switch between tools all the time to perform minor pattern tweaks.

As we have seen, there are three handles available for editing patterns:

▶ The cross handle that shifts (translates) the pattern inside the object

▶ The square handle that resizes the pattern

▶ The circle handle that rotates the pattern

Moving the cross handle also moves the square and circle handles so we can always expect them to appear together. Things do get a bit tricky when the pattern is scaled to a much larger size. In this case, the handles will end up far in between.

Moving the circle handle rotates the pattern, and it also rotates the handles positions. This is also something to be aware of when you have trouble locating the handles.

The editing handles are usually positioned at the top-left corner of the page. If a pattern was created from an object the handles will appear on that object.

What to do when handles are far away from the object

When working on an object that is far away from where the pattern handles appear it is useful to move the handles closer to the object by dragging the cross handle closer to the object. Circle and square pattern handles will move along with the cross handle.

There's more...

Probably the most fun we can have with patterns is creating our own. To illustrate this, we used an object from an example in the recipe with the radial gradients and converted it to a pattern by going to **Object | Pattern | Objects** (*Alt + I*):

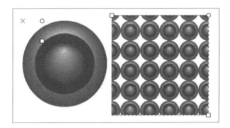

The object on the left is the original one that got converted to a pattern. After that step the handles are positioned at the object's corners, cross at top left, circle at top right, and square handle at the bottom-right corner of the object. After applying the newly created pattern to a rectangle the pattern was the same size as the original object which seemed a little too large so we used the square handle to make it smaller. This is the result seen in the image above.

Moving patterns along with objects

Just like with gradients if we want to make the pattern move along with the object it is applied to, we have to make sure that the button **Move patterns (in fill or stroke) along with the objects** is enabled. This button is located on the right-hand side of the **Selector** toolbar, so you have to switch to the **Selector** tool to use it, or you can set this option in **Inkscape Preferences** (*Shift + Ctrl + P*) | **Transforms** | **Transform patterns**.

Pattern edges visible

Inkscape will smoothen object edges by applying an antialiasing effect to them. This can cause problems in patterns and clones where objects are placed one next to another; there is an unwanted thin but visible crack between the objects.

Although it is not currently possible to disable antialiasing, we can suppress it when we generate a bitmap image. The way to do it is to assure that all object edges are perfectly snapped to a 1x1 grid, then export our drawing at the default resolution of 90 DPI.

See the Inkscape FAQ for more information:

`http://wiki.inkscape.org/wiki/index.php/FAQ`

Clipping bitmaps using patterns

Even though clipping is a separate option in Inkscape and in most cases it's easier to use clipping than patterns. It isn't supported by all SVG viewers so sometimes you'll want to use patterns instead.

The procedure is the same as with any other pattern. First we must turn an imported bitmap image into a pattern, then apply that pattern to an object. The object shape will determine the "clipping" area, as in the following image:

See also

For more information, refer to the recipe on *Creating a button to use with the CSS Sliding Doors technique* in *Chapter 10*.

Picking and assigning colors with the Dropper tool

It's hard to imagine any graphics application without a **Dropper** tool (often also called **color picker**). In Inkscape, you simply select an object, select the **Dropper** tool, and click anywhere on canvas to assign the color under the cursor to the object fill (or stroke if you hold *Shift* while clicking). This works as expected if the object you are picking from is fully opaque.

There are more options when picking the color from a partially transparent object and this is what we will investigate in this recipe.

Getting ready

Having the **Fill and Stroke** dialogue window open helps with tracking how different **Dropper** tool options interact with object opacity so make sure you open it (*Shift + Ctrl + F*).

How to do it...

The following steps show the various interactions of the **Dropper** tool with different objects:

1. Select the rectangle tool (*F4*) and create a tall rectangle. Set its fill to **Green (#008000)**, and its **Opacity, %** to 50.

2. Create three squares on the right-hand side of the tall rectangle and make sure their **Opacity, %** is set to 100.

3. Select the first square. Select the **Dropper** tool ![dropper icon] (*F7* or *D*); the first square will remain selected. Make sure that neither **Pick** nor **Assign** opacity options are active on the **Dropper** toolbar. Click anywhere on the tall rectangle.

4. Switch to **Selector** tool (*Space* or *F1*). Select the second square. Select the **Dropper** tool (*Space*, *F7* or *D*) and make sure that the **Pick** option is active but **Assign** is not. Click anywhere on the tall rectangle. The square will remain unchanged.

5. Switch to the **Selector** tool (*Space* or *F1*). Select the third square. Select the **Dropper** tool (*Space*, *F7* or *D*) and make sure that both **Pick** and **Assign** options are active. Click anywhere on the tall rectangle.

The following image displays the workflow and the result of this recipe:

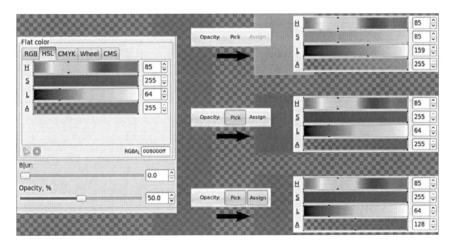

How it works...

When using the **Dropper** tool to pick colors from partially transparent objects there are two options: **Pick** and **Assign** that can be combined in three different ways that influence the outcome.

The checkerboard pattern was applied to the background of the earlier image so it's more clear which areas are partially transparent and which are opaque. The transparency information can also be read from the screenshots of color information for each object. The squares all have full overall opacity so their transparency is only governed by the **A** (alpha) box as seen in the screenshots. The following are the results:

▸ For the first square, the opacity wasn't picked, so Inkscape use the same color that the rectangle appears to have due to the transparency: a lighter shade of green.

▸ For the second square, the opaque color is picked but the 50% opacity isn't assigned. Therefore, the square remained unchanged with the same color and no transparency.

▸ For the third and last rectangle, both color and opacity were picked and applied, therefore the style appears to be copied and pasted, as if we were using the **Paste Style** option (*Shift + Ctrl + V*). The dropper, however, only modified the RBGA values of the color, not the object's opacity. Use **Edit | Paste Style** to paste all the attributes of the style.

There's more...

So far we have only been clicking on the canvas to pick color, but clicking and dragging is also available. Dragging with the **Dropper** tool creates a circular selection, the average color of that region is picked to be applied to the object:

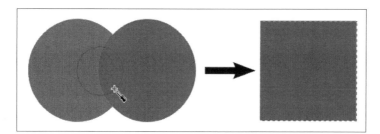

This can especially be useful with bitmap textures. Here we are selecting the average color of all the pixels inside the circular selection:

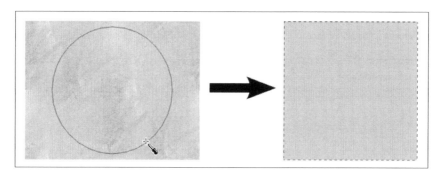

Inverse picked color

Holding the *Alt* key while using the **Dropper** tool inverts the color:

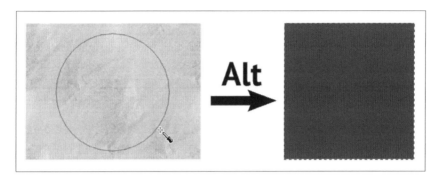

Copy color under cursor

One other useful feature of **Dropper** tool is that with *Ctrl + C* we can copy the color that is under the cursor into the clipboard. No objects need to be selected for this to work.

Once we have a color in our clipboard we can select an object to paste the color with *Ctrl + V*.

If the object that is under the cursor when copying is partially transparent all the Dropper option combinations we tested earlier will influence the result, so we have to pay attention to which options are active.

Adjusting hue, lightness, saturation, and stroke width using Color Gestures

Mouse gestures are a way of accomplishing certain tasks simply by moving or dragging your mouse in a certain manner, and are often employed in applications and games to improve the user experience. Inkscape comes with mouse gestures available in the style indicator at the bottom-left of the screen. This is where the dragging to change hue, lightness, or saturation begins.

Most often we will want to change the lightness and saturation of a color. Website color palettes often include several colors that vary only slightly in lightness or saturation, and in illustrations we often add highlights and shadows that use the same base color with modified lightness.

Color Gestures offer a way to do this interactively so we see the changes in real time on screen. It's much easier to hit the correct shades this way, unburdened with numbers and only relying on visual feedback.

In this recipe we will go through several gestured color changes on the same object to see what it feels like to use the gestures in an ordinary workflow.

Getting ready

Color boxes in the **Fill and Stroke** dialogue also update in real time with Color Gestures so open it (*Shift + Ctrl + F*) and take notice while making the gestures. Seeing the indicators move as you gesture across the screen can be a very direct and simple method of understanding how the program is interpreting the motion of the pointer.

Generally speaking, Web designers and pixel artists prefer to use **RGB** for compatibility reasons, while photographers and printing industry professionals tend to work exclusively in the **CMYK** color space. However, many computer artists prefer using the **HSL** (**Hue – Saturation – Lightness**) color space, striking a good balance between computational speed and perceptual relevance. We will use it in this recipe, so make sure you select it in the **Fill and Stroke** dialogue.

How to do it...

The following steps will show you how to use Color Gestures:

1. Select the **Rectangle** tool (*F4*) and draw a rectangle.
2. Color its fill **Red (#FF0000)** and stroke **(#A02C2C).**
3. Click and hold the fill box in the Style indicator, and drag away towards the middle of the window under the angle of approximately 45°.
4. Still not releasing the mouse move it slowly towards the top left corner of the window and back towards the bottom right corner. Keep an eye on the **Fill and Stroke** dialogue as you drag.
5. Release the mouse when over green area of the **H** box in the **Fill and Stroke** dialogue window, this will turn the object fill to lime green.
6. Hold *Ctrl* while dragging on the fill box, move it away towards the window center and move back and forth like in Step 4, keeping an eye on the **Fill and Stroke** dialogue.
7. Release the mouse when in the lower part of the window to change the fill color to a dark green.
8. Switch to the **Stroke paint** tab in the **Fill and Stroke** dialogue window.
9. Hold *Shift* while dragging the stroke box, move it away towards the window center, and move back and forth like in Step 4, while keeping an eye on the **Fill and Stroke** dialogue.
10. Release the mouse when in the top part of the window to change the stroke color to dark red.
11. Click and drag away from the stroke width box in the Style indicator, move it slowly towards the top-left corner of the window and back towards the bottom-right corner to see the stroke width change.

12. Release the mouse when in the top part of the window to make the stroke width larger.

Here is a screenshot of some of the steps from this recipe:

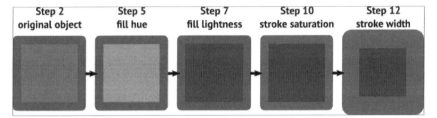

How it works...

There is an imaginary line that goes from the Style indicator towards the canvas under the angle of 45°. Moving the mouse above that line increases the property value and moving it below decreases it.

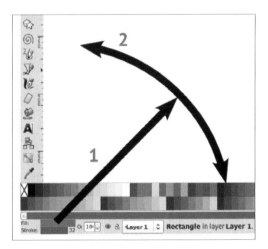

With no modifier key hue is adjusted, *Ctrl* changes the lightness, *Shift* changes the saturation, and clicking on the stroke width box changes the stroke width.

There's more...

It isn't necessary to stop between different value changes. Try dragging the mouse diagonally from top-left to bottom-right while interchangeably releasing and holding the *Ctrl* and *Shift* keys.

Hold *Alt* while dragging to freeze the changes for a moment so you can reposition the mouse to a better spot. This is especially useful when encountering the window border while dragging.

You might be wondering about the opacity box in the Style indicator since this is the only option we haven't mentioned. This box doesn't react to click-dragging but you can put your mouse wheel to use here. Hover over the box with the mouse pointer and scroll the wheel up or down to change opacity.

Different color icon sets using RGB Barrel

"Do a barrel roll!" – Peppy, in 'Star Fox' for the 90's SNES gaming console..

Inkscape comes with several extensions that change the object color according to a certain set of options and conditions. These extensions can be found under the menu **Extensions | Color**. It is easy to guess from their names what each of them does (**Grayscale, Less Light, More Saturation**).

In this recipe we will use the RGB Barrel extension to very quickly create several copies of the same icon but with a different overall color palette.

Getting ready

The icon we are going to experiment on is a group of two objects, one is the icon background in the shape of a rectangle with rounded corners, and the other is the icon sign itself. The background object is styled with a three-stop blue gradient to give it more depth and the icon is white so it will be intact after the encounter with the RGB Barrel.

Open the `RGBbarrel.svg` file accompanying this chapter, the icon is there ready to be RGB-barreled.

How to do it...

The following steps will show you how to copy an icon, using RGB Barrel:

1. Select and hold the blue icon with the **Selector** tool (*F1*) and hit *Space* to make a copy.
2. Drop the original icon next to the new one (it will stay selected).
3. Go to **Extensions | Color | RGB Barrel**.
4. Select and hold the red icon with the **Selector** tool (*F1*) and hit *Space* to make a copy.
5. Drop the icon next to the new one (it will stay selected).
6. Go to **Extensions | Color | RGB Barrel**, the end result should look like the following:

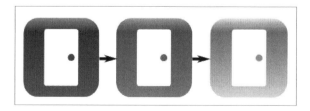

How it works...

The RGB Barrel extension takes the object colors and changes their hue by shifting it 120° around the color circle. This way blue colors turn into red, red into green, and green back into blue, so there are never more than three different items in a RGB Barrel set.

If the object is styled with a gradient all gradient stops will be transformed one by one. Since icons are often made according to this principle, this tool makes it easy to create an icon set with a large range of colors. Our icon is styled with the shades of the same color, but it works the same on all kinds of color combinations:

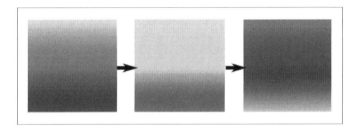

There's more...

If you don't like the colors you end up with you can tweak them with other tools and try RGB Barrel again. Other color extensions can help with the tweaking as well as the **Tweak** tool (Jitter colors).

See also

For more information refer to the recipe on *Changing icon colors using tiled clones* in *Chapter 4*.

3

Speeding Up Your Workflow

In this chapter, we will cover:

- ▶ Autosaving documents
- ▶ Designing plate rims using Layers
- ▶ Creating geometric illusions using Grids
- ▶ Creating a simple flashlight using Guides
- ▶ Creating a stylized flower using Snapping
- ▶ Designing a leaflet using Align and Distribute
- ▶ Creating your own custom color swatches
- ▶ Creating your own color palette
- ▶ More time-saving tips
- ▶ Importing drawings from **OpenClipArt**

Introduction

Most veterans of the computer graphics industry will tell you that the secret to producing high quality visuals doesn't necessarily depend on natural talent.

Rather, it's a matter of planning a strategy and putting dedication and hard work into executing it. No matter how complex, any problem can be fragmented into a set of more digestible parts. Deadlines, the bane of all professionals, are easier to meet if you have your work carefully planned out for you beforehand.

In this chapter, we will introduce and explore some commonly used workflows, which will soon become second nature to us. With time and experience, we will develop our own workflows to deal with new and unexpected situations.

Keyboard shortcuts play an important part of speeding up our activities. So we will mention them often in recipes. The Inkscape developers took great care in providing intuitive keyboard shortcuts, making the easier to remember; for example, * for the **Star** tool or # for toggling grid visibility. You can find the list under **Help | Keys and Mouse Reference** or by visiting the following site:

`http://inkscape.org/doc/keys047.html`

Autosaving documents

Although Inkscape is a mature and stable software product, why take the risk of losing our work due to an unexpected, catastrophic event? The **autosave** feature takes away the need to manually save every now and then, letting us concentrate on our task. If a disaster should occur, we can revert to our most recent autosave, losing at worst 10 minutes of our time.

How to do it...

Follow these steps to enable **autosave**:

1. Create a folder somewhere on your system where you intend to keep the autosaved versions of your files.

2. Open **File | Inkscape Preferences** (*Shift + Ctrl + P*) | **Save**.

3. Tick the **Enable autosave (requires restart)** option.

4. Enter the number 5 into the **Interval (in minutes):** box.

5. In the **Path:** field, enter the *relative* path (to your home directory) or *absolute* path to the folder you created in Step 1.

6. Enter the number 10 into the **Maximum number of autosaves:** box.

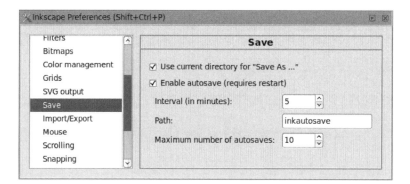

7.   Close **Inkscape Preferences**, close Inkscape, and restart it.

How it works...

We had to close the Inkscape window so it would pick up the new preferences the next time it starts; only certain preferences require this.

If we leave the **Path:** field empty with **autosave** enabled, the autosaved files will be stored in the temporary folder of your system.

The **Maximum number of autosaves** limits the number of autosaved files in the folder. Older files get deleted when the maximum is reached.

There's more...

Next to **autosave** there are some other saving-related options to consider.

If you use the **Save As...** option ![] (*Shift + Ctrl + S*) to save in the folder where the currently open file is located, tick the **Use current directory for "Save As ..."** option in the **Save** preferences. Otherwise, the **Save As...**option will remember the folder where we last saved a file and open it.

Exporting to formats other than SVG

As with any other application, it's always best to save the file in the native format (Inkscape SVG) and only export into other formats as necessary. This is because only the native format can save every feature or editing method we used in our document. Saving to other formats may lose some editing options or object properties, so we won't be able to edit them the same as if we had saved them in native format. If our end product is a PNG, EPS, or a PDF file, we should create and save it as Inkscape SVG and save the drawing in a different format when we are done with it.

 Take particular care when saving your work in formats other than Inkscape native format, such as the Plain SVG format. Some Inkscape-specific information might be removed and the drawing might not look the same when we reopen it.

Using the **Save a Copy...** (*Shift + Ctrl + Alt + S*) option during editing, we can save the current state of the file under a different name and continue editing it without interrupting our workflow. This option is also useful if we want to make document copies in another format during editing.

Designing plate rims using Layers

If you have worked with a raster graphics program such as The Gimp or Photoshop, you might have used the layers system to view and manipulate different parts of a picture.

In Inkscape, we will find that there is less emphasis on this concept and more on objects. Still, using layers can prove quite handy in some situations and therefore Inkscape provides a system to create and manage them.

In this recipe, our goal will be to draw a kitchen plate with two options for the pattern rim design. This is the drawing with one of the patterns active:

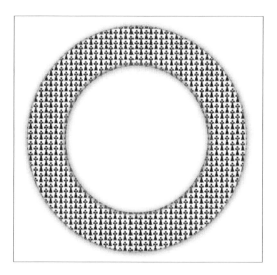

How to do it...

The following steps will show you how to design your plate rims:

1. Open the **Fill and Stroke** (*Shift + Ctrl + F*) and **Layers** 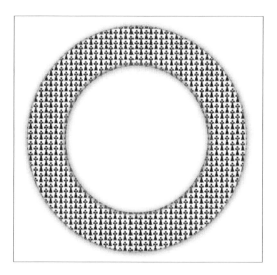 dialogs (*Shift + Ctrl + L*).

2. Create a circle using the **Ellipse** tool (*F5* or *E*) while holding *Ctrl*, make it as large as the page. Set its fill to none, its stroke to **White** (it will blend with the background), and set the stroke width to 150.

3. Duplicate the circle (*Ctrl + D*). Set its stroke color to **30% Gray** and **Blur:** slider to 3.

4. Press the *Esc* key once. The focus will shift from the **Fill and Stroke** dialog window and back to the object.

5. Move the duplicated circle to the bottom of the stack using the *End* or *Page Down* key on your keyboard.

6. Move the duplicated circle a little to the bottom and right with the bottom and right arrow keys.

7. Open the **Layers** dialog (*Shift + Ctrl + L*). Click on the current layer and rename it to "Plate Shadow".

8. Click on the **Plus** button ⊞ on the **Layers** dialog to add a new layer (*Shift + Ctrl +N*). In the pop-up window, enter "Plate pattern" as the name for the new layer. Select **Above current,** and click **Add**.

9. Click on the **Plus** button on the **Layers** dialog to add a new layer (*Shift + Ctrl +N*). In the pop-up window, enter "Plate 3D" as the name for the new layer. Select **Above Current** and click **Add.**

10. Click on the white stroke of the visible circle to select it. Duplicate it twice using *Ctrl + D*. Press the *Shift + Page Up* twice to move the object two layers up; it will end up in the **Plate 3D** layer.

11. Hold *Alt* while clicking on the white stroke to select the object below the one that is currently selected. Press the *Shift + Page Up* once to move the object one layer up; it will end up in the **Plate pattern** layer.

12. On the **Stroke paint** tab in the **Fill and Stroke** dialog, click on the **Pattern** button, select the **Polka dots, large** pattern from the drop-down menu. It won't be visible because the object from the **Plate 3D** layer is covering it.

13. Click on the white stroke on the canvas to select the object from the **Plate 3D** layer. Change its stroke color to **Black**.

14. Select the **Gradient** tool (*Ctrl + F1* or *G*) and create a symmetric radial gradient in the stroke, and set the end stop to **30% Gray**.

15. Edit the gradient to create a 3D illusion on the plate rim edges. To do this, create a new stop close to the start stop and move it towards the inner stroke edge, release before you reach the edge. Then create another one near the end stop, select it and lower the **Opacity, %** slider to 2. Finally, create the third stop within the stroke near the inner edge. Then select it, change its color to **White**, and set the **Opacity, %** slider to 0.

16. Right-click on the **Plate pattern** layer in the **Layers** dialog and select **Duplicate Current Layer**.

17. In the **Stroke paint** tab in the **Fill and Stroke** dialog, select the **Ermine** pattern from the drop-down menu.

18. Toggle **Plate pattern copy** layer visibility by clicking on the **Eye** icon 👁.

How it works...

To improve the photorealism of our kitchen plate, we used a couple objects, one below the drawing and one on top. In between lies the actual pattern. This kind of a "sandwich" can be achieved in one layer by stacking objects on top of each other.

But what happens when we need to create a different pattern? We can reuse all of the objects and only change the object with the pattern. However, this way we lose the pattern we first created. We can duplicate the pattern object but then switching between which pattern object is currently used can be somewhat difficult When drawings become complex, micromanaging the objects can be time consuming.

That is why we separated objects into different layers. Bottom and top layers hold the bottom and top shadows, while in between we can have as many patterns as needed. Layer visibility can be easily toggled so making sure that only one pattern is visible at a time is a matter of a few simple clicks.

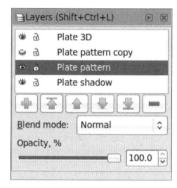

In this recipe, we created two patterns for our plate; each is on its own layer so we can easily switch between them by toggling their visibility. The examples from this recipe can be found in the `LayersPlate.svg` file. More fun with plates can be had by checking out `LayersPlateFull.svg`, where plates can be optionally filled with treats through the use of layers:

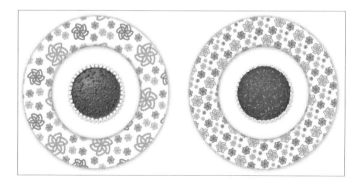

There's more...

Some operations involving layers can be done without having the **Layers** dialog open. In the bottom-left of the Inkscape window there are some layer options: switch layer with the current layer selected, layer visibility, and lock icons. If you don't need to duplicate layers or use blends, you can do everything with these options and a few memorized shortcuts that can be found on the **Layer** menu.

If you are working with many different layers and objects, and things are becoming confusing, you can use the lock button to *freeze* that particular layer and prevent any changes from being made to it, or the eye button to *hide* that layer from view.

XML editor as textual layers dialog

The SVG file format is based on XML (Extensible Markup Language) and can be edited using a simple text editor, such as Notepad or TextEdit. Inkscape parses the textual data and renders it in graphical elements on the canvas, while also providing a WYSIWYG editing environment. Additionally, it also provides a specialized text editor that can manipulate XML/SVG markup.

To open the XML editor, we can use the *Shift + Ctrl + X* shortcut or the **View and edit the XML tree of the document** button <> on the toolbar. Open it when viewing the LayersPlate. svg from this recipe and expand the layer elements using the little triangle icons next to them:

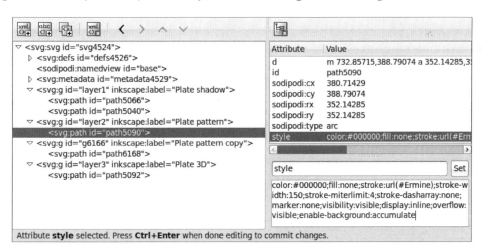

We can see that the position of layers and objects in an SVG document resembles the graphical z-order we see on the Canvas—the sooner they appear in markup, the lower they appear visually.

Selecting an object in the XML editor (by clicking on it) also selects it on the Canvas and vice-versa. This can be used to select objects that appear below others in complex drawings with lots of objects stacked on top of one another.

We also see the objects are enclosed within the tags of the layers they belong to. Elements can be dragged and dropped so we can use this editor to rearrange where layers and objects appear within the vertical stack or move objects between different layers.

SVG format and layers—Root layer

SVG doesn't have layers as part of its specification. To introduce this functionality into Inkscape, the already existing SVG group element was used, with an additional label defining the name of the layer. In other words, we must always remember that layers are Inkscape-only features and when saving a document into Plain SVG, our labels will be deleted and our layers will turn into plain SVG groups;

The area in the document that holds objects and layers if they exist is generally referred to as the "root".

Blend modes

You're probably familiar with layer blend modes as many graphics editing applications provide support for them. Inkscape comes with four layer blend modes in addition to Normal: Multiply, Screen, Darken, and Lighten. As expected, the Blend mode selector can be found in the **Layers** dialog.

The file `LayersBlends.svg` accompanying this chapter provides a convenient playground for testing blend modes:

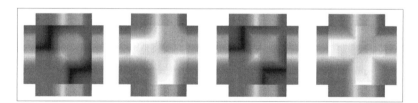

Geometric illusions using Grids

When working with a lot of geometric shapes or objects of predetermined sizes and positions, it is useful to use a grid to make drawing and positioning easier.

In this recipe, we will recreate a famous geometric illusion: Curry's Missing Square Puzzle, also known as Curry's paradox.

In Curry's paradox, a right triangle is divided into several shapes, and those shapes are then rearranged to again form a right rectangle of seemingly the equal surface, but something doesn't add up!

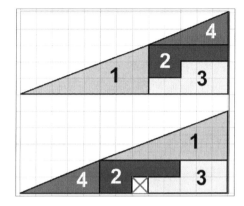

Where did that extra square come from? We will investigate and solve the mystery in this recipe.

How to do it...

The following recipe will illustrate the use of grids:

1. In the **Document Properties** (*Shift + Ctrl + D*) under the **Grid** tab, create a new rectangular grid by hitting the **New** button. Change the **Spacing X:** and **Spacing Y:** from the default 1 to 50 and close the **Document Properties** dialog:

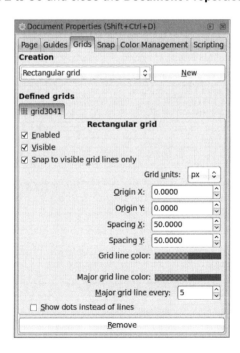

2. Select the **Pen** tool (*Shift* + *F6* or *B*) and, on the toolbar, set the **Mode:** to **Create a sequence of straight line segments** and **Shape:** to **None**.

3. Make sure that **Snap to grids** is enabled on the **Snapping** toolbar, so that when you're moving your mouse over grid intersections, you see snapping tooltips.

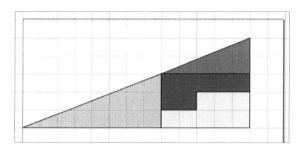

4. Start drawing the green right rectangle by clicking on the left page border (the grid is aligned with it) on the second major horizontal grid line from top (major grid lines appear thicker) like in the preceding image, the mouse pointer will snap there.

5. Move to the right along the horizontal direction counting eight grid intersections. Click there to create the second triangle corner, the pointer will snap to the grid.

6. Move straight to the top counting three grid intersections, click there to create the third triangle corner, the pointer will snap to the grid.

7. Go back to the first point and click there to close the triangle, set the triangle fill to **Lime (#00FF00)**, stroke to **Black**, and width to 2.

8. Start drawing the smaller right triangle by clicking on the top-right corner of the lime triangle.

9. Create the second corner by clicking five grid units to the right.

10. Create the third corner by clicking two grid units straight up.

11. Finish the triangle by clicking on the first triangle corner, set its fill to **Red (#FF0000)**, stroke to **Black**, and stroke width to 2.

12. Draw the blue L-shaped object by clicking on the point where triangles meet, click again on the bottom-right corner of the red triangle, five more clicks—one unit down, three left, one down, two left, and the last one to the starting point to close the shape. Set its fill to **Blue (#0000FF)**, stroke to **Black**, and stroke width to 2.

13. Draw the second L-shaped object to make the complete drawing a right triangle. Start at the bottom-left corner of the blue L-shaped object, then click 2 units right, 1 unit up, 3 units right, 2 units down, 5 units left, and 1 up to close the shape. Set its fill to **Yellow (#FFFF00)**, stroke to **Black**, and stroke width to 2.

14. Select **Selector** tool (*F1* or *S*). Select all objects in the drawing (*Ctrl + A*), duplicate the selection (*Ctrl + D*). Move the selection by clicking on it and dragging downwards, it will snap to the grid.

15. Rearrange the duplicated objects; move the red triangle left and down so its left corner aligns with the left corner of the green triangle, move the green triangle so its left corner aligns with the top corner of the red triangle, and finally move the blue shape left and down so it aligns with the red triangle. You will end up with the following figure:

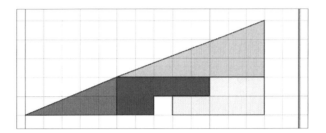

How it works...

If you're wondering about how the illusion works, the hint is in the last step when moving the red triangle over the green one. Have fun figuring it out!

 Hint: try zooming on the hypotenuse of the composite shape, with the grid enabled.

Each document in Inkscape can have its own set of grids. When we zoom out, the grid lines become hard to distinguish so Inkscape hides some of them to improve legibility, only leaving the major ones. As we zoom in more, grid line levels appear. It is recommended to set the grid spacing to the minimum unit you want to deal with in your drawing.

As seen in this recipe, grids are normally used with snapping to the grid to speed up the drawing process or arranging objects on the canvas.

There's more...

Our blue object had the same fill hue as grid lines so they seem to disappear over the object. Depending on the predominant colors in the drawing, the grid color can be changed to a color that stands out more. If you think the lines stand out more than necessary, you can reduce their opacity or use the **Show dots instead of lines** option. Check the **Document Properties** panel 📄 (*Shift + Ctrl + D*) in the **Grid** section.

Anti-aliasing and snapping to pixel grid

The Inkscape renderer applies anti-aliasing to object edges which can cause the edges to look blurry. This can be suppressed by snapping to the pixel grid. It is helpful to create two rectangle pixel grids, one with no origin shift and the other one with 0.5 pixel origin shift for both X and Y axes. Changing the second grid color or lines/dots option can help with separating them visually.

To suppress anti-aliasing on horizontal and vertical lines, all stroke widths must be a whole number (integer), the objects without a stroke or with an even-number stroke should be snapped to the grid without origin shift, and the objects with odd-number stroke widths should be snapped to the 0.5 origin shift grid. When exporting, make sure the dpi is set to 90, which is Inkscape default.

PixelSnap extension

There is an automatic way to snap to the pixel grid with stroke widths considered: **PixelSnap** extension. Simply select all the objects you want aligned this way and go to **Extensions | Modify Path | PixelSnap...**

Axonometric grid

To help with creating axonometric drawings, we can use **Axonometric grid**. When creating a new grid, in the **Document Properties**, there is an option to choose between rectangular and axonometric grid. The default settings are for isometric grid:

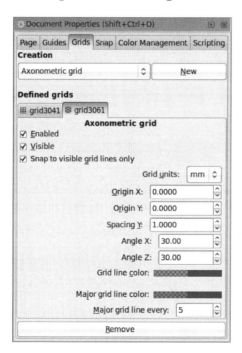

In an additional file accompanying this chapter, you can find another optical illusion example made with a help of the axonometric grid. The file's name is `GridAxonometric.svg` and the illusion is the Penrose Triangle illusion; try to recreate it yourself:

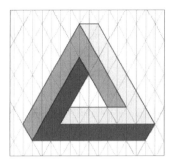

Just a couple of hints: you should use the **Pen (Bezier)** tool and draw *three* objects.

See also

For more information, refer to *Creating a stylized fower using Snapping* and *Creating a simple fashlight using Guides*, that can be found in this chapter.

Creating a simple flashlight using Guides

Guides are helper lines that aren't part of the drawing but help with creating and aligning objects. In this recipe we'll create a simple flashlight drawing to illustrate common options when using guides.

How to do it...

The following steps will show you how to create a flashlight using guides:

1. Click on the left ruler and drag to the canvas to create a vertical guide, double-click on the guide to get the options pop-up, and set **X:** to 280.

2. Click on the left ruler and drag to the canvas to create another vertical guide, double-click on the guide to get the options pop-up, and set **X:** to 480.

3. Click on the top ruler and drag it to the canvas to create a horizontal guide, double-click on the guide to get the options pop-up, and set **Y:** to 130.

4. Click on the top ruler and drag it to the canvas to create another horizontal guide, double-click on the guide to get the options pop-up, and set **Y:** to 470.

5. Create a rectangle by snapping to the guides intersections (the **Snap to guides** toolbar button must be selected). Set its fill to a gray linear gradient for a slight 3D effect, set the stroke to **70% Gray**.

6. Click near the top of the left rule and drag to the canvas to create an angled guide, snap it to the top-right corner of the rectangle. Double-click on the guide to get the options pop-up, set **Angle (degrees):** to 70.

7. Click near the top of the left rule and drag to the canvas to create another angled guide, snap it to the top-left corner of the rectangle, set **Angle (degrees):** to 110.

8. With the **Pen** tool (*Shift + F6* or *B*), draw a four-point object by snapping to the top rectangle corners and angled guides near the top of the page.

9. Set its fill to **Yellow (#FFFF00)** and remove stroke.

10. Use the **Gradient** tool (*Ctrl + F1* or *G*) to create a yellow radial gradient inside the four-point object.

11. Use the |key to turn off the guides and see your drawing:

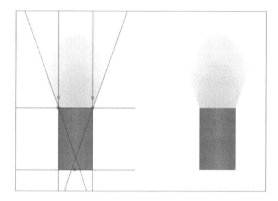

How it works...

If we click on a ruler and drag the pointer to the Canvas, we can conveniently create and deploy horizontal and vertical guides. If we need an angle of 45°, we can click and drag from the ruler corners. Dragging a guide back to the ruler deletes it. All guides can be angled at arbitrary angles and moved to different positions either using the options pop-up window or simply by selecting and dragging them with the **Selector** tool.

Using guides is most effective when **Snap to guides** is active. Every guide has a special point called the origin represented with a small circle on the guide. The origin can be used to snap to other guides or objects while dragging and the guide can be rotated around it. Guide information as well as available keyboard shortcuts are displayed in the Status bar when hovering over a guide.

There's more...

If the guides aren't easily visiblein their background context, we can change their color in the in the **Document Properties** (*Shift + Ctrl + D*), **Guides** tab.

The **Relative change** in the options pop-up can be useful when we need to make a new guide with an offset from an existing guide. The offset can be a shift in any specified direction or rotation.

Creating guides from objects

Guides can also be created from objects, by using using the **Menu | Objects | Object to Guides** command (*Shift + G*). The object is deleted in the process unless set otherwise in **Inkscape Preferences | Tools**. To get predictable results it's best to use objects with straight lines and convert shapes and text to paths. Here are a couple of examples (the object was duplicated before converting to guides so you can see the original):

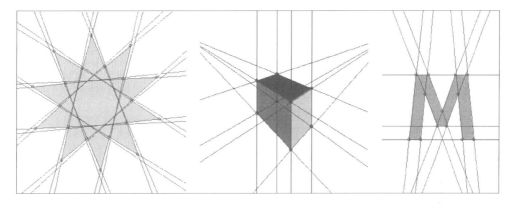

See also

For more information, refer to the recipe on *Geometric illusions using Grids*, seen earlier in this chapter. Also, in the last chapter of this book, we will create an extension that will split any object in sections using Python generated guides.

Creating a stylized flower using Snapping

This recipe is a little exercise in snapping. We'll try out different snapping options while arranging objects into a composite image of a stylized flower.

How to do it...

The following steps show you how to use the snapping option to create a flower:

1. Create a 300 x 300 pixel square, having rounded corners with a radius of 100 px. Set its fill to **Purple (#800080)** and its opacity to 50.

2. Convert it to a path (*Shift + Ctrl + C*).

3. Create three more copies by stamping with *Space* three times while holding it with your mouse.

4. Make sure that **Enable Snapping** is on. You can toggle it using the % key. **Snap nodes or handles**, **Snap to cusp nodes**, and **Snap to smooth nodes** on the **Snapping** toolbar.

5. Move the squares one by one so they overlap a bit and make their nodes snap so they form a flowery shape:

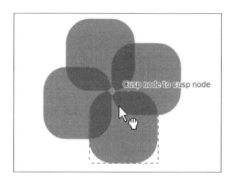

6. Select the **Star** tool (*Shift + F9* or ***) and set the options on the toolbar to: **Star**, **Corners:** 4 , **Spoke ratio:** 0.95, **Rounded:** 0.1, and **Randomized:** to 0.

7. Click near the center of the "flower", hold *Ctrl*, and drag away to create the star object, release when the star is larger than the "flower".

8. Lower the star to the bottom using *Page Down* four times or *End*, set its fill to **#FFB380**, and make sure the opacity is 50.

9. Select the **Ellipse** tool (*F5* or *E*) and draw a circle by clicking at the "flower" center to snap to it and holding *Ctrl* and *Shift* while dragging outwards to create a circle around the "flower" center. Set the circle fill to **#D40000** and make sure the opacity is set to 50.

10. Select the **Star** tool (*Shift + F9* or ***) and set the options on the toolbar to: **Star**, **Corners:** 7, **Spoke ratio:** 0.4, **Rounded:** 0, and **Randomized:** to 0.

11. Create a small star somewhere on canvas, set its fill to **Yellow (#FFFF00)**, stroke to **Fuchsia (#FF00FF)**, stroke width to 1, and opacity to 100.

12. Stamp the star seven times using the **Selector** tool (*Space* or *F1* or *S*) to get eight stars in total.

13. On the **Snapping** toolbar enable **Snap bounding box corners** ⬚ and **Snap to bounding box corners** ⬚.

14. Move each star towards a corner of the rectangles until their bounding box corners snap together:

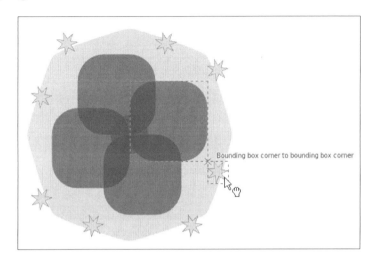

How it works...

With snapping enabled moving an object across Canvas or moving the mouse pointer triggers snapping indicators to appear and enables us to snap to the registered point.

The trick is to activate appropriate snapping settings for each situation and disable the rest so they don't interfere. Sometimes it's necessary to zoom in for snapping to be precise.

There's more...

Snapping occurs with a slight delay that can be adjusted in the **Inkscape Preferences** (*Shift + Ctrl + P*) under **Snapping**. If you prefer to make the snap immediate set the **Delay (in ms):** to 0.

Enabling the **Only snap the node closest to the pointer** option can help us to be more precise when snapping by grabbing the object close to the point we want to snap.

Under **Document Properties** (*Shift + Ctrl + D*) there is the **Snap** tab where we can change the option as to whether snapping should always occur or only when within a certain distance.

Snapping can sometimes get in the way; for example, we might want to disable it temporarily so we can move a particular object with precision, and this can be done by holding *Shift* while moving the object. The % key toggles snapping on or off so we can use this too as a quick snapping switch.

See also

For more information, refer to *Geometric illusions using Grids* and *Creating a stylized fower using Snapping*, in this chapter.

Leaflet design using Align and Distribute

Grid and snapping are excellent ways to get your drawing elements in the correct position, but they can sometimes be too much and in those cases the **Align and Distribute** options speed things up more.

We will design a simple leaflet to test this functionality. You can use similar colors as in the example or choose your own, as we won't focus much on colors in this recipe.

Let's take a look at what we will create in a few moments:

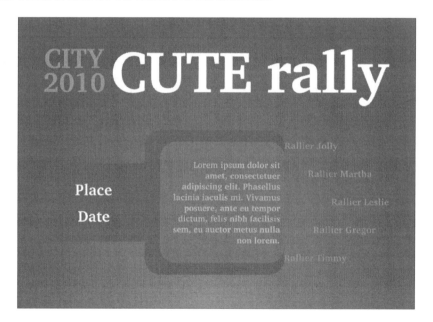

How to do it...

The following steps will show you how to create the preceding leaflet using **Align and Distribute**:

1. Switch the page orientation to **Landscape** in the **Document Properties** (*Shift + Ctrl + D*).

2. Create a page sized rectangle and fill it with a slight gradient to serve as the leaflet backdrop.

3. Create three text objects: "CUTE rally", "CITY", and "2010". Text size depends on the particular font, in my case 150, 72, and 72 seemed to work best.

4. Open the **Align and Distribute** dialogue ▤ (*Shift + Ctrl + A*).

5. Select "2010" and "CUTE rally" (in that order) objects and align their text baselines using the **Align baselines of texts** ▤ option. Make sure the **Relative to:** option is set to **Last selected**.

6. Move "2010" while holding the *Ctrl* key, and position it to the left of "CUTE rally".

7. Select "CITY" and "CUTE rally" (in that order) and align their top edges using the **Align top edges** ▤ option.

8. Select "CITY" and "2010" (in that order) and center them using the **Center on vertical axis** ▤ option.

9. Select all three text objects and center them horizontally on the page by setting **Relative to:** to **Page**, ticking the **Treat selection as group:** option and pressing the **Center on vertical axis** button.

10. Move the selection up near the top page edge, holding the *Ctrl* down to constrain the movement vertically and not lose the centering we just set.

11. Create a 370 px square with rounded corners of radius 40 px. Center the square by using the **Center on vertical axis** button. Use the **Rectangle** toolbar to set these exact values.

12. Create a rectangle that is 330 px wide and 310 px tall with rounded corners of 40 px radius.

13. Select both the rectangle and the square (in this order), in the **Align and Distribute** dialogue set **Relative to:** Last selected, untick the **Treat selection as group:** option, and use the **Center on horizontal axis** ▤, and **Align right sides** ▤ options.

14. Select the **Text** tool (*F8* or *T*) and click and drag inside the rectangle to create a flowed text object, paste some dummy text inside and right-align the text.

15. Select the flowed text and the rectangle (in that order) and align them by using the **Center on horizontal axis**.

16. Create a 260 x 200 px rectangle and make its corners sharp.

17. Select the new rectangle and the larger rounded corner square (in that order), center them by using the **Center on horizontal axis** option, and align their edges with the **Align right edges of objects to the left edge of the anchor** ▤ option.

18. Create two text objects: "Place" and, underneath it, "Date". A text size of 40 worked for me.

19. Select "Place" and "Date" and the new rectangle and center them by using the **Center on horizontal axis** option. Move the "Place" and "Date" by holding *Ctrl* so they are completely inside the rectangle.

20. Create five short text objects that represent names on the right-hand side of the squares, text size of 24 worked in my case.

21. Select the top-most name and add the smaller rounded corner rectangle to the selection; align them using the **Align top edges** and **Align left edges of objects to the right edge of the anchor** options.

22. Select the bottom most name and add the smaller rounded corner square to the selection; align them using the **Align bottom edges** and **Align left edges of objects to the right edge of the anchor** options.

23. Select all five name objects and use the **Distribute baselines of text vertically** option.

24. Select the middle name object and add "CUTE rally" to the selection; align them with **Align right sides** option.

25. Select the first top three name objects and use the **Distribute baseline anchors of text horizontally** option.

26. Do the same for the bottom-most three name objects. If some objects don't appear to be aligned as in the picture, you might have to shuffle them, as the distribution is influenced by order and position.

How it works...

Text baseline alignment is a very useful property when manipulating any kind of structured layouts featuring text. It is sophisticated enough to make arrangements for certain letters, such as the "y" in "rally", which takes the correct baseline into consideration (see Step 5).

The **Relative to:** option has several choices to choose from but it's probably the best practice to use the same option by default and only change it when absolutely needed. The default option should be the one that feels most natural to you, probably being either **Last selected** or **First selected**.

When we have several objects already lined up the way we want them but need to position them in relation to some other object we can use the **Treat selection as group:** option, without really grouping them. This doesn't work for the entire **Relative to:** options, as some combinations don't make sense.

The file `AlignDistribute.svg` contains our leaflet example. In case you don't have the font that has been used installed on your computer there is an additional layer in the document with all text objects converted into paths so it will look exactly as in the screenshot. Note that text baseline alignment only works on text objects.

There's more...

There are some more options on the **Align and Distribute** dialogue that we haven't used, such as the option to randomize objects positions, and another one to equalize their edge distances, which can be useful when creating designs with many duplicates or clones and we need to tidy them a bit. The **Remove overlaps** option can also help in a similar way.

Align and Distribute nodes

When **Node** tool is active the **Align and Distribute** dialogue shows four options to align and distribute selected nodes. These options only move the nodes without changing the handles positions so interesting effects can be achieved when using them.

Rows and Columns

The **Rows and Columns** dialogue offers several very useful options for arranging objects into a grid. The dialogue can be found under **Object | Rows and Columns**. Here is a simple example:

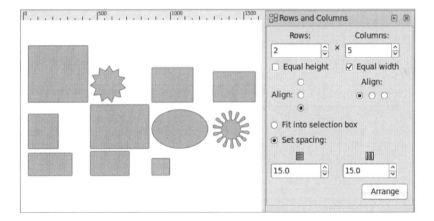

Creating your own custom color swatches

Certain projects will require strict adherence to a specific color theme. In these cases, creating a new palette might be overkill, so Inkscape lets us specify custom swatches and save them along with our drawings.

Swatches also support gradients: another advantage over color palettes. These features can be of great assistance when producing websites or promotional material that requires a coherent look and feel.

Getting ready

Open the **Swatches** dialogue (*Shift + Ctrl + W*). Switch the color palette from **Inkscape default** to **Auto**. You can also use the small button with the a black arrowhead pointing left, on the right of the currently selected swatch.

How to do it...

The following steps will show you how to create a custom color swatch:

1. Create a small rectangle in the center of the page.

2. Bring up the **Fill and Stroke** (*Shift + Ctrl + F*) dialog, set the **Fill** to **Flat color** and choose a color from the HSL color picker. Adjust the **H**, **S**, **L**, and **A** settings as you see fit.

3. Click on the **Swatch Fill** button 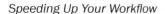, right next to the **Unset fill** button . The color will be added to the current palette swatch.

4. Change the color by modifying the **H**, **S**, **L**, **A** sliders. Any changes will also update the color in the swatch.

5. Create another rectangle.

6. Select the **Gradient** tool and apply a linear gradient to the rectangle.

7. Select the start stop and choose a starting color for the gradient in the **Fill and Stroke** dialog, using the **HSL** color picker.

8. Select the end stop and choose an ending color for the gradient, using the **HSL** color picker.

9. Click on the **Swatch Fill** button again. The gradient will be added to the **Auto swatch**.

10. Right-click on the gradient in the swatch. A special window will pop up. You can modify the gradient stops here.

11. Close the pop-up window and save the document in the native Inkscape format, naming it `swatch-test.svg`. The **Auto swatch** will be saved together with the document.

How it works...

As we add swatches to the **Swatches** dialogue window we can see that the **Auto color** palette at the bottom of the window also updates in real time. Once we are finished with creating new swatches we can close the **Swatches** dialogue and continue to use the **Auto palette**. This is especially useful on small screens.

When an existing swatch is changed, every object that was styled with it will be updated. This is another way to save time when dealing with color changes in addition to gradient sharing and clones.

See also

For more information, refer to *Creating your own color palette*, the recipe that follows.

Creating your own color palette

Color palettes are sets of predefined color swatches. They are used as a way to speed up color editing process. Also there are projects that always use the same colors to make their designs consistent. Examples of those projects are the Tango and Echo icon themes, for graphical user-interfaces that are part the Freedesktop and GNOME initiatives.

Inkscape comes with several useful color palettes we can use to make our workflow easier, but there are cases when we need to create our own color palette, and this recipe will explain how.

Getting ready

Palettes are saved in a specific directory, according to your operating system. On Windows it is usually `C:\Program Files\Inkscape\share\palettes`; on Linux you will find it in your `~/.config/inkscape/palettes` directory; on Mac OS X it is `~/inkscape/palettes`.

How to do it...

The following steps will show you how to create your own color palette:

1. Create several objects and style them with colors you want in your palette. You can create as much as you want. If you style objects with gradients the color stops will be used to create chips in the palette.

2. Save the file in your usual documents directory as an Inkscape SVG file and name it as you would like to name the new palette.

3. Save the file as a **GIMP Palette** file (`*.gpl`), use the same name you used in Step 2. Save it in the folder where Inkscape keeps custom palettes on your system.

4. Restart Inkscape and choose your newly created palette from the **Palettes** fly-out menu (*Shift + Ctrl + W*), or select it directly from the swatch panel.

How it works...

We saved the document before exporting it as a GPL file (GIMP Palette) in order to specify name for it. That will be the name that will be used for the palette.

There's more...

GPL (GIMP Palette) files are simple lists of RGB values. You can change the name of the palette by opening the file with a simple text editor. This also lets you tweak the RGB values by hand, or include additional ones.

If you have some other software, such as The GIMP, that can create color palettes and save them in the GPL file format, you can also use it to add more palettes to Inkscape, simply save them in the correct directory.

See also

For more information, refer to *Creating your own custom color swatches* recipe in this chapter.

More time-saving tips

This recipe lists some of the useful shortcuts that aren't obvious to new users but are very easy to remember and can speed up the drawing process.

The Notification region in the Statusbar

This region shows miscellaneous information about the selected objects or options available for currently selected tools. Since it changes depending on the context it is useful to glance at it often, new users can learn from the tips shown and some necessary information can only be found there. If you can't see the whole message because the region is too small you can hover over it with the mouse and read the tooltip.

Space bar to switch between Selector and other tools

Pressing the *Space* key on the keyboard will switch between the **Selector** tool and the tool that was last used. For example you can have an object selected and use the **Dropper** tool to pick a color for the object. Now you want to do the same for a lot of other objects, the easiest way is to press the *Space* key to get to the **Selector** tool and select a different object; press *Space* to get to the **Dropper** and change colors, press *Space* to select yet another object, press *Space* again to get the **Dropper**, and so on.

This shortcut doesn't work with the **Text** tool when a text object is selected.

Panning and zooming using the mouse wheel

A favorite of many graphical editors is the drag and pan functionality of the middle mouse button/wheel. Just click anywhere in the canvas and drag to move the canvas around. Once you get used to it, you may want to remove the scrollbars (*Ctrl + B*) for additional canvas space.

Paste in place

This option can be found in the **Edit** menu and there is a shortcut associated with it—*Ctrl + Alt + V*. It is useful when copying objects between documents or working with groups.

For example, if you need to copy an object from a group, but want it at the exact same place, just enter the group or select the object directly by using *Ctrl* then select **Edit | Paste in Place** (*Ctrl + Alt +V*).

Maybe you have a really cluttered scene in your drawing you want to clear up, but you don't want to mess up the good bits: just cut the objects you want to keep in the same position, rearrange everything as you see fit, and then **Paste in Place.**

The most typical use is copying objects to and from documents in different Inkscape windows, preserving their position. This way you can avoid saving an intermediate version of your drawing.

Paste style

This option can also be found in the **Edit** menu and there is a shortcut associated with it—*Shift + Ctrl + V*. It is done by copying the object with the desired style and using the **Paste style** option on another object. The second object will take on the style attributes from the first one.

Paste size

Paste size has several options that can be used. **Paste size** changes the object's width and height to the width and height of the copied object. If more objects are selected the selection is treated as one object. **Paste Width** and **Paste Height** only change the object size in the specified dimension, unless the lock ratio button on the **Selector** toolbar is active, in which case the value in the chosen dimension is pasted and the other dimension is scaled proportionally.

The options that end with "Separately" are used when we want to affect many objects at the same time pasting the same size to each object separately.

Stamping—copying objects while dragging them across the screen

Stamping works with the **Selector** tool where you simply drag the object across the screen and press the *Space* key when ever the object is over the place where you want a copy of it. You can rapidly create and position multiple clones of a shape inside the Canvas in this way.

Showing/hiding open dialogues

On small screens, dialogs can take up a lot of the screen so there isn't much space to see the drawing. We can temporarily hide all the dialogs, then bring them all back using *F12*. This works whether the dialogs are docked or not and they appear at the same positions we left them in.

Hiding everything except dialogues

The *F11* key toggles fullscreen as in many other applications, but Inkscape comes with another option—*Shift + F11* that doesn't hide the window borders and decorations but hides everything inside the window except open dialogs. This can be very useful on small screens, especially if you know your keyboard shortcuts! Another possible use for this is when showing someone else your drawing so you can quickly show it off without interface distractions.

Changing the focus from dialogue to canvas

The *Esc* key is a quick way to deselect objects and cancel various actions, but it also has one other use that comes in very handy when keyboard shortcuts are a part of the workflow. When editing options within a dialog we can't edit objects on canvas even when they are selected. For example if we changed the **Blur** on the **Fill and Stroke** dialog and now want to move that object with arrow keys, simply pressing the arrow keys will change the blur value because it is still in focus. That when we can use *Esc* to defocus the dialogue so we can use the arrow keys on our selection.

Toggling display modes

One of the display modes Inkscape offers is the **No Filters** mode. Filters can be a performance hog so it can slow down the workflow significantly. Working in the **No Filters** mode can help by showing the filtered objects as if they weren't filtered. This way you're still aware of the objects and their positions although they temporarily look a bit different from expected, which might be a better solution than keeping all the filtered objects in a separate layer and hiding the layer.

The **Outline** mode shows the drawing structure; styles aren't shown. It can be used to select objects that are hard to select in **Normal** mode.

Importing drawings from OpenClipArt

OpenClipArt is an online library of SVG clipart licensed under the Public Domain license. This project was started by Inkscape developers to provide clipart that is free for any kind of use. To new Inkscape users this can be a valuable source of drawings to dissect and learn from.

This recipe shows us how to import the drawings directly from Inkscape. If you need to sample the offer in more detail visit the website and do a search there, the URL is `http://www.openclipart.org`.

 At this time of writing, the **Import drawings from OpenClipArt.org** functionality has not been added to the official Windows distribution of Inkscape yet. Check the Inkscape website for the current status of the integration.

How to do it...

Follow these steps to import drawings from OpenClipArt:

1. Open the dialogue by going to **File | Import From Open Clip Art Library**.
2. Enter the search phrase "bug" into the search box and press **Search**.
3. Click on some of the search results so see their preview.
4. Select **ladybug** and click **Open**.
5. Explore!

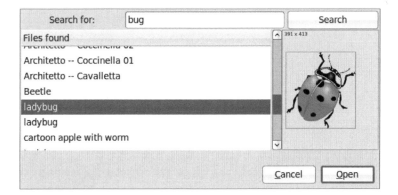

There's more...

Once you feel confident using Inkscape, consider donating your art to **OpenClipArt.org**. It's a big community with very talented and dedicated people, where you'll be able to receive comments, suggestions, and gratification for your work.

4
Creating and Editing Clones

In this chapter, we will cover:

- ▸ Drawing clock dial markers using clones
- ▸ Drawing a colorful grid of tiled clones
- ▸ Changing icon colors using tiled clones
- ▸ Drawing clock dial markers using tiled clones
- ▸ Creating halftones using tiled clones
- ▸ Creating a bokeh effect using tiled clones
- ▸ Creating kaleidoscopic patterns using tiled clones
- ▸ Drawing a tree with cloned leaves using the Spray tool
- ▸ Clipping using clones

Introduction

"Repetita iuvant" (Repetition is useful), ancient Latin saying.

Cloning objects does not only reduce the size of SVG files, but also creates some very interesting effects with little effort. This chapter will demonstrate some common uses of clones in illustrations.

Drawing clock dial markers using clones

This recipe will teach us the basics of clone manipulation through the example of a very simple clock dial where the hour marks are created using clones.

How to do it...

Carry out the following steps to create clock markers using clones:

1. Select the **Rectangle** tool (*F4* or *R*) and create a narrow vertical rectangle.

2. Unset its fill by using the **Unset fill** option from the menu popup in the Style indicator or by using the **Fill and Stroke** (*Shift + Ctrl + F*) dialog. It will then appear black. Now remove its stroke.

3. Switch to the **Selector** tool (*Space* or *F1* or *S*) and bring up the rotation handles on the rectangle by clicking on it *twice* (not the same as double-clicking).

4. Drag the rotation center (displayed as a crosshair) downwards while holding *Ctrl* to constrain movement to the vertical axis and drag down, past the bottom edge of the rectangle until you reach a distance roughly equal to the height of the rectangle itself.

5. Clone the rectangle by clicking on the **Create a Clone (a copy linked to the original)** of selected object 🔗 (*Alt + D*, or **Edit | Clone | Create Clone**). It will appear exactly on top of the rectangle.

6. Drag one of the rotation arrow handles to the right while holding *Ctrl* to constrain the angle to 30°.

7. Duplicate the clone by using *Ctrl + D* or the duplicate button 🔍 on the Control toolbar. It will appear exactly on top of the clone. Check which object is the original of the duplicated clone by using *Shift + D*.

8. Drag one of the rotation arrow handles to the right and down while holding *Ctrl* to constrain the angle to 30°.

9. Repeat Steps 7 and 8 until you have twelve rectangles in total that make up the full clock dial.

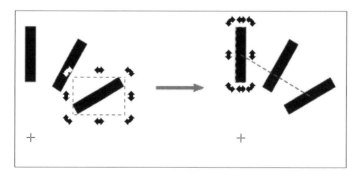

10. Color each clone's fill (but not the original rectangle) with a different color.

11. Select the original rectangle and color its fill with **Lime (#00FF00)**. Notice how all the clone fills will automatically match the new color.

12. Select one of the clones and check what their fill color is in the Style indicator or in the **Fill and Stroke** dialogue (*Shift + Ctrl + F*). Notice it isn't **Lime (#00FF00)**.

13. Select the original rectangle again (*Shift + D*) and unset its fill. Notice how all the clones change their fill color back to the ones we assigned:

14. Rotate the rectangle, notice how all the clones get rotated by the same amount.

15. Move the rectangle away from its position; this time, the clones will not be affected by the change.

16. In the **Inkscape Preferences** (*Shift + Ctrl + P*) under **Clones** change the movement setting from **Stay unmoved** to **Move in parallel**.

17. Move the rectangle again; notice how clones will now shift their position on the Canvas, but maintain their relative placement to each other.

18. Now change the movement setting from **Move in parallel** to **Move according to transform**.

19. Move the rectangle again; notice how the clones don't follow the rectangle movement with respect to the rectangle but instead with respect to themselves. Try resizing it and see what happens. We can product some pretty interesting effects by manipulating our clones in this manner, although we'll probably have distanced ourselves from the original clock replica.

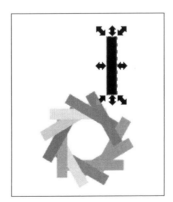

How it works...

Clones are affected by their original objects although some of their properties can be edited independently and applied directly to clones. For example, it is possible to resize a clone without resizing the original. Still, when the original object is resized each and every linked clone will also change proportionally.

A clone's colors are identical to the original object unless we set the original colors to **Unset**, only then can different colors be assigned to clones.

When a clone is duplicated it keeps the link to the same original object, so if we need to have more than one clone of the same object we don't have to clone the original many times, we can duplicate the first clone we made if it's more convenient that way.

The default settings specify that any movement of the original does not affect any clones, but feel free to change this or any other settings in order to achieve the result you expect - or even an unexpected one! We can use those options in turns, move the clones according to transform when needed, then switch back to no movement.

There's more...

One other useful clone feature is that they can be relinked to a completely different object.

Relinking clones

To relink clones we first copy the object we want to use as the new original, select all the clones we want to relink, and go to **Edit | Clone | Relink to Copied**. After relinking, the clones will be moved from their position in the same direction and distance that the new original is positioned with respect to the old original. So if you want the relinked clones to remain in place after this operation make sure to center the new original over the old one; you can always move it away later. If the new object has a different shape than the previous, the clones will experience a Kafkaesque metamorphosis and match it.

Copying clones between documents

Clones are totally dependent on their original object, just as if they were multiple shadows of the same physical being. If you copy a clone and paste it in another document it won't appear, at least not visually. If you inspect the document structure with XML editor (*Shift + Ctrl + X*) you will see that the pasted clone is there; the statusbar notification tips tell us that it's an **Orphaned clone**. It doesn't visually appear on canvas because it doesn't have the necessary information from its original. So when copying clones from one document to another make sure you also include the original.

It is also possible to relink the orphaned clone to an object in the new document. Use the XML editor to select the orphaned clone because it's not possible to select it on canvas.

Unlinking clones

If we don't need the clones to be dependent on their original any more so that we can perform edits not possible on clones, we can unlink them using **Edit | Clone | Unlink clone** 🔳 (*Shift + Alt + D*). The clones will now be fully independent objects. We can also simply delete the original objects, the clones will be automatically unlinked.

If the original colors were unset, the clones will keep their own colors, otherwise they take on the colors of the original.

See also

For more information, refer to the *Drawing a clock dial using tiled clones* recipe that follows.

Drawing a colorful grid of tiled clones

In art, an intelligent use of repetition evokes a sense of elegant complexity in the viewer. By using the powerful tiled clones feature present in Inkscape, we can leverage this technique to produce beautiful backgrounds and textures.

In this recipe we will create a grid of equally spaced squares in different ranges of colors.

How to do it...

The following steps will show you how to draw a colorful grid of tiled clones:

1. Create a 10 x 10 px rectangle, unset its fill, and remove its stroke.

2. Go to **Edit | Clone | Create Tiled Clones...** 🔳 to open the dialog.

3. Set **Rows, columns:** boxes both to 20 to create 20 rows and 20 columns grid of 400 clones in total.

4. On the **Symmetry** tab, choose **P1: simple translation**.

5. On the **Shift** tab set **Shift X: Per column:** and **Shift Y: Per row:** to 10. This means that the gap between the clones will be (10 * 10) / 100 = 1 pixel wide.

6. On the **Color** tab set the **Initial color:** to ff8787ff, **H: Per row:** to 1, and **H: Per column:** to 5. This will make the color hue change faster from one column to the next than from one row to the next.

7. Leave all the other settings as default and press the **Create** button. The following is what we get:

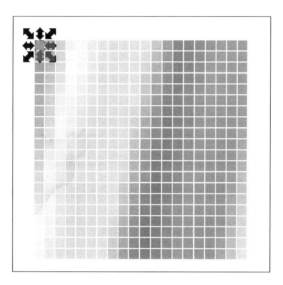

8. Press **Remove** on the **Tiled clones** dialog to undo the last step.

9. On the **Color** tab of **Tiled clones** dialog change **H: Randomize:** to 5. Leave everything else as it is, and press **Create**:

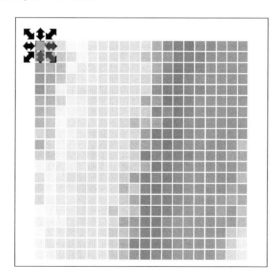

10. Press **Remove** on the dialog to undo the last step.

11. On the **Color** tab of the dialog, change **H: Randomize:** to 50. Leave everything else as it is, and press **Create**:

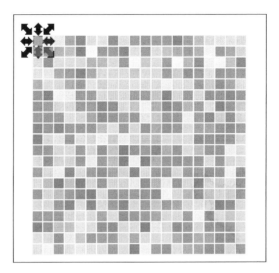

How it works...

When tiled clones are created, the first clone is positioned over the original. In our case it means that we have 401 objects in total on the Canvas; the original with the unset fill is hidden below the first clone.

> If you accidentally deselect and lose focus of the original, you can select it again by holding *Alt* while clicking on the first clone to select what is behind it.

The default settings for the **Shift** option are to tile clones one next to another in a grid (**Shift X:** and **Shift Y:** are 0). Setting the shift to a number greater than 0 will make gaps between tiles, and setting it to a number lower than 0 will make the tiles overlap.

Sometimes we need to make the clones tile one on top of another instead of one next to another. This can be done by setting the **Shift X: Per column:** and **Shift Y: Per row:** to -100, but there is also a useful option that can do that for us—**Exclude tile:**. Using the **Exclude tile:** option makes it easier to manipulate the shifting percentages when we need the base position of the clones to be over the original.

> When tiling rectangles, make sure to snap the original to grid (toggle grid visibility with # and snapping with %) and calculate the gap to be a whole (and not fractions of) pixels. This will make the rectangle edges appear sharp when looking at the Canvas with a 100% zoom or when exporting the drawing at the default 90 dpi resolution.

In order to mess around with the colors as we did before, we first had to unset the fill of the original rectangle. If we change the color of the original all the clones will take on that color, but if we unset the original fill again the clones will go back to the colors they were originally. Clones have good memory and remember the colors that they have during the time the original is unset.

There's more...

There are many more options available when tiling clones than what we used in this recipe. You probably noticed the other tabs in the tile clone dialog that we didn't use: **Scale**, **Rotation**, **Blur & Opacity**, and **Trace**. We also didn't mention many other settings available on the tabs we did use; for example randomizing isn't available only for colors, but most of the other tabs have it too. Try playing with them yourself to discover new possibilities of the tile clones feature, or wait until we try them together later in this and the following chapters.

Use saved size and position of the tile

This option from the tiled clone dialog is useful when modifying the size of the original object. If we want the clones grid to stay in place unaffected by the change in size of the original object we need to use this option. One of the examples where to use it is when creating seamless patterns of groups of objects where some objects protrude out of the pattern box.

See also

For more information, refer to the *Changing icon colors using tiled clones* and *Drawing clock dial markers using tiled clones* recipes in this chapter.

Changing icon colors using tiled clones

When creating icon sets we often want to change their base color without affecting the overall look, so we can use them on different background colors, website themes, or in other contexts. This can easily be done with tiled clones, in a way similar to how we did in the last recipe. In this recipe we will create an icon using several objects in a group and create tiled clones of it to get different icon colors.

Getting ready

Usually we want to achieve various effects in our drawings with as few objects as possible so it's easier to manage the drawing. In this case though we will have to separate our icon color information from the highlights into two objects. The goal is to unset the fill of the color-bearing object so when tiling the clones of the icon we can use the **Color** tab to change it without affecting the highlights.

If you already know how to create a simple icon, or you don't want to warm up by creating one, you can use the one already available in the file `ClonedIcons.svg` and skip to Step 14.

How to do it...

The following steps will show you how to clone an icon:

1. Create a rounded rectangle that will serve as our base object. Duplicate it (Ctrl + D) three times so you have a total of four objects. One will serve as the icon shadow, the other as the base color and edge 3D shadow, the third will be used as a clipping object, and the fourth will serve as highlights.

2. Move the rectangles away so they aren't stacked on top of one another.

3. Select one rectangle and set its stroke to **Black** with stroke opacity (**A:** box on the **Stroke** tab) set to 150. Make it thicker, temporarily set its fill to some color so we can later adjust the stroke to make it look like a 3D edge.

4. Center this rectangle below the one from Step 1 using the **Align and Distribute** dialog (*Shift + Ctrl + A*).

5. Clip the centered rectangles (**Object | Clip | Set**). You might want to color the fill of the clipping rectangle differently and remove its stroke before clipping so it's more clear what parts will be clipped out.

6. Blur the resulting rectangle using the **Fill and Stroke** dialog (*Shift + Ctrl + F*) so the fill and stroke colors blend. Clipping will keep the rectangle edges sharp. Adjust the stroke width and blurring to get a nice 3D shading effect.

7. Select the clipped and blurred rectangle together with another one and center them. If the clipped and blurred rectangle ends up on top, select it and send it to the bottom using *Page Down* or *End*.

8. Select the rectangle on top and color its fill **White**, this will be our highlights object. Make it smaller by holding *Shift + Ctrl* while resizing it using resize handles to keep it centered and to keep the same aspect ratio.

9. Create a white to transparent gradient on the fill of the white object. Modify the gradient by adding stops and changing their opacity to get the highlight effect you like.

10. Select the remaining rectangle, set its fill color to **70% Gray** and center it behind (*Page Down* or *End*) the clipped and blurred rectangle. We now have a shadow for our icon.

11. Blur the gray rectangle, press *Esc* to shift the focus back to the canvas from the dialog, and use the arrow keys to move the shadow to the right and down.

12. Create another object that will represent the icon function and color it white. Center it over the icon.

13. Select the clipped and blurred rectangle and unset its fill color. It will appear black so the blurred stroke won't be visible.

14. Select all objects (*Ctrl + A*). There should be four of them. Group them using *Ctrl + G*.

15. Open the tiled clones dialog by going to **Edit | Clone | Create Tiled Clones...**.

16. Set the **Rows, columns:** boxes both to 10 to create ten rows and ten columns, a grid of 100 clones in total.

17. On the **Symmetry** tab choose **P1: simple translation**.

18. On the **Shift** tab set **Shift X: Per column:** and **Shift Y: Per row:** to 20.

19. On the **Color** tab set the **Initial color:** to d40000ff, **H:** to 8, **S:** to 1 with **Randomize:** set to 15, and **L:** to 1 with **Randomize:** set to 15.

20. Leave all the other settings as default and press the **Create** button. We should now be looking at something quite similar to the following image:

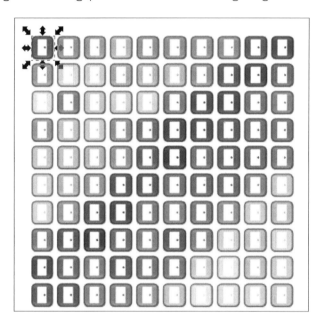

How it works...

We didn't have to create a separate object for the 3D edge shadow because stroke and fill can be unset separately. So we were able to use the fill of an object as the base icon color that will change when cloned and its stroke as the 3D edge that won't change.

The **Hue** property was instrumental in changing our clones' base color, but we also added a very slight change in saturation and lightness to get more options because we have enough rows and columns to achieve it. We also applied randomization in order to make the changes less predictable, although we are always increasing the Saturation and Lightness.

See also

For more information, refer to the recipe on *Drawing a colorful grid of tiled clones* in this chapter.

Drawing clock dial markers using tiled clones

In this recipe we will rehash the simple clock dial design seen in the first recipe of this chapter, and recreate it in fewer steps using tiled clones.

How to do it...

The following steps will show you how to easily draw clock dial markers:

1. Select the **Rectangle** tool (*F4* or *R*) and create a narrow vertical rectangle.

2. Unset its fill by using the **Unset fill** option from the menu popup in the Style indicator or using the **Fill and Stroke** (*Shift + Ctrl + F*) dialog. It will appear black. Remove its stroke.

> **What's the difference between a Removed and an Unset fill or stroke?**
>
> Good question. If you take a look at the SVG XML of an object, you will see that *removing* will set the relative style—fill/stroke attribute of the object to None. Whereas *unsetting* it will remove the attribute entirely, thus permitting the object to acquire this attribute from a parent.

3. Switch to the **Selector** tool (*Space* or *F1* or *S*) and bring up the rotation handles on the rectangle by clicking on it twice (not the same as double-clicking).

4. Drag the rotation center downwards while holding *Ctrl* to keep it vertical. Release it when you've reached a distance roughly equal to the rectangle's height.

5. Go to **Edit | Clone | Create Tiled Clones...** to open the dialog.

6. Press the **Reset** button on the dialog to set all the tiled clone options to their defaults.

7. Set **Rows, columns:** boxes to 1 and 12. This setup will create 12 clones aligned in 1 row and 12 columns.

8. On the **Symmetry** tab choose **P1: simple translation**.

9. On the **Shift** tab, tick the **Exclude tile:** for columns (**Per columns:**) so that the columns are all positioned one on top of another instead of one next to another.

10. On the **Rotation** tab set the **Angle: Per column:** to 30 (360/12=30).

11. On the **Color** tab set the **Initial color:** to ff8787ff, **H: Per column:** to 15, and **Randomize:** to 20.

12. Leave all the other settings as default and press the **Create** button; this is what I got (your colors will vary):

How it works...

The Tiled clones option can be used to avoid repetitive operations when creating many clones, therefore reducing our work. In this example each marker is created the same way so this can be automated with the tiled clones feature. In addition we also get the automatic color randomization, all without having to select each clone and manipulate it separately.

The **Exclude tile:** in columns during **Shift** makes sure the clones aren't moved away from the original so all the rotation centers are in the same place. This way when the rotation comes into place the clones are arranged in a circle.

The only difference between this and the first recipe is that in this one we have an extra clone, because the tiled clones feature creates one on top of the original. Move away the original or delete the clone on top of it if it makes it easier for you

See also

For more information refer to *Drawing clock dial markers using clones*, *Drawing a colorful grid of tiled clones*, and *Changing icon colors using tiled clones* discussed in this chapter.

Creating halftones using tiled clones

Halftone images are especially popular in abstract, hi-tech or sci-fi images and backgrounds, but can be used in many other situations.

In this recipe we will create a halftone image out of a drawing using tiled clones. Usually grayscale photos with a lot of gray shades are used, but in this recipe we will create our own drawing to trace into a halftone.

How to do it...

The following steps will show you how to create halftones:

1. Create a complex star shape of any color and blur it. Resize it to about 750 px in height and width and position it at the top of the page.

2. Zoom in right on the top-left corner of the page.

3. Create a 10 px circle there, set its fill to black and remove the stroke.

4. Open the tiled clones dialog by going to **Edit | Clone | Create Tiled Clones...**.

5. Press the **Reset** button on the dialog to set all the tiled clone options to their defaults.

6. Set **Width, height:** boxes both to 750 to make sure the trace is over the size of the complex star shape we created in Step 1.

7. On the **Trace** tab enable the **Trace the drawing under the tiles** option. Under **Pick from drawing:** select **Opacity**, under **Apply the value to the clones:** select **Size**.

8. Leave all the other settings as default and press the **Create** button. Depending on your CPU power you may have to wait a bit for the command to finish executing.

9. Remove the star shape from under the tiled clones:

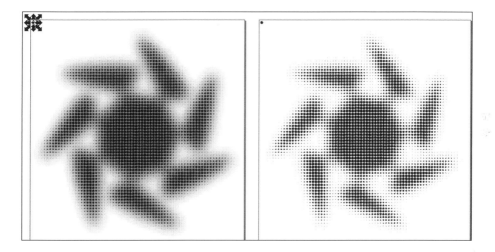

How it works...

We used the **Opacity** property of the original drawing as the trace input because parts of our drawing have different opacity (created by blurring). If we had used an imported photo we couldn't have used **Opacity** because Inkscape would interpret the whole photo area as opaque and our circle tiled would come out all the same. Using **Color** or any of the other options will work better with photos.

Of the available options for tiled clones we chose **Size** as the affected attribute. That is why the tiled clones change in size depending on the opacity of the object behind them.

See also

For more information, refer to *Creating and editing 2D geometric shapes* in *chapter 1* and *Drawing a colorful grid of tiled clones* in this chapter.

Creating a bokeh effect using tiled clones

Bokeh effects seem very popular among wallpapers and other art used on computers, and are even starting to make their appearance in real-time 3D graphics for consumer hardware. The word seems to derive from the Japanese "*boke*", which means "*haze*". This recipe shows us how to create this effect quickly and easily using tiled clones.

How to do it...

The following steps will show you how to create a bokeh effect:

1. Open the **Document Properties** (*Shift + Ctrl + D*) and change the page orientation to **Landscape**. Zoom and fit the drawing in the canvas by pressing the *5* key.

2. Use the **Calligraphy** tool (*Ctrl + F6* or *C*) to create two wavy lines across the page using the **Dip pen** mode (select it from the left-hand list in the **Calligraphy** toolbar) and a width of 64 px. Hold *Shift* while drawing the second line to combine it with the first into one object.

3. Create a multicolor gradient in the fill of the object.

4. Use the **Ellipse** tool (*F5* or *E*) to create a 90 px circle in the top-left corner of the page. Lower its opacity to 70, unset its fill, set its stroke to white and stroke width to 3.

5. Open the tiled clones dialog by going to **Edit | Clone | Create Tiled Clones...**.

6. Press the **Reset** button on the dialog to set all the tiled clone options to their defaults.

7. Set **Width, height:** boxes, both to 1000 x 700 to trace approximately over the page area.

8. On the **Shift** tab, set **Shift X:** and **Shift Y:** to 10, and **Randomize:** to 30 in **Per Row:** and **Per Column:**.

9. On the **Blur & opacity** tab set **Blur:** and **Fade out:** to 2, and **Randomize:** to 15, in **Per Row:** and **Per Column:**.

10. On the **Trace** tab enable the **Trace the drawing under the tiles** option. Under **Pick from drawing:** select **Opacity**. Under **Tweak the picked value:** set **Gamma-correct:** to 5. Under **Apply the value to the clones':** select **Size**, **Color**, and **Opacity**.

11. Leave all the other settings as default and press the **Create** button. If you don't like the pattern you got you can get a new one by clicking the **Create** button again.

12. Duplicate the original circle (*Ctrl + D*).

13. In the tiled clones dialog **Blur & opacity** tab, change **Blur:** and **Fade out:** to 0, and **Randomize:** to 5.

14. Leave all the other settings as default and press the **Create** button. The drawing should now resemble the one in the following picture:

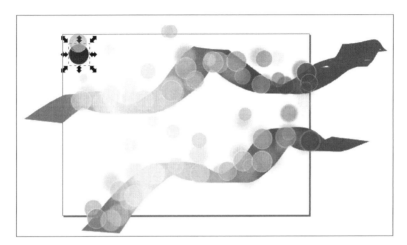

15. Use the **Rectangle** tool (*F4* or *R*) to create a page sized or larger rectangle. Use snapping to page border if you like to make it precise.

16. Make sure the opacity of the rectangle is set to 100, remove stroke, and send it to the back of the drawing (*End*).

17. Set the rectangle fill to the same gradient we used for wavy lines in Step 3 by choosing it from the drop-down list on gradient toolbar and aligning it so the colors match.

18. Change each of the gradient color stops by lowering their saturation to 200 and lightness to 50 while keeping the hue intact.

19. Select the wavy object we created in Step 2, the original circles with unset fills, and if they exist clones that were created near the original circles so they ended up being gray. Send the selection to back (*End*). The following is what our final image looks like:

How it works...

We randomized the shift of the tiled clones so we don't get a uniform layout of the cloned objects, and we used the wavy lines object to limit the clone positions to that area at least up to a point.

We used two sets of tiled clones, one for the more blurred objects and that appear in the background and the one in the foreground so we can better control of the blur amount.

The rectangle in the background hints the sources of the bokeh circles, and that's why we made the colors match.

See also

For more information, refer to the recipe on *Creating halftones using tiled clones* in this chapter.

Creating a kaleidoscopic pattern using tiled clones

Throughout this chapter we've only used simple symmetry in our tiled clone examples which is the one we usually need, but Inkscape can also be used to arrange objects in seventeen different symmetries. This recipe will show us how to create a kaleidoscopic pattern using one of those symmetries.

Most kaleidoscopes are created using three equal size mirrors positioned so their edges form an equilateral triangle. That layout dictates that we create an equal sided triangle as our base object, and use P3M1 symmetry to tile the clones so they are positioned one next to the other without gaps or overlaps.

Getting ready

For this recipe, close and restart your Inkscape session, so we can start a new drawing with all the default options reset.

How to do it...

The following steps will show you how to create a kaleidoscopic pattern:

1. Create an upright triangle (three corners) using the **Polygon mode** of the **Star** tool (*Shift + F9* or ***), by holding *Ctrl* and dragging upwards.

2. Set its fill to **White** and stroke to 1 px **Black** so we can easily distinguish the clones once they are created.

3. Duplicate it (*Ctrl + D*), remove stroke on the duplicate and set its fill to red so it's easy to distinguish it from the white one.

4. Switch to the **Selector** tool (*Space* or *F1* or *S*), and select the bottom (white) triangle by pressing *Alt* while clicking.

5. Group the white triangle (*Ctrl + G*). This group will be our cloning original.

6. Add the red triangle to the selection by clicking on it while holding *Shift* and clip the group with the red triangle by going to **Object | Clip | Set**.

7. Open the tiled clones dialog by going to **Edit | Clone | Create Tiled Clones...**.

8. Press the **Reset** button on the dialog to make sure that all the tiled clone options are set to their defaults.

9. Set **Rows, columns:** boxes to 5 and 12 to create 60 clones in total.

10. On the **Symmetry** tab, select **P3M1: reflection + 120° rotation, sparse**.

11. Leave all the other settings as default and press the **Create** button. The following is what we have so far:

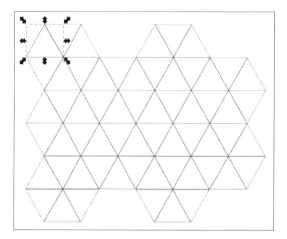

12. Select the clone that is on top of the original group by clicking on it, and delete it (*Delete* or *Backspace*) so we can access the original more easily.

13. Select the original group and enter it by double-clicking or holding *Ctrl* while clicking on it. Select the white triangle.

14. Press the **Zoom to fit selection in the window** 🔍 (or the *3* key).

15. Create a lot of colorful transparent objects inside the group. These are the beads the kaleidoscope usually comes with. Use the **Spray** tool to disperse duplicates or clones once you create a bead you're happy with.

16. Select the white triangle and remove its stroke, and you're done! Here is what I got after playing around with the beads:

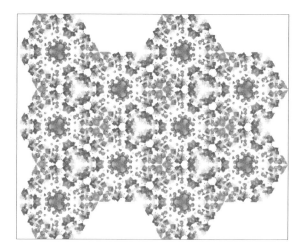

How it works...

Inkscape uses the geometric bounding box as a reference when tiling, so having a stroke doesn't cause unexpected clone positions.

We had to clip the original object in addition to grouping it because otherwise because otherwise the beads would have protruded from the triangle area into the adjacent ones, and that is not what happens in a kaleidoscope—unless it is a broken one! The following image zooms into the original drawing so we can try to spot where the "mirrors" are positioned:

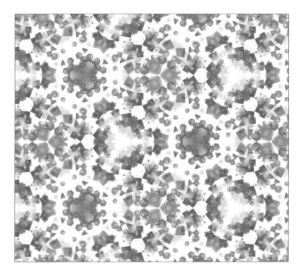

We didn't have to use an equal sided triangle shape to use this symmetry, but other shapes wouldn't be positioned without gaps or overlaps between them. Try to use this symmetry on some other shape and see what interesting results you get.

See also

For more information, refer to the *Drawing a tree with cloned leaves using the Spray tool* recipe in this chapter.

Drawing a tree with cloned leaves using the Spray tool

The **Spay** tool provides another way of rapidly creating clones and placing them in a pseudo-random fashion, with several options that adjust the clones position, size, and rotation. In this recipe we will "spray" leaf clones on a tree as an example of its usefulness.

How to do it...

The following steps will show how to use the **Spray** tool to clone leaves:

1. Create a tree trunk and branches using Spiro spline mode in **Pencil** (*F6* or *P*) or the **Pen** (*Shift* + *F6* or *B*) tool. I used the **Pencil** tool with **Smoothing:** set to 34 and **Shape:** to **Triangle in**. Change the fill color to **#552200**.

2. Convert the main trunk to a path and use the **Node** tool to modify its thickness.

3. Create a green leaf that will be used as an original to create all the other leaves as clones. I created an ellipse, converted it to a path (*Shift* + *Ctrl* + *C*). Then converted the top node to a cusp (*Shift* + *C*), filled it with a radial gradient, and added some lines as veins on top of it. I then grouped all leaf objects (*Ctrl* + *G*) so the whole leaf is in one group.

4. Shift the group rotation center to the "bottom" of the leaf. Click on the group twice (not double-clicking) to get to rotation handles, drag the rotation center.

5. Select the leaf group and switch to the **Spray** tool. Set the **Mode:** to **Spray clones of the initial selection**, **Width:** to 15, **Amount:** to 15, **Rotation:** to 15, **Scale:** to 30, **Scatter:** to 1, and **Focus:** to 0.

6. Click and drag with **Spray** tool to "paint" leaf clones along branches where the current leaf rotation makes sense. Use the *Up* and *Down* arrow keys to continually make the clones larger or smaller.

If you hold the *Down* arrow for some time the clones will be created so small that you can't even see them. So don't forget to get them back holding the *Up* key while spraying.

7. Switch to the **Selector** tool (*Space* or *F1* or *S*).

8. If the angle of the leaves we just created needs to be corrected, rotate the original group to adjust the clones to a better angle.

9. Duplicate the original (*Ctrl + D*) and rotate it to an angle that is suited for the other side of the branches.

10. Switch back to the **Spray** tool (*Space*) and "paint" more leaf clones.

11. Repeat Step 6 to Step 9 as many times for different leaf rotations.

12. Switch to the **Selector** tool (*Space* or *F1* or *S*) and duplicate the original (*Ctrl + D*) once more. Change the colors of the objects inside to brown.

13. Skew the brown group a bit and scale it down. This will be our dead leaf original; it is skewed to look differently "on the ground" than the leaves on the tree.

14. Switch back to the **Spray** tool (*Space*) and "paint" dead leaf clones along the bottom of the page around the tree trunk.

15. Optionally to make the drawing more complete create a page sized rectangle (*F4* or *R*), fill it with a "horizon" gradient, and send it back using the *End* key to create a backdrop for the drawing.

16. To make the tree trunk and branches more realistic select them all (use Outline mode (*Ctrl + 5*) if necessary to make it easier).

17. Duplicate them (*Ctrl + D*).We will work on the duplicates while keeping the original Spiro spline objects for possible later editing.

18. Convert to paths to remove the Spiro spline effect (*Shift + Ctrl + C*).

19. Union them into one path (*Ctrl + +*) and duplicate it (*Ctrl + D*).

20. Clip the two paths we just created (**Object | Clip | Set**).

21. Add a 6 px dark brown stroke to the remaining clipped object and blur it.

22. Send it back (*End*) then keep sending it forward one object at a time using *Page Up* until it's positioned just over the original Spiro spline objects.

How it works...

We used the **Rotation:** and **Scale:** options to add randomness to our sprayed on leaves, to make them appear more natural.

The **Width:** option works in combination with **Scatter:** and **Focus:** determining the area limits where to create new objects if the objects are smaller than the **Width:** value. We wanted to arrange leaves in such a way that it's possible to tell which branch they belong to, so we needed both **Scatter:** and **Focus:** to be at their minimum.

There's more...

In addition to clones, the **Spray** tool has a mode to create independent copies of the selected object, and another one where a union is performed on all the objects after we stop drawing, so we get a single object (not a group) as the final result. Let's take a quick look at a couple of options:

> ▶ **Focus:** always puts objects on a circle. This isn't noticeable when dragging the mouse across canvas but you can see it when spraying over one spot which can be done by clicking and using the mouse wheel (don't move the mouse).

> ▶ **Scatter:** places clones in a random position around the mouse pointer.

See also

For more information, refer to the recipe on *Creating a kaleidoscopic pattern using tiled clones* in this chapter.

Clipping with clones

After an object has been clipped we can still edit its clipping object by using the **Node** tool. However, it may sometimes be inconvenient if there are a lot of nodes, resulting in an unclear drawing or if we wish to have a more clear visualization of the clipping path.

This can be done by using a clone as a clipping path on another object, so we end up with the clone original next to the clipped object free to show us the clipping path.

How to do it...

Clipping can be performed by carrying out the following steps:

1. Create a star using the **Star** tool (*Shift + F9* or ***) and choose a color for its fill and stroke.

2. Convert it to a path (*Shift + Ctrl + C*, or **Path | Object to Path**).

3. Duplicate the star (*Ctrl + D*). Remove its stroke and make its fill **Lime (#00FF00)**. Move it away from the original star.

4. Clone the duplicated star (*Alt + D*) and position the clone over the original star.

5. Select the clone and the original star (*Shift + Alt* and left-click) and clip them by going to **Object | Clip | Set**.

6. Select the original lime star and edit it using the **Node** tool (*F2* or *N*). Notice how the clipping area of the ellipse object changes as we edit the clipping clone original:

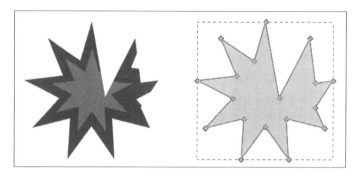

For more information, refer to *Clipping* from *Chapter 1*, and *Drawing clock dial markers using clones* in this chapter.

5
Live Path Effects

In this chapter, we will cover:

- ▶ Bending paths
- ▶ Using Patterns along path
- ▶ Using Envelope Deformation
- ▶ Interpolating Sub-Paths
- ▶ Stitching Sub-Paths
- ▶ Creating gears
- ▶ Creating hatches (rough)
- ▶ Sketching shapes
- ▶ Constructing grids
- ▶ Creating rulers
- ▶ Creating knots
- ▶ Generating VonKoch fractals

Introduction

So far we have used Inkscape's main tools to assemble primitives into a variety of shapes. The process of creating these building blocks can be fully automated using features known as Live Path Effects (LPEs). They are very useful, easy to use, and ubiquitous that we couldn't resist the temptation of using one in the very first chapter of the book: Spiro Spline.

In a nutshell, LPEs twist, replicate, transform, and apply many other modifications to shapes in a sequential and repeatable way. There are many different types of LPEs available for Inkscape 0.48, and even more are being developed. In this chapter we will cover some of the most interesting ones available for this release.

Bending paths

In this recipe we will go through the basic **Live Path Effect** options using the Bend path effect. We will create a simple rectangle and morph it into a waving flag. We will also bend some letter shapes directly and through linking to objects to use as bending paths.

How to do it...

The following steps show how to use bending paths:

1. Create a rectangle using the **Rectangle** tool (*F4* or *R*), set its fill to **#D5D5FF**, stroke to **60% Gray**, and stroke width to 1.

2. Open the **Path Effect Editor** by using *Shift + Ctrl + 7* or by going to **Path | Path Effect Editor...**.

3. Under the **Apply new effect**, choose **Bend** and press **Add**, this will apply the Bend LPE to the rectangle but the rectangle won't change as a result of it.

4. We now have several options available under **Current effect**. Select the **Edit on-canvas** option, and notice the bending line on the rectangle that appeared.

5. Click on the green line (the **Bezier segment**) and drag slightly to bend the rectangle. Adjust more precisely using handles on the end nodes, and click on a node to show the handles. Here is what we have so far:

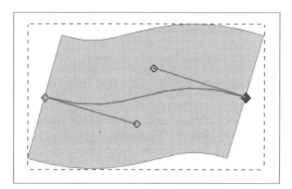

6. Duplicate the rectangle (*Ctrl + D*) and move it away. Notice that the duplicated object will keep the LPE applied.

7. Switch to the **Node** tool (*F2* or *N*) and notice the four corner nodes of the original rectangle appear. The rectangle was automatically converted to a path when applying the LPE.

8. Turn on the **Show path outline (without path effects)** 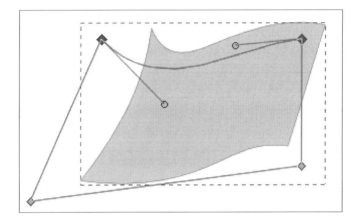 and **Show Bezier handles of selected nodes** to see the original shape and its node handles. Move the nodes with the **Node** tool and notice how the bent shape updates accordingly:

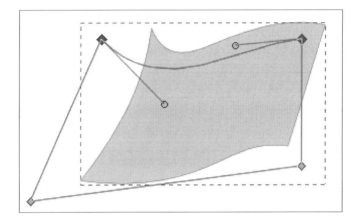

9. Press the *7* key to switch to the edit LPE bending path mode; if more adjustments are necessary, switch back to the **Node** tool using *F2* or *N*.

10. Select the other rectangle (the one we got in Step 6), click on the **Copy path** button in the **Path Effect Editor** and paste somewhere on canvas (*Ctrl + V* or right-click and choose **Paste** from the pop-up menu). Remove the fill and add a stroke to the pasted path for more clarity. This is a copy of the rectangle bending path but it is in no way connected to the rectangle or its LPE.

11. Create an "S" using the normal mode of the **Pencil** tool (*F6* or *P*) with **Smoothing:** set to 50.

12. Switch to the **Selector** tool (*Space* or *F1* or *S*) and copy the "S" (*Ctrl + C*).

13. Select the rectangle with Bend applied to it and press the **Paste path** button in the **Path Effect Editor** to bend our rectangle in the form of the "S".

14. The shape might look a bit weird if our rectangle length and width are similar; this can be corrected in the Bend LPE by changing the **Width** value. In this case, reducing the width from 1 to 0.2 produces the desired results:

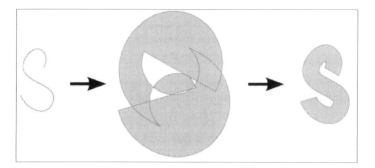

15. Create a "C" using the normal mode of the **Pencil** tool (*F6* or *P*) with **Smoothing:** set to 50 and copy it (*Ctrl + C*).

16. Select one of the objects with Bend applied to it and press the **Link to path** button in the **Path Effect Editor** in order to bend our rectangle in the form of the "C". The LPE object will be positioned over the "C" and the "C" shape will still be available for editing.

17. Change the **Width** value if necessary. In our case, a value of 0.2 proved adequate.

18. Select the "C" shape and edit it using the **Path** tool (*F2* or *N*). Notice how editing the "C" shape automatically updates the LPE linked to it:

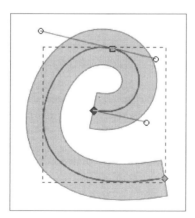

There's more...

Unexpected results can happen if the shape we're trying to bend is vertical (taller than wide); the Inkscape developers, in their wisdom, have provided a special **Original path is vertical** option that will adapt the bending effect accordingly.

Bending groups

We bent only one object in this recipe but bending groups is also possible. Just make sure the objects within the group are converted to paths before the bending is applied.

Stacking LPEs

It's possible to apply more than one LPE to a single object. You can preview what the shape looks like with or without a particular LPE applied by toggling the "eye" ![icon] icon in the **Effect list**.

Removing Path Effects

Live Path Effects change the shape of an object while keeping the original shape information intact (these changes are made "Live", as in real time). This means that LPEs can be undone, and the **Remove Path Effect** option under the **Path** menu does exactly that. You have to remove the object from the selection and then select it again to update the Path Effect Editor display.

See also

For more information, refer to the recipes on *Using Pattern Along Path* and *Using Envelope Deformation*, which will be discussed later in this chapter.

Using Pattern Along Path

We have already used the **Pattern Along Path** effect without even knowing it by choosing a shape in the **Shape:** option of the **Pen** and **Pencil** tools (we told you LPEs are ubiqitous!). This LPE takes a path and applies it along another one, like a reverse Bend LPE. In this recipe we will learn another method to widen the outline of a tree trunk created using **Spiro Spline** and explore some other options of this LPE.

How to do it...

The following steps will show how to widen an outline using **Pattern Along Path**:

1. Create a tree trunk using the **Spiro spline** mode with the **Pencil** (*F6* or *P*) tool. Set the **Smoothing:** to 34 and the **Shape:** to **Triangle in**.

2. Open the **Path Effect Editor** by using *Shift + Ctrl + 7* or by going to **Path | Path Effect Editor....**You will see two LPEs listed: **Spiro spline** and **Pattern Along Path**.

3. Select the **Pattern Along Path** by clicking on it to get to its options.

4. Use the arrow handles to widen the shape. Notice how this affects only the skeleton path and the "tree trunk" remains the same width because it's governed by the LPE shape.

5. To make the "tree trunk" appear wider change the original triangle using the **Edit on-canvas** option of the Pattern source. It will appear as a green path near the top-left corner of the page.

6. Move the top triangle corner upwards and the bottom one downwards. Notice how the "tree trunk" appears wider.

7. There is also another way to achieve the same result—using the **Width** option. Change it to 5 and see how the "tree trunk" gets even wider. This time the original triangle shape isn't modified.

8. Tick the **Pattern is vertical** option. Notice how the shape changes depending on what base triangle orientation is taken as the pattern.

9. Change the **Pattern copies** from **Single, stretched** to **Single**. Notice we only see a small triangle at the beginning of the skeleton path because the original triangle shape is much smaller than the skeleton path, and we're only using a single one without stretching it.

10. Change the **Pattern copies** to **Repeated, stretched**. The triangles are "copied" along the skeleton and positioned one next to the other. If there is a small part of the skeleton path not covered using the original triangle size they are stretched a bit to compensate for it. Since they are so small compared to the skeleton path there isn't much difference between using the **Repeated, stretched** and **Repeated** option. Notice the **Pattern is vertical** is still enabled.

11. Untick the **Pattern is vertical** option. Notice the change in triangles.

12. Change the **Spacing** option to 25. Notice how the triangles are now spaced out.

13. Tick the **Pattern is vertical** option. The triangles change shape again based on the orientation but now the spacing between them is noticeable.

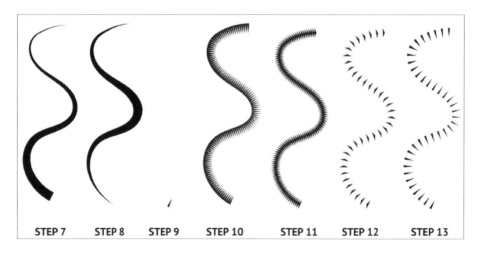

STEP 7   STEP 8   STEP 9   STEP 10   STEP 11   STEP 12   STEP 13

How it works...

The **Pattern Along Path** LPE uses one path as a pattern that is to be stretched and/or repeated along a skeleton path. Other than using the **Shape:** option of the **Pen** and **Pencil** tools we can create separate patterns and skeletons to be combined through the **Path Effect Editor** just like with any other LPE. The usual options to edit, copy, paste, and link are available, and both the pattern and the skeleton can be edited live.

Pattern Along Path also has some specific options to determine how the pattern is applied along the skeleton. We can choose to stretch it or repeat it, therefore increasing the separation between the repeated items.

There's more...

Normal and Tangential offsets are also specific options that influence the positions of the patterns in relation to the skeleton path. Normal offset moves the patterns away from the skeleton, and the tangential offset moves them along its tangent.

The difference between **Pattern along Path** and the other LPEs is that we can't use groups as patterns or skeletons.

Pattern along Path extension

Another (and older) way to achieve the same effect is by using the **Pattern along Path** extension found under the **Extensions | Generate from Path** menu. The extension also offers to choose between **Snake** and **Ribbon** as the **Deformation type**. Groups can be used as patterns, but the changes made to the pattern cannot be undone. The z-order determines which object is used as the pattern—the top-most one.

The extension doesn't always give the same results as the LPE; the straight segments stay straight when the extension is used, but the LPE bends them.

See also

For more information refer to the recipes that follow in this chapter.

Using Envelope Deformation

Envelope Deformation is often used to create interesting effects on text so this is the example we'll use in this recipe.

How to do it...

The following steps will show you how to use **Envelope Deformation**:

1. Select the **Text** tool (*F8* or *T*) and create a text object by clicking on the Canvas and typing "INKSCAPE". Set the font size to 144.

2. Open the **Path Effect Editor** by using *Shift + Ctrl + 7* or by going to **Path | Path Effect Editor....** Notice that we have the message **Item is not a path or shape** in the **Current effect** area. This means we can't use Envelope LPE on text objects.

3. Convert the text to a path (*Shift + Ctrl + C*). We will get a group.

4. Under **Apply new effect**, choose **Envelope Deformation** and press the **Add** button. Notice that the group hasn't changed.

5. Untick the **Enable left & right paths** option because if we're deforming text, results are better using only two opposite envelope edges.

6. Select the **Edit on-canvas** option for the **Top bend path** and edit it by dragging it or its handles.

7. Select the **Edit on-canvas** option for the **Bottom bend path** and edit it by dragging it or its handles:

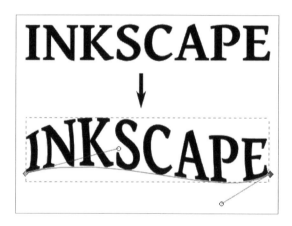

8. Tick the **Enable left & right paths** option to see how the shape changes ; the text deformation is now less elegant.

There's more...

We don't always have to use only two envelope edges. Sometimes it will be necessary to edit all four of them.

Envelope extension

Another (and older) way to achieve the same effect is by using the **Envelope** extension found under the **Extensions | Modify Path** menu. The path we want to morph this way must be converted to a path (*Shift + Ctrl + C*), and we have to create a four-node path to act as the envelope. For best results create the left-bottom node first, then move clockwise. The skeleton path must be selected second.

See also

For more information, refer to the *Bending paths* recipe seen earlier in this chapter.

Interpolating sub-paths

Interpolate Sub-Paths is an effect that can help us "blend" two sub-paths of an object. The interpolation in this LPE only affects the shape of the paths and not their style, since sub-paths cannot be styled separately.

This effect can create various 3D surface illusions, hair, hatches, and engravings, or it can be used to create shape variations so it's easier to choose the perfect one.

How to do it...

The following steps will show how to interpolate sub-paths:

1. Select the **Pencil** tool (*F6* or *P*). Set it to normal mode, set **Smoothing:** to 35, and create a horizontal wavy line. Hold *Shift* while creating another similar line so it's added to the same object. Create the second line drawing in the same direction so their path directions are parallel.

 If you forgot to press *Shift* and created two separate paths, you can still combine them into one object by selecting both of them using *Ctrl + K* or by going to **Path | Combine** so they become object sub-paths.

2. Open the **Path Effect Editor** by using *Shift + Ctrl + 7* or by going to **Path | Path Effect Editor...**.
3. Under **Apply new effect**, choose **Interpolate Sub-Paths** and press the **Add** button. Notice the additional three lines that have been interpolated between the sub-paths.
4. Under **Current effect** set **Steps** to 20 to increase the number of interpolated lines.
5. Select the **Edit on-canvas** button. Notice the green trajectory path appears over the object. This is the control path for this LPE.

6. Edit the trajectory by dragging its outline or node handles with the mouse. Notice how the interpolated lines change accordingly:

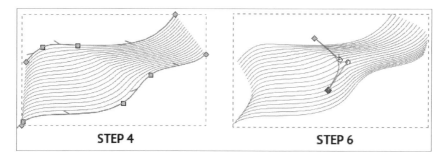

7. Add a new node on the trajectory next by double-clicking on the path.

8. Untick the **Equidistant spacing** option so the middle node now controls how interpolated paths are positioned. There is an equal number of lines between nodes but since the amount of space is not the same they appear thicker in area with less space between nodes.

9. Select the **Node** tool (*F2* or *N*) and edit the original two sub-paths just as you would any path by dragging them or their nodes and handles. Notice how the interpolated paths automatically adjust with the changes.

There's more...

The sub-paths we want to interpolate can also be closed paths.

The path direction affects the interpolation: if we reverse the direction of one sub-path the interpolation results will be different. You can enable displaying path direction in the **Inkscape Preferences** (*Shift + Ctrl + P*), by ticking the **Tools | Node | Show path direction on outlines**.

The following is an example of the same sub-paths being interpolated, only the top sub-path has the direction reversed in the second example:

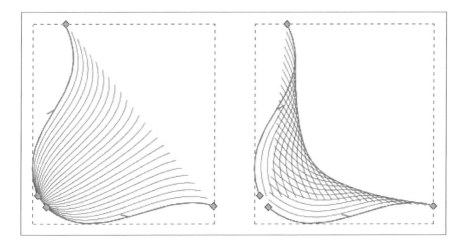

If we need our interpolated objects to become normal paths we can use the **Object to Path** option (*Shift + Ctrl + C*) but this way we lose the ability to edit it further as a LPE.

Interpolate extension

The option to interpolate also exists as an extension that can be found under **Extensions | Generate from Path | Interpolate...** but there are differences between the extension and LPE features. The extension can be applied to two objects (they don't have to be sub-paths of a single object) and the styles can also be interpolated which can give very dramatic results. The **Exponent** option controls the spacing between interpolated objects. The disadvantage of the extension is that you can't monitor the live results. Here is a simple example of two spirals converted to paths with interpolated styles, and another one that simulates a complex gradient:

You can find these examples in the `InterpolateSubpaths.svg` file accompanying this chapter.

See also

For more information, refer to the recipe on *Using Pattern Along Path* seen earlier in this chapter.

Stitching sub-paths

Stitch Sub-Paths LPE is almost like an opposite of **Interpolate Sub-Paths** LPE. It can create 3D surface effects, hair, hatches, and engravings but instead of generating additional paths "parallel" to the sub-paths, it creates them "orthogonally" to the original sub-paths.

Stitch Sub-Paths LPE also has some additional randomizing options and the possibility to use a custom path shape as "stitches".

In this recipe we will use **Stitch Sub-Paths** LPE to create a stitched effect on an alphabet. With a little practice, we can fashion a textual logo from a brand name using the very same technique.

How to do it...

The following steps will show how to stitch sub-paths:

1. Select the **Text** tool (*F8* or *T*) and write the letter "C". Choose your favorite font family, set the font size to 500. Remove the fill, set stroke to **Navy (#000080)**, stroke width to 8px, and miter cap to Round cap in the **Stroke style** tab of the **Fill and Stroke** dialog (*Shift + Ctrl + F*). This style will later be inherited by the stitches.

2. Convert the text object to a path (*Shift + Ctrl + C*) and ungroup it (*Shift + Ctrl + G*).

3. Select the **Node** tool (*F2* or *N*). Break the path (that is currently closed) into two sub-paths by breaking the paths at two selected nodes or deleting the segment between the selected nodes. Make sure to break it at the ends of the letter "C" so we get similarly shaped sub-paths.

4. Open the **Path Effect Editor** by using *Shift + Ctrl + 7* or by going to **Path | Path Effect Editor...**.

5. Under **Apply new effect**, choose **Stitch Sub-Paths** and press the **Add** button. Notice the straight lines that appear and our original path is not visible any more.

6. Enter 30 in the **Number of paths** option. Notice that the "stitches" aren't confined inside the "C" shape. We didn't get the effect we were looking for because the sub-paths directions are opposite.

7. Reverse one of the sub-paths direction by first breaking it apart (*Shift + Ctrl + K*)— the stitches will disappear temporarily. Select only one of the resulting objects and reverse it by going to **Path | Reverse**. Then select them both and combine (*Ctrl + K*). You will see the stitches properly positioned.

8. Press the **Edit on-canvas** button and notice the green control path. Edit it by dragging it or its nodes and handles to change the shape of the stitches.

9. To randomize the start and end points' positions, and the spacing between the stitches, set all the **Spacing variance** randomizing boxes to 0.20.

10. If you don't like the result you got by randomizing, click on the dice icon next to the value you want to rearrange in a new random order. The following image shows some of the steps:

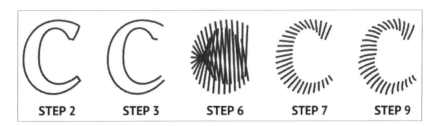

There's more...

As with the other LPEs it is possible to edit the original object with the **Node** tool and switch to editing the control path by pressing 7.

In addition to using the green control path we can change the stitch path shapes by copying a path and using the **Paste path** button in the **Current effect** area. Here is an example of a star converted to a path and pasted as a stitch on our "C" object:

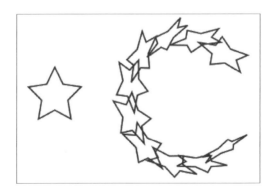

For more examples of stitched sub-paths check out the `inkscape046StitchedGold.svg` file, a submission to the About screen contest for 0.46 Inkscape version when this LPE was first introduced.

See also

For more information, refer to *Using Pattern Along Path*, *Stitching sub-paths*, and *Creating hatches (rough)* in this chapter.

Creating gears

The Gears LPE creates gears around each node of a skeleton path and adjusts the gear radius and the number of teeth , in order to make the device realistic. This effect can be employed, for example, to add a busy, mechanical look to a background In this recipe we will take the LPE for a spin (no pun intended!) and create a very simple array of gears.

How to do it...

The following steps will show how to create gears around a path:

1. Use the **Pen** tool (*Shift + F6* or *B*) to create a path with seven nodes by clicking on the canvas. Zigzag the nodes' positions (it doesn't matter if the segments are straight or curved).

2. Open the **Path Effect Editor** by using *Shift + Ctrl + 7* or by going to **Path | Path Effect Editor...**.

3. Under **Apply new effect**, choose **Gears** and press the **Add** button. Notice that gears appear around some of the nodes. Things don't look quite right: such a machine would probably crash and burn as soon as it is operated!

4. Enter 20 in both the **Teeth** and the **Phi** (Pressure angle) boxes.

5. There are probably nodes without their gears and some gears might overlap. To correct this use the **Node** tool (*F2* or *N*) to move the nodes so that gears connect correctly. Notice how gears are adjusted automatically as we move the nodes.

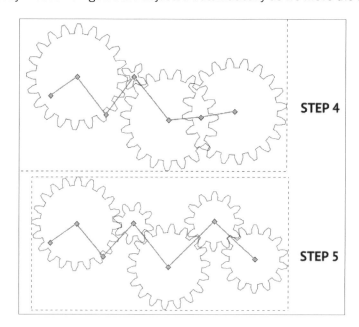

STEP 4

STEP 5

There's more...

There is also an extension that can create single gears. It can be found under **Extensions |
Render | Gear...** and it can be used to create a single gear with somewhat more control over
the gear properties.

See also

For more information, refer to *Using Pattern Along Path* in this chapter.

Creating hatches (rough)

The Hatches (rough) LPE fills an object's fill with lines that look hand-drawn. It comes with a
variety of options to adjust the line properties, which we'll explore in this recipe.

How to do it...

To create rough hatches, carry out the following steps:

1. Select the **Star** tool (*Shift + F9* or ***) and create an upright star by clicking and
    dragging upwards while holding *Ctrl*. Set the star stroke to **Black** and width to 8.

2. Open the **Path Effect Editor** by using *Shift + Ctrl + 7* or by going to **Path | Path
    Effect Editor...**

3. Under **Apply new effect**, choose **Hatches (rough)** and press the **Add** button. Notice
    the star shape becomes invisible and is replaced by squiggly lines inside its fill.

4. Set **Frequency randomness**, **Magnitude jitter**, and **Parallelism jitter** to 0 to get a
    more symmetric pattern.

5. Set **Half-turns smoothness 2nd side in** and **out** to 2 to make the top hills more
    curved.

6. Set **Thickness: at 2nd side** to 40. This is where it becomes obvious that the lines
    are actually created by two parallel paths, like a calligraphy path, and with certain
    settings we can make them separate to reveal the fill color between them.

7. Set **Thickness: from 2nd to 1st side** to 10, to make the stroke thickness vary
    depending on the direction of the curve.

8. Select the **Node** tool (*F2* or *N*) and notice the hatches handles that appear. Hover
    over the diamond ones and read the statusbar tips to find out which one controls
    bending and which one controls direction and frequency.

9. Drag the handle for direction and frequency up and to the left to make the hatches
    diagonal and thicker.

10. Drag the handle for bending up and to the right to make the hatches curve.

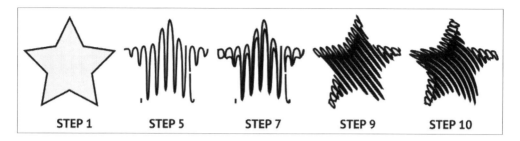

See also

For more information, refer to *Bending paths* in this chapter.

Sketching shapes

The Sketch LPE simulates a hand-created sketch drawing with multiple attempts to "correct" the line, in a style somewhat resembling the famous blueprints of the inventor and polymath Leonardo Da Vinci. This LPE comes with a number of options that can be used not only to adjust the sketch effect but to also produce some less sketchy patterns. We will explore these options in this recipe.

How to do it...

The following steps will show how to simulate a sketch:

1. Select the **Spiral** tool (*F9* or *I*) and create a spiral, set the stroke width to 2 and fill it with some color.

2. Open the **Path Effect Editor** by using *Shift + Ctrl + 7* or by going to **Path | Path Effect Editor...**.

3. Under **Apply new effect**, choose **Sketch** and press the **Add** button. Notice the sketch effect gets applied with the default settings.

4. To make the sketch appear less cluttered set **Strokes** to 2.

5. Loosen the strokes by increasing the **Average Offset** to 15.

6. Increase **Max. tremble** to 15 and **Tremble frequency** to 7 to make the lines squiggly.

7. To make the construction lines more prominent set **Scale** to 150 and **Max. length** to 300.

8. If you don't like the result you got by randomizing, click on the dice icon next to the value you want to rearrange in a new random order.

| STEP 1 | STEP 3 | STEP 5 | STEP 7 |

How it works...

Sketch LPE traces paths with two kinds of lines:

- ▸ **Strokes** that follow the path curvature
- ▸ **Construction lines** that are straight shorter segments

The settings allow us to choose how many lines to use so it's possible to turn either line type off by setting its number to 0. There are a lot of options to control the appearance of lines creating different patterns, making the lines appear more regular or randomizing their properties.

See also

For more information, refer to *Using Pattern Along Path*, *Stitching sub-paths*, and *Creating Hatches (rough)* in this chapter.

Constructing grids

Construct grid is a very simple LPE that creates a grid using a path's first three nodes to determine the grid parameters.

How to do it...

The following steps show how to construct grids:

1. Select the **Ellipse** tool (*F5* or *E*) and create a narrow ellipse at the bottom of the page.

2. Open the **Path Effect Editor** by using *Shift + Ctrl + 7* or by going to **Path | Path Effect Editor...**.

3. Under **Apply new effect**, choose **Construct grid** and press the **Add** button. Notice the ellipse becomes invisible and the grid is created using the ellipse handles position as grid parameters.

4. Enter 3 in both the **Size X** and **Size Y** boxes to reduce the number of grid fields.

5. Change the grid width and height by dragging the ellipse width and height handles (still using the **Ellipse** tool).

6. Use the ellipse circle handles to skew the grid as you see fit.

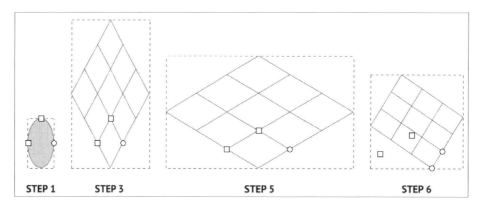

See also

For more information, refer to *Creating rulers* in this chapter.

Creating rulers

The **Ruler** LPE is a simple effect that applies ruler markers to paths. As the path is edited the ruler markers adjust automatically as we'll see in this recipe.

How to do it...

The following steps show how to create a ruler:

1. Select the **Rectangle** tool (*F4* or *R*) and create a rectangle.

2. Open the **Path Effect Editor** by using *Shift + Ctrl + 7* or by going to **Path | Path Effect Editor...**.

3. Under **Apply new effect**, choose **Ruler** and press the **Add** button. Notice ruler marks that appear outside of the rectangle.

4. Set **Mark distance** and **Major length** to 30, and **Minor length** to 15 to change the ruler scale and make it more readable.

5. Change the **Mark direction** to **Both** to center the ruler marks on the path stroke.

6. Select the **Node** tool (*F2* or *N*) and make all nodes smooth by selecting them all (*Ctrl + A*) and using the appropriate button on the toolbar or *Shift + S*. Notice how the ruler marks adjust to the path shape.

7. Edit the path by dragging it or its nodes and handles. Notice how the ruler marks adjust automatically.

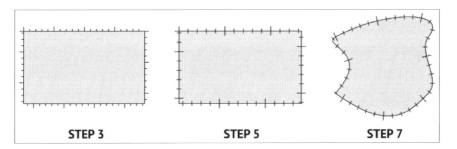

| STEP 3 | STEP 5 | STEP 7 |

See also

For more information, refer to *Using Pattern Along Path* in this chapter.

Creating knots

The **Knot** LPE creates visual gaps at the points where a path intersects itself as if the path is tied into a knot, with certain path segments running over others.

How to do it...

The following steps will show how to create knots in a path:

1. Select the **Star** tool (*Shift +F9* or ***), press the **Reset the shape parameters to their defaults** button and create a complex star shape with nine corners and rounded base radius with a value that gets an effect you like. Remove the star fill to keep it aligned with the goal of creating a knot out of a path and increase the stroke width to 6. You should get a shape similar to the one shown in the picture.

2. Open the **Path Effect Editor** by using *Shift + Ctrl + 7* or by going to **Path | Path Effect Editor...**.

3. Under the **Apply new effect**, choose **Knot** and press the **Add** button. Notice the gaps in the stroke around the intersection points.

4. Select the **Node** tool (*F2* or *N*) and notice that a diamond handle appears over one of the intersections. Drag the handle to an intersection of your choice whose gap type you wish to change.

5. Click on the diamond handle once or twice to change which path segment goes over or under, or remove the gap altogether. Repeat if necessary on other intersections.

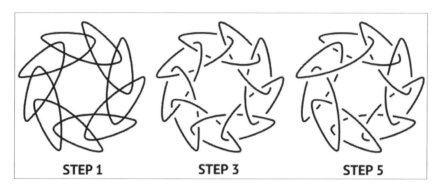

STEP 1   STEP 3   STEP 5

See also

For more information, refer to *Using Pattern Along Path* in this chapter.

Generating VonKoch fractals

The **VonKoch** LPE (named after the Swedish mathematician Helge Von Koch) creates a *fractal* pattern out of the object it is applied to by repeating it in a scaled form and positioning it according to control paths available in this LPE. In this recipe we will create a simple pattern using the VonKoch LPE.

How to do it...

The following steps will show how to create VonKoch fractals:

1. Select the **Ellipse** tool (*F5* or *E*) and create a wide ellipse at the page center.

2. Open the **Path Effect Editor** by using *Shift + Ctrl + 7* or by going to **Path | Path Effect Editor...**.

3. Under **Apply new effect**, choose **VonKoch** and press the **Add** button. Notice the two additional ellipses beneath the original one.

4. Create an angled guide by dragging with the mouse out of the top-left corner of the ruler on to the Canvas. Change the guide angle to 60° by double-clicking on it to get a pop-up and position it so it touches the original ellipse's right edge.

5. Press the **Generating path** button. Notice the two green controlling paths over the smaller ellipses.

6. Move each controlling path separately so they touch the guide with their right-hand edges, one ellipse above and the other below the original ellipse.

7. Increase the **Nb of generations** to 3 to generate more fractal steps.

8. Press the **Reference segment** button. Notice the green controlling paths over the original ellipses.

9. Switch the focus back to the canvas from the dialog by pressing *Esc*.

10. Select both nodes (*Ctrl + A*) and move them to the left using the *Left* arrow key (it is easier to do it using the keyboard because ellipse handles cover the control path nodes making them hard to select using a mouse). Move the green control path until its right node reaches the left edge of the original ellipse. Notice how the generated objects shift automatically to satisfy the position condition in relation to the object in the previous generation.

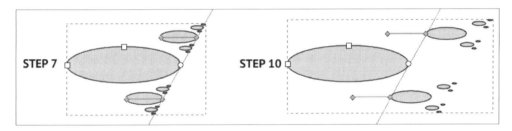

There's more...

Some VonKoch effects can also be created using the L-system extension found under **Extensions | Render | L-system**. This extension will be covered in more detail in the next chapter.

See also

For more information, refer to *Rendering L-system patterns* in *Chapter 6*.

6
Extensions

In this chapter, we will cover:

- ► Coloring Markers to Match Stroke
- ► Using Whirl
- ► Rendering 3D polyhedrons and wireframe spheres
- ► Rendering barcodes
- ► Rendering calendars
- ► Using Render Grid, Cartesian Grid, and Polar Grid
- ► Rendering spirographs
- ► Rendering L-systems
- ► Plotting functions and parametric curves
- ► Rendering Printing Marks
- ► Playing "Connect the dots" with Number Nodes
- ► Creating irregular edges

Introduction

As we have seen in the previous chapters, Inkscape's standard tools are both flexible and powerful. However, there are many situations in which building everything from scratch is repetitive, time consuming, and prone to errors.

Many modern programming languages provide a standard set of libraries with ready-made functions and classes for connecting to networks, creating user-interfaces, and so on. Similarly, Inkscape follows a "batteries included" (to quote a popular Python motto) philosophy, and ships with a vast library of extensions that are ready to be used immediately.

Extensions can rapidly create complex shapes and guides, manipulate object attributes (such as color), format text, and even perform raster image enhancing. Inkscape 0.48 provides an extensive collection of more than a hundred extensions, and we will explore some of the most useful ones in this chapter.

Setting Color Markers to Match Stroke

Markers applied to paths are like other objects in Inkscape. They have their own styles. One of the most common tasks when using markers is adjusting their style to match the one of the path they are applied to. The extension **Color Markers to Match Stroke** changes the fill and stroke of the markers applied to a path, applying the color of the path stroke.

How to do it...

The following steps will show how to set the color of stroke markers:

1. Select the **Create regular (Bezier) path** mode of the **Pencil** tool (*F6* or *P*) and create a short wavy line.

2. Assign **Arrow1Lstart** as the **Start Markers:**, **DotL** as the **Mid Markers:**, and **Arrow1Lend** as the **End Markers:** on the **Stroke style** tab of the **Fill and Stroke** dialog (*Shift + Ctrl + F*).

3. Change the path stroke color to **Red (#FF0000)**.

4. Go to **Extensions | Modify Path | Color Markers to Match Stroke**. The extension will be executed immediately and the markers' fill and stroke will be assigned the color of the path stroke (**Red (#FF0000)**).

There's more...

Besides using this extension the marker colors can be edited directly using the XML editor (*Shift + Ctrl + X*). Each path with markers applied has them listed under the `style` attribute. This is where we can take note of the marker name. Then we expand the `svg:defs` element in the XML tree (usually found near the top) and find the marker under an `svg:marker` element that has an `id` attribute the same as the marker name. The path found inside the `svg:marker` is the actual marker object and any modification made to its style will be immediately visible in the Canvas.

Here I changed the start marker fill color to blue and stroke width to 0.8. The mid marker's fill was removed, stroke set to lime, and width was increased to 2. The end marker was scaled using the `transform:scale()` attribute and under `style` attribute stroke color was changed to black and fill to aqua. These changes produced the following result:

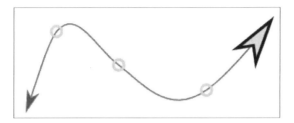

Object to markers

More flexibility can be achieved by creating our own markers using the **Object | Objects to Marker** command. The marker size will scale together with the path stroke, so you might need to use the tips in the previous section to set it back to the desired size.

See also

For more information, refer to the *Creating freehand and straight lines* and *Editing paths* with *the Node tool* recipes in *Chapter 1*.

Using Whirl

This recipe will show us how to use the **Whirl** extension to deform an object to look like it was melted and rotated. The effect is similar to what happens when you stir the soft foam of a cappuccino, whirling the pattern made by the barista.

How to do it...

The following steps demonstrate how to use the **Whirl** extension:

1. Select the **Star** tool (*Shift + F9* or ***) and create a star with nine corners and a **Spoke ratio:** of 0.2. Don't move the object from its original position until **Whirl** is applied to get expected results.

2. Convert the star to a path (*Shift + Ctrl + C*) because the extension can only be applied to a path.

3. Increase the number of nodes in the path by selecting the **Node** tool (*F2* or *N*). Then, select all the nodes (*Ctrl + A*) and press the *Ins* key (or press the **Insert new nodes into the selected segments** button ⊞) several times.

4. Zoom to selection by pressing *3* so the star now fills the screen as much as possible. This step is important because the **Whirl** extension makes the changes with respect to the currently visible Canvas.

5. Open the **Whirl** dialog by going to **Extensions | Modify Path | Whirl...**, set the **Amount of whirl** to 10, and press **Apply**.

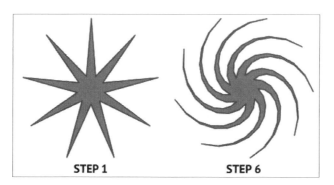

6. Repeat Step 1 through Step 3, or simply go back using the **Undo** button [icon] (*Ctrl + Z*). Zoom out and pan the Canvas so that the star is positioned in the bottom part of the visible Canvas.

7. Open the **Whirl** dialog by going to **Extensions | Modify Path | Whirl...**, set the **Amount of whirl** to 4, and press **Apply**. The star will be moved away from its original position and deformed, as in the following image:

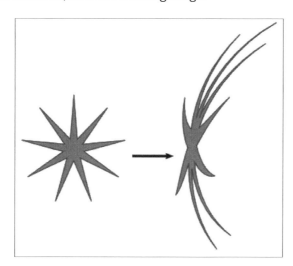

How it works...

The **Whirl** extension is calculated with respect to the visible Canvas. The object shouldn't be moved to position it on the Canvas; instead the Canvas must be panned because the deformation will take into consideration the original position and the results might not be what we expect if we move the object.

There's more...

As we have seen there are a couple of "arcane" factors that influence the outcome of the extensions, that is, the number of nodes and the zoom factor of the shape with respect to the Canvas. By taking a look at the source code of the extension, written in Python, we can see that the method that generates the whirl effect takes these two factors into consideration. We will learn how to modify and create our own extensions in the last chapter of this book.

Adding nodes

Almost all extensions require the objects to be converted to paths and adding more nodes gives better results. In this case, the deformation was smoother.

This can also be accomplished with the **Add Nodes** extension found under **Extensions | Modify Path**. This extension can be used instead if the insert function of the **Node** tool when dealing with complex shapes to get a more even distribution of nodes.

See also

For more information, refer to the *Bending paths*, *Using Pattern Along Path*, and *Using Envelope Deformation* recipes in this chapter.

Rendering 3D polyhedrons and wireframe spheres

This recipe will show us how to render 3D geometric objects using the 3D Polyhedron and Wireframe sphere extensions.

How to do it...

The following steps will show you how to render 3D objects and wireframes:

1. Open the **3D Polyhedron** dialog by going to **Extensions | Render | 3D Polyhedron...**.
2. Under **Object:** select **Truncated Cube** from the drop-down menu.
3. Under **Object Type** select **Face-Specified**.

4. On the **View** tab set **Rotate around:** to **Y-Axis** and **Rotation, degrees** to 20.

5. Set the following **Then rotate around:** to **X-Axis** and **Rotation, degrees** to 20.

6. Under the **Style** tab set **Fill opacity, %** to 60, **Stroke width, px** to 4. Make sure **Shading** is ticked. Set **Light Z** to -1, **Show:** to **Faces** and tick **Draw back-facing polygons**.

7. Leave the other options as default and press **Apply**. The truncated cube will be created in the center of the visible Canvas.

8. Open the **Wireframe Sphere** dialog by going to **Extensions | Render | Wireframe Sphere...**.

9. Under **Lines of latitude** and **Lines of longitude** enter 12. Set **Tilt [deg]** to 30, **Rotation [deg]** to 10, and **Radius [px]** to 160.

10. Leave the other options as default and press **Apply**. The wireframe sphere will be created at the center of the visible Canvas. To make it more visible increase the stroke to 2.

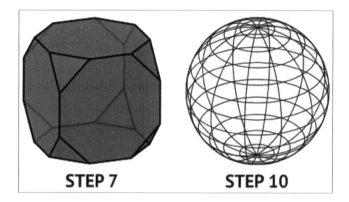

How it works...

As we saw, all we have to do to use one of the rendering extensions is to select the desired options and press **Apply**.

The **3D Polyhedron** extension offers sixteen different objects to be rendered, but you can also choose your own file to describe the object. The files must be in the **Wavefront Obj** format (see http://en.wikipedia.org/wiki/Wavefront_.obj_file).

While the 3D polyhedron consists of faces of the polyhedron, the wireframe sphere consists of ellipses. If there's a need to style the back-facing lines of the sphere differently, create a sphere with those lines hidden, duplicate such a sphere, flip it horizontally and vertically, and send it to the back (*End*):

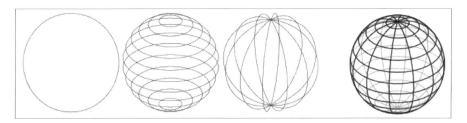

See also

For more information, refer to the recipe *Plotting functions and parametric curves* in *Chapter 6*.

Rendering barcodes

This recipe will show us how to use the **Render | Barcode** and **Render | Barcode - Datamatrix** extensions to generate... you guessed it, barcodes!

How to do it...

Carry out the following steps to create barcodes:

1. Open the **Barcode** dialog by going to **Extensions | Render | Barcode...**.
2. Under **Barcode Type:** select **EAN13**, under **Barcode Data:** enter a 12-digit number (I used 123456789123), and under **Bar Height:** enter 80.
3. Press **Apply**, and the barcode will be rendered at the center of the visible Canvas.
4. Open the **Barcode - Datamatrix** dialog by going to **Extensions | Render | Barcode - Datamatrix...**.
5. In the **Text** box enter "Inkscape", set **Rows** and **Cols** to 20, and **Square Size / px** to 5.
6. Press **Apply**, and the barcode will be rendered at the center of the visible Canvas.

Although only one barcode type is used in this recipe there are ten types in total supported by the **Barcode** extension.

Rendering calendars

What would a graphics package be without the option of rendering pretty calendars to print and keep at home or at the office? This recipe will show us how to generate a calendar using the **Calendar** extension.

How to do it...

Carry out the following steps to create a fancy looking calendar:

1. Open the **Calendar** dialog by going to **Extensions | Render | Calendar...**.
2. Under the **Colors** tab set **Year color** to #0000ff and **Weekend day color** to #d40000.
3. Leave the other options as default and press **Apply**. The calendar will be rendered near the top of the page. Here is what the first three months look like:

2010

January

Sun	Mon	Tue	Wed	Thu	Fri	Sat
27	28	29	30	31	1	2
3	4	5	6	7	8	9
10	11	12	13	14	15	16
17	18	19	20	21	22	23
24	25	26	27	28	29	30
31	1	2	3	4	5	6

February

Sun	Mon	Tue	Wed	Thu	Fri	Sat
31	1	2	3	4	5	6
7	8	9	10	11	12	13
14	15	16	17	18	19	20
21	22	23	24	25	26	27
28	1	2	3	4	5	6
7	8	9	10	11	12	13

March

Sun	Mon	Tue	Wed	Thu	Fri	Sat
28	1	2	3	4	5	6
7	8	9	10	11	12	13
14	15	16	17	18	19	20
21	22	23	24	25	26	27
28	29	30	31	1	2	3
4	5	6	7	8	9	10

There's more...

Calendar creation doesn't stop here! The **Calendar** extension has a lot of configuration parameters that can change the language, the starting and ending months, the rendering of the greyed out numbers, the days of the next months, and lots more.

By rendering each month on a separate Canvas and adding decorations, such as photos or clipart, you can easily produce a professional looking calendar for home or commercial use.

Using Render Grid, Cartesian Grid, and Polar Grid

In this recipe we will see how we can render different kinds of grids using **Render | Grid**, **Render | Cartesian Grid** and **Render | Polar Grid** extensions.

The grids rendered in this recipe are objects in Inkscape and are not to be confused with the helper grid lines set in **Document Properties** (*Shift + Ctrl + D*). In other words, these grids are meant to be part of the drawing content, and not to be used as drawing aides.

How to do it...

The following steps will show how to render grids:

1. Open the **Grid** dialog by going to **Extensions | Render | Grid...**.

2. Set both **Horizontal Spacing** and **Vertical Spacing** to 50.

3. Leave the other options as default and press **Apply**. The page area will be filled with lines 50 px apart.

4. Open the **Cartesian Grid** dialog by going to **Extensions | Render | Cartesian Grid...**.

5. In the dialog set the parameters according to the following table:

Major X Divisions	3
Major Y Divisions	3
Major X Division Spacing [px]	300
Major Y Divisions Spacing [px]	300
Subdivisions per Major X Division	2
Subdivisions per Major Y Division	2
Subsubdivs. per X Subdivision	3
Subsubdivs. per Y Subdivision	3

6. Leave the other options as default and press **Apply**. The Cartesian grid will be rendered at the center of the visible Canvas.

7. Open the **Polar Grid** dialog by going to **Extensions | Render | Polar Grid...** and set the parameters according to the following table:

Major Circular Divisions	3
Major Circular Division Spacing [px]	150
Subdivisions per Major Circular Division	10
Logarithmic Subdiv.	On
Angle Divisions	30
Angle Divisions at center	4
Subdivisions per Major Angular Division	2
Minor Angle Division End 'n' Divs. Before Centre	2
Centre Dot Diameter [px]	20
Circumferential Labels	Degrees
Circumferential Label Size [px]	20
Circumferential Label Outset [px]	22

8. Leave the other options as default and press **Apply**. The Polar grid will be rendered at the center of the visible Canvas

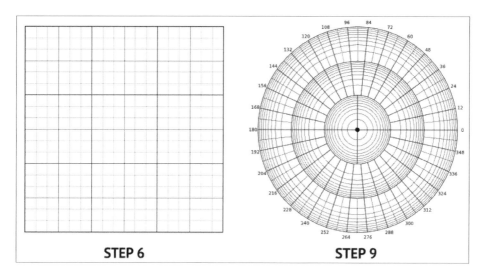

STEP 6   STEP 9

How it works...

As we can see from this recipe the **Grid** extension can be used for the simplest grid of equally distant lines of the same thickness. For more control we can use the **Cartesian Grid** extension, where three levels of divisions can be set and line thickness can be different for each of them. There is even the option to make logarithmic divisions.

The **Polar Grid** is very similar to the **Cartesian Grid** extension, only it renders polar coordinates. Two levels of circular and angular divisions are available with a separate angular division for the first circular division.

The option **Minor Angle Division End 'n' Divs. Before Centre** determines between which circle divisions to stop/start showing minor angle divisions. In our example the value is set to 2, which means that minor angle divisions will not be shown in the first two major circle divisions, but they will be shown in the third major circle division. This option is very useful when using a lot of divisions to make the smaller circle divisions less cluttered.

See also

For more information, refer to the recipe on *Geometric illusions using Grid* in *Chapter 3*, and *Rendering 3D polyhedrons and wireframe spheres* in this chapter.

Rendering spirographs

In this recipe we will play with the **Spirograph** extension to create some interesting patterns.

How to do it...

The following steps will show how to render spirographs:

1. Open the the the **Spirograph** dialog by going to **Extensions | Render | Spirograph....**

2. Set **R (Ring radius)** to 100, **r (Gear radius)** to 81, **d (Pen radius)** to 70, and **Gear Placement** to **Outside (Epitrochoid)**.

3. Leave the other options as default and press **Apply**, the spirograph will be rendered at the center of the visible Canvas. Don't close the dialog yet!

4. Pan the Canvas so that the spirograph isn't in the center any more.

5. Change the **Gear Placement** to **Inside (Hypotrochoid)**.

6. Press **Apply**. The second spirograph will be rendered at the center of the visible Canvas, but it will be smaller than the first one.

7. On the **Selector** toolbar, turn off the **Scale stroke width** button and turn the lock ratio button between the width and height boxes on.

8. Copy the first spirograph (*Ctrl + C*), select the second, and go to **Edit | Paste size | Paste size** to make the second spirograph the same size:

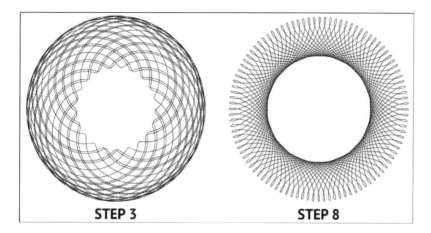

STEP 3   STEP 8

9. Change the **R**, **r**, and **d** parameters from Step 2 to different values and see what kind of results you get.

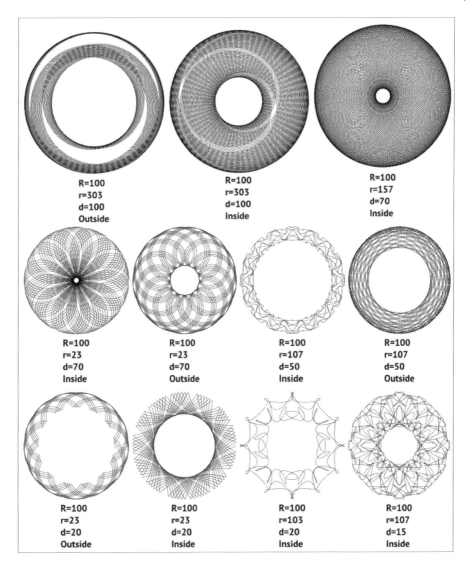

R=100
r=303
d=100
Outside

R=100
r=303
d=100
Inside

R=100
r=157
d=70
Inside

R=100
r=23
d=70
Inside

R=100
r=23
d=70
Outside

R=100
r=107
d=50
Inside

R=100
r=107
d=50
Outside

R=100
r=23
d=20
Outside

R=100
r=23
d=20
Inside

R=100
r=103
d=20
Inside

R=100
r=107
d=15
Inside

How it works...

The maximum number of generated nodes is hardcoded in the extension as 1000. In case of very complex drawings it might run out of nodes, so reducing the **Quality** value might help.

There are more spirograph examples with their respective spirograph values in the `Spirograph.svg` file accompanying this chapter.

For more information, refer to the *Rendering L-systems* recipe that follows.

Rendering L-systems

This recipe will show us how to play with the **L-system** extension to render some very interesting patterns. This extension uses the *Lindenmayer* formulas, but no previous knowledge of L-systems is required to successfully follow this recipe. We will continue our venture in the fascinating world of spirographic shapes by using this extension to produce a similar drawing.

The L-system grammar was invented by Hungarian biologist, *Aristid Lindenmayer* to describe the growth of plants, so our second example will show how to create a bush-like object. Finally, in our third example we will generate a complex geometrical pattern resembling a labyrinth. Isn't it amazing how these three different objects are related by the same mathematical formulas?

How to do it...

Carry out the following steps to build L-system objects:

1. Open the **L-system** dialog by going to **Extensions | Render | L-system...**.
2. Open the **Help** tab in the **L-system** dialog and read the explanation.
3. Go back to the **Axiom and rules** tab and enter F in the **Axiom** box, F=F+F-F+F in the **Rules** box. Set **Order** to 5, **Step length (px)** to 20, **Left angle** to 20, and **Right angle** to 80, and leave the randomizing boxes at 0.
4. Press **Apply**. The object will be rendered at the center of the visible Canvas.

> As more generations of the L-system formula are calculated Inkscape will need more nodes to create the object, and calculating will take more time, sometimes using 100% of your CPU. When testing out a new formula it's always safe to first calculate and draw a small number of generations. The number of generations is controlled by **Order** so use 2, 3, or 4 as values to see how much resources they need before generating more complex generations.
>
> Also, when dealing with a large number of nodes that this extension can generate, switch to the Outline view to speed up rendering using *Ctrl + 5*.

5. Create a bush-like object by setting **Axiom** to ++++F, **Rules** to F=FF-[-F+F+F]+[+F-F-F], **Order** to 4, **Step length (px)** to 5, both **Left angle** and **Right angle** to 22, and leave the randomizing boxes at 0.

6. Press **Apply**. The object will be rendered at the center of the visible Canvas, but it will look like it's been rotated. To make it conform to gravity better, rotate it 90° counter-clockwise using *Ctrl + [* or the button on the Selector toolbar.

7. Create a Peano-Gosper curve by setting **Axiom** to A, **Rules** to A=A+BF++BF-FA--FAFA-BF+;B=-FA+BFBF++BF+FA--FA-B, **Order** to 3, **Step length (px)** to 6, both **Left angle** and **Right angle** to 60, and leave the randomizing boxes at 0.

8. Press **Apply**. The object will be rendered at the center of the visible Canvas.

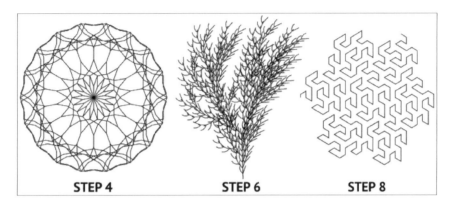

How it works...

L-system formulas are recursive and each time they are executed the end result is different, more complex with each new generation. In some formulas angles are important and using different ones won't give a meaningful result, while in others changing the angles modifies the result, creating new patterns. **Step length (px)** determines the size of the basic line used to build the pattern on, and together with the number of generations (**Order**) determines what the size of the final object will be. **Randomize step (%)** and **Randomize angle (%)** options are usually very helpful when creating realistic plant drawings.

The first two examples in the following image are created with the same formula, only randomizing is applied to both step and angle. Other examples are available in the L-systemMoreExamples.svg file accompanying this chapter.

Don't forget to also check out the screenshot on inkscape.org showing more examples together with their formulas:

`http://www.inkscape.org/screenshots/gallery/inkscape-0.44-lindenmayer.png`

See also

For more information, refer to *Rendering spirographs* and *Rendering functions and parametric curves* in this chapter.

Rendering functions and parametric curves

In this recipe we will plot an example of under-damping curve and some attractive examples of parametric curves such as the Teardrop Curve by using the **Function plotter** and **Parametric curves** extensions.

How to do it...

The following steps will show how to render functions and curves:

1. Select the **Rectangle** tool (*F4* or *R*) and create a 600 x 400 rectangle. Make its fill **White**, stroke **Black**, and stroke width 1. Make sure it stays selected.

2. Open the **Function Plotter** dialog by going to **Extensions | Render | Function Plotter...**.

3. Read the **Use** and **Functions** tabs in the **Function Plotter** dialog and read the explanations.

4. Go back to the **Range and sampling** tab and change the **End X value** to 50. Make sure that **Multiply X range by 2*pi** isn't ticked, set **Y value of rectangle's bottom** to -1, **Y value of rectangle's top** to 1, and **Number of samples** to 50. Make sure that **Isotropic scaling** and **Use polar coordinates** are unticked.

5. In the **Function** box enter `exp(-x/8)*cos(sqrt(63)*x/8)`. Make sure **Calculate first derivative numerically** and **Draw Axes** are ticked and untick the **Remove rectangle** option.

6. Press **Apply**. The function will be plotted inside the rectangle.

7. Close the **Function Plotter** dialog and create another 600 x 400 rectangle.

8. To create a Teardrop curve, open the **Parametric Curves** dialog by going to **Extensions | Render | Parametric Curves...**.

9. Read the **Use** and **Functions** tabs in the **Parametric Curves** dialog and read the explanations.

10. Go back to the **Range and sampling** tab and change the **End t-value** to 1. Make sure that **Multiply t-range by 2*pi** is ticked, set **x-value of rectangle's left** to -1, **x-value of rectangle's right** to 1, **x-value of rectangle's bottom** to -1, **x-value of rectangle's top** to 1, and **Samples** to 30. Make sure that **Isotropic scaling**, **Remove rectangle**, and **Draw Axes** are unticked.

11. In the **x-Function** box enter `cos(t)` and in the **y-Function** box `sin(t)*pow(sin(t/2),2)`.

12. Press **Apply** to plot the curve inside the rectangle.

13. Select the same rectangle again and change the **y-Function** to `sin(t)*pow(sin(t/2),5)` (only the exponent changed).

14. Press **Apply** to plot another Teardrop curve on top of the one we created in Step 12.

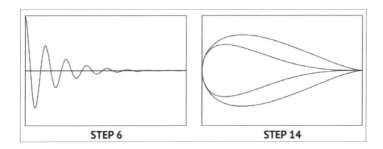

STEP 6   STEP 14

How it works...

Before the functions can be plotted, **Function Plotter** and **Parametric Curves** extensions require a rectangle to be selected that will determine over which area of the Canvas to plot. This will only work on rectangles created by the **Rectangle** tool; it won't work if the rectangle is converted to an object.

If the curve doesn't look as expected it may be because the number of nodes from the **Number of samples** box (or **Samples** in **Parametric Curves**) isn't big enough to create an accurate plot. Increase this number to get more accurate results.

If you need to use functions not listed under the **Functions** tab in the **Function Plotter** dialog you can find the correct syntax in Python documentation online:

`http://docs.python.org/library/math.html`

See also

For more information, refer to *Rendering spirographs* and *Rendering L-systems* in this chapter.

Rendering printing marks

In this recipe we will create *printing marks*, those colorful and sometimes mysterious symbols you will have encountered numerous times on cardboard boxes or paper prints. We will use the **Printing Marks** extension, on a custom template format.

How to do it...

Carry out the following steps to render printing marks:

1. Open **Document Properties** (*Shift + Ctrl + D*) on the **Page** tab and change the **Default units:** to **in**. Under **Page size** set **Custom size** to use **in** as **Units:** and set **Width:** to 11 and **Height:** to 4.

2. Open the **Printing Marks** dialogue by going to **Extensions** > **Render** > **Printing Marks...**.

3. On the **Marks** tab select all the options so they are all rendered.

4. On the **Positioning** tab, select **Canvas** under **Set crop marks to** option, select **in** as **Unit**, set **Offset:** to 0.2, and all **Bleed Margin** boxes to 0.2.

5. In the **Current layer** drop-down menu at the bottom left of the Inkscape window choose **[Printing Marks]** and unlock it by clicking on the padlock icon next to it.

6. Open **Inkscape Preferences** (*Shift + Ctrl + P*) and under **Tools** tick **Keep objects after conversion to guides** and make sure **Treat groups as a single object** is unticked.

7. Open the **XML Editor** (*Shift + Ctrl + X*) and select the `BleedMarks` subgroup found in the `printing-marks` group. Create guides out of them by pressing *Shift + G* or **Object | Objects to Guides in the menu**.

8. Lock the **Printing Marks** layer by clicking on the padlock icon next to it.

How it works...

Printing marks should be applied to the drawing right after we have set the dimensions of our document, and should be rendered after the document size is set and before drawing starts. We do this in case there are any areas where colors reach the edge of the paper/medium , in order to make it easier to create background color bleeds. It is useful to convert the bleed marks to guides straight away so we can align background elements to them.

See also

For more information, refer to the *Creating a simple flashlight using Guides* recipe in *Chapter 3*.

Playing "connect the dots" with Number Nodes

In this recipe we will create a simple "connect the dots" template using the **Number Nodes** extension.

How to do it...

The following steps will demonstrate how to create a "connect the dots" template:

1. Select the **Star** tool (*Shift + F9* or ***). Create a complex star with five rounded corners, remove its fill and set stroke to **Black** and stroke width to 2.

2. Convert the star to a path (*Shift + Ctrl + C*).

3. Increase the number of nodes in the path by selecting the **Node** tool (*F2* or *N*), selecting all the nodes (*Ctrl + A*), and pressing *Insert* several times.

4. Open the **Number Nodes** dialog by going to **Extensions | Visualize Path | Number Nodes...**. Set **Font size** to 24 and **Dot size** to 10 px.

5. Tick **Live preview** to see what the effect would look like when applied. If the font or dots sizes aren't nice, then edit them directly in the boxes and press *Enter*. The drawing will be updated automatically.

6. When you're happy with the sizes, press **Apply**. The path will be removed from the drawing and nodes will be marked with numbered dots.

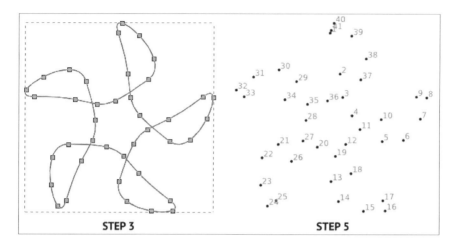

STEP 3   STEP 5

See also

For more information, refer to *Creating and editing 2D geometric shapes* and *Editing paths using the Node tool* in *Chapter 1*.

Creating irregular edges

In this recipe we will use the **Fractalize**, **Jitter nodes**, and **Straighten Segments** extensions to make the object edge irregular. These effects can be used when creating the burned paper edge look.

How to do it...

The following steps will demonstrate creation of irregular edges:

1. Select the **Rectangle** tool (*F4* or *R*) and create a 400 x 500 px rectangle. Open the **Fill and Stroke** (*Shift + Ctrl + F*) editor and set its fill to `#fff7d5ff`, stroke to `#2b1100ff`, and stroke width to 16.

2. Convert it to a path (*Shift + Ctrl + C*).

3. Increase the number of nodes in the path by selecting the **Node** tool (*F2* or *N*), selecting all the nodes (*Ctrl + A*), and pressing *Insert* several times.

4. Select (just press the *Space* key) and duplicate the rectangle by stamping with the *Space* key twice so there are three objects in total.

5. Select one of the rectangles and open the **Fractalize** dialog by going to **Extensions | Modify Path | Fractalize...**.

6. Set **Subdivisions** to 2, **Smoothness** to 3, and press **Apply**. The object's edge will get deformed.

7. Select the remaining two rectangles and open the **Jitter nodes** dialog by going to **Extensions | Modify Path | Jitter nodes...**.

8. Set **Maximum displacement in X, px** and **Maximum displacement in Y, px** to 20. Untick **Shift nodes**, and tick **Shift node handles** and **Use normal distribution**.

9. Press **Apply**. Both of the object's edges will be deformed.

10. Select only one of the rectangles treated with **Jitter nodes** extension and open the **Straighten Segments** dialog by going to **Extensions | Modify Path | Straighten Segments...**.

11. Set **Percent** to 40 and **Behavior** to 1, and press **Apply**. This will reduce the "irregularities" in the object's edge.

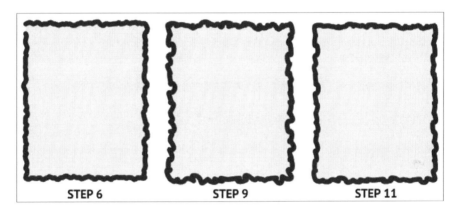

STEP 6   STEP 9   STEP 11

How it works...

As shown in the examples, both **Fractalize** and **Jitter nodes** extensions can create irregular edges, while the **Straighten Segments** extension can help reduce the jitter when necessary.

The **Fractalize** extension creates more nodes when **Subdivisions** is set to a larger number, so it may be very CPU intensive at times. This extension retains the object shape more if there are more nodes in the path before applying the extension. *Jittered* nodes retain the object shape better if we only shift the handles.

There's more...

One of many uses for irregular edges is creating a burned paper effect. Here is what our examples might look like after a bit of clipping and blurring:

Irregular edges can also be achieved with the **Tweak** tool (*Shift + F2* or *W*) while using the **Roughen parts of paths** mode. However, this can produce a large number of nodes so it's best to set **Fidelity:** to a low number.

SVG filters can also be used to roughen edges. **Torn edges** is one that is very similar to our example. However, since filters are much more resource intensive it's better to use extensions and raw node manipulation when the outcomes don't differ a lot.

See also

For more information, refer to the recipes on *Creating and editing 2D geometric shapes* and *Editing paths with the Node tool* in *Chapter 1*, and *Creating irregular edges using filters* in *Chapter 7*.

7
SVG Filters

In this chapter, we will cover:

- ▸ Blurring
- ▸ Creating irregular edges using filters
- ▸ Using lighting effects
- ▸ Creating a red wax seal
- ▸ Creating a brushed steel effect
- ▸ Creating a water surface effect
- ▸ Filtering all objects in a layer
- ▸ Creating your own filter from scratch

Introduction

Solid color and gradient vector objects can only get us so far when trying to create realistic shading and other complex effects. SVG filters give us the ability to achieve such effects on vector objects by combining various filter primitives.

Inkscape comes with a many different preset filters (all listed under the **Filters** menu) we can use straight away, although a few tweaks might be necessary to produce the intended result. This chapter will show us how to make those tweaks on some of the filters, and in the final recipe we will create our very own filter.

Due to the large number of filters available, trying to find the one closest to our needs using a trial and error process can be time consuming. To compare all the filter outcomes on the same object you can open the file `filters.svg` that comes with your Inkscape installation in the folder `share/examples`. When testing filters, be sure to use objects having strokes, gradient fills, and transparency as specimens, as some filters produce varying results depending on the object's attributes.

Filter rendering is quite CPU intensive and once they stack up they can reduce the Canvas update rate, so you might want to disable them temporarily by selecting the **Menu | View | Display Mode | No filters** mode, if you need to concentrate on another part of the drawing. To remove all filters from an object, select it and choose **Menu | Filters | Remove Filters**.

Blurring

The blur effect is versatile and has many possible applications in the realm of vector graphics. It is frequently used to enhance depth perception in a drawing, and to make certain elements stand out. It has its own section in the Inkscape menu (**Menu | Filters | Blurs**), where you will find several filter presets with descriptive names, such as "Apparition" and "Noisy". These presets combine different effects to produce a particular blur, and can be modified using the **Filter Editor**.

This recipe will show us how to use the **Gaussian Blur** filter and introduce us to some basic filters related options.

How to do it...

The following steps will demonstrate how to use **Blurs**:

1. Select the **Ellipse** tool (*F5* or *E*) and create an ellipse inside the page area. Set its fill to **Lime (#00FF00)**, stroke to **Green (#008000)**, and stroke width to 32.

2. Open the **Fill and Stroke** dialog (*Shift + Ctrl + F*) and increase the blur to 7 using the **Blur:** slider. Notice how the edges of the ellipse (outside edge and the one between the fill and the stroke) get more and more blurred, and how the object bounding box is now larger.

3. Open the **Filter Editor** by going to **Filters | Filter Editor...**. Notice that there is one filter listed in the **Filter** list. This is the blur filter applied to the ellipse, and under **Effect** there is one filter primitive, namely **Gaussian Blur**.

 Sometimes the filter selection in the **Filter** list isn't updated automatically, to refresh it simply deselect the object (*Esc*) and select it again.

4. Under the **Effect parameters** tab make sure that the **Link** under **Standard Deviation:** is pressed and move the top slider to the right until you reach 25. Notice how the blur of the ellipse changes as the slider is moved, and also notice how the **Blur:** slider in the **Fill and Stroke** dialog changes with it (it will end up on 12.5). The object bounding box changes too.

5. Press the **Link** button to unlink the X from the Y standard deviation slider and change the second (Y) slider to 0 to only blur the object in the X direction.

6. Select the **Filter General Settings** tab and change the X box of the **Coordinates:** to 0.2 and the Y to 0.25. Set X box of the **Dimensions:** to 0.6 and the Y box to 0.5. Notice how the object gets clipped as we change the settings.

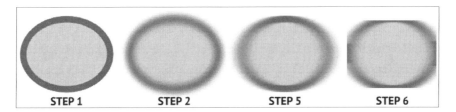

| STEP 1 | STEP 2 | STEP 5 | STEP 6 |

How it works...

We can apply the **Blur** filter to the currently selected object by using the slider in the **Fill and Stroke** dialog (**Blend** can also be applied to layers). If we want to apply blurring through the **Filter Editor** we can use the **Simple blur** that can be accessed from the menu, under the **Filters | ABCs** category.

The **Blur:** slider is actually the standard deviation property of the blur although the scale is doubled. Changing one automatically updates the value of the other.

If we want to apply a more complex blurring effect we have to open the **Filter Editor** and unlink the X and Y standard deviation options.

The size of the filter region is a common setting to all filters and is defined by the **Dimensions** parameters in the **Filter General Settings** tab found in the **Filter Editor**. It is obvious from our blur example how the filter region needs to be larger than the original object size to avoid clipping at the original bounding box edges and get the expected result. A predefined, finite region is necessary because the standard deviation function is calculated using an infinite plane, which is both impractical and unnecessary in this context.

A more "natural selection"

Selecting filtered objects using the rubber-band selection is a hit-and-miss affair because the bounding boxes are usually larger compared to the unfiltered state. Another way of selecting can be very helpful in that case. First empty your selection in case you have anything selected (*Esc*), hold *Alt*, and start dragging over the objects you want selected. A red line appears when we start dragging and all objects it touches are selected. The selection must be empty otherwise *Alt* triggers the movement of the selection. The *Shift* key can also come in handy to add any objects we missed.

Using the **Blur:** slider in the **Fill and Stroke** dialog adjusts the filter region automatically so the object isn't clipped at any side. If we want to change the region manually we can do so through the **Filter Editor**.

Having only one filter primitive inside the filter structure makes it the simplest filter we'll encounter. More complex filters consist of more than one filter primitive and those primitives are usually of different types.

There's more...

Many different blur presets are present in the **Blurs** section, such as **Motion blur, horizontal** and **Motion blur, vertical,** which we learned how to do manually. Using the presets can be a bit quicker but they always apply the same amount of blurring so if it doesn't turn out to be the right amount you will need to adjust that manually.

A lot of filters from other categories also use the **Gaussian Blur** filter primitive as part of their structure and although most of them can't be labeled as blur effects some could easily be listed under the **Blurs** category. Examples are the **Feather** filter under the **ABCs** category, **Soft colors** under the **Color** category that produces the well-known *Ortoneffect*, used in photo manipulation to produce hazy, dreamlike landscapes, **Soft focus lens** under **Image effects**, and **Fuzzy Glow** under **Shadows and Glows**.

See also

For more information, refer to the *Creating irregular edges using filters*, *Using lighting effects*, *Creating a red wax seal*, and *Creating a water surface effect* recipes that can be found later in this chapter.

Creating irregular edges using filters

In the previous chapter, we created an object with irregular edges using extensions. In this recipe we will further enhance this effect by creating a sheet of paper with burnt edges, using the **Roughen** and **Blur content** filters.

How to do it...

The following steps will demonstrate how to create burnt paper edges:

1. Select the **Rectangle** tool (*F4* or *R*) and create a 400 x 500 px rectangle. Set its fill to **#fff7d5ff**, stroke to **#2b1100**, and stroke width to 16.

2. Apply the **Roughen** filter by going to **Filters | ABCs | Roughen**. Notice how all the edges (outside edge and the one between the fill and the stroke) turned irregular.

3. Now all that's left is to blur the edge between the fill and the stroke, which can be done by going to **Filters | Blurs | Blur content**.

4. Change the stroke width to 8.

5. Open **Filter Editor**, select the **Turbulence** primitive from the **Effect** list, change the **Type:** to **Fractal Noise**, and change the **Base Frequency:** to 0.025.

6. Select the **Displacement Map** primitive from the **Effect** list and change the **Scale:** slider to 30. We now have our burnt sheet of paper.

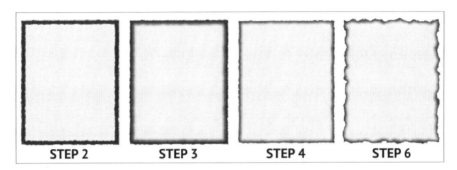

How it works...

Applying **Roughen** and **Blur content** brings us close to our goal but some tweaks to the filters are necessary to replicate the look from the last chapte, where te stroke was halved because we clipped the object using its duplicate. Since no clipping occurs when applying **Roughen** or **Blur content** we had to compensate by halving the stroke in this recipe.

The **Turbulence** filter primitive is used when our object has a property that is chaotic and random up to a point. It is often used when creating realistic textures. There are two types of **Turbulence** primitive filters and it can be hard sometimes to predict which one is better for our current case and it's the same with a lot of settings. Try experimenting with the different options available before settling on one.

As you can guess from the name, the **Displacement Map** shifts parts of the object from their positions. Although this description is overly simplified we can deduce why its **Scale:** slide changes the object edges to be more or less irregular.

The amount of blurring we got using the **Blur content** filter seems to be right for our example. Else, we would be able to tweak the amount in the **Gaussian Blur** primitive.

Compare the burnt paper example from the previous chapter with the one from this recipe, especially the "shading" of the edges. Which do you prefer? As you can see, filters can introduce a dose of randomness, making it look more realistic. If we wanted to recreate it manually it would take a lot of custom styled objects and much more time than when using filters.

There's more...

Roughen isn't the only filter that can be used to create irregular edges, but it proved itself as a good choice for the burnt paper edges look we expected to achieve. Most of the other filter presets that make the object edges irregular can be found under **Distort**, **Protrusions**, and **Textures**.

See also

For more information, refer to *Creating irregular edges using filters* and *Creating a water surface effect* from this chapter.

Using lighting effects

Lighting effects can make a flat object, such as a label, acquire the three dimensional look of a button through the use of highlights and shadows. Inkscape comes with **Diffuse light** and **Specular light** filters that create soft light sources, such as those produced by rays of sunlight shining on a wall, or reflected light sources.

This recipe will show us how we can use those filters to give our viewer an illusion of three dimensions.

How to do it...

The following steps will demonstrate how to use lighting effects:

1. Select the **Star** tool (*Shift* + *F9* or ***) and create a star with four corners. Set **Spoke ratio:** to 0.477 and **Rounded:** to 0.14. Set its fill to a color you like (we used **#0066FF** in the picture) and remove the stroke. Stamp it three times (*Space*) to get four stars in total.

2. Select one star and apply the **Diffuse light** filter to it by going to **Filters | ABCs | Diffuse light**. Notice how the object appears to be three dimensional, being lit by a distant light source coming from the upper-left corner.

3. Select the second star and apply the Specular light filter to it by going to **Filters | ABCs | Specular light**. Notice that the highlight appear to be reflected from the object.

4. Select the third star and apply the **Combined lighting** filter to it by going to **Filters | Bevels | Combined lighting**. Notice how our star now has a more realistic 3D look.

5. Select the fourth star and apply the **Combined lighting** filter again, like we did in Step 4.

6. Open the **Filter Editor**. Notice that the filter applied to the fourth star is active. Select the first **Gaussian Blur** primitive by clicking on it and increase the **Standard Deviation:** to 16.

7. Select the **Diffuse Lighting** primitive by clicking on it and change the **Surface Scale:** to 30 on the **Effect parameters** tab. Notice how the object looks less flat.

8. Select the **Specular Lighting** primitive by clicking on it and change the **Exponent:** to 40 and **Elevation** to 66.

9. Select the second **Gaussian Blur** primitive by clicking on it and increase the **Standard Deviation:** to 10. Notice how the highlight now appears to be reflected from an object that is more plump.

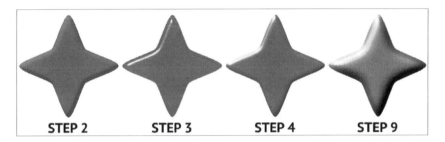

How it works...

If you take a look at the structure of the **Diffuse light** and **Specular light** filters and compare it to the **Combined lighting** filter, you'll see that the **Combined lighting** is simply diffuse and specular light filters applied to an object at the same time. There are some minor differences in the filter settings and they are visible in our examples. Which filter you use is completely up to the case you're working on, although using **Combined lighting** might be a quicker and simpler way of reaching a more complete 3D look.

Tweaking the settings of the **Combined lighting** filter enabled us to make the object appear more plump. You probably noticed that the settings for diffuse and specular primitives only differ in **Exponent:** option which is present only in **Specular lighting** and makes the object appear more shiny.

However, to get the look we wanted we also had to tweak the **Gaussian Blur** primitives that feed into the diffuse and specular primitives. Here we can see how filter primitives work together. Most often they do their bit and pass the result to the next primitive. Understanding of the inner workings of filter primitives helps to guess which options and which primitives to tweak to achieve a certain result, although we can often get by with the trial and error method. If you are curious about what's going on "behind the scenes", refer to the SVG filters working draft: `http://www.w3.org/TR/SVG/filters.html`.

Notice that we didn't have to touch the **Composite** primitives. They are there simply because of the nature of the lighting filters. Lighting filters are applied to the whole filter region, shading them completely. But our intention is to confine the shading to the object edges and **Composite** primitives enable us to do just that. The last **Composite** primitive applied to an independent effect (such as diffuse or specular lighting) always uses the **Source Graphic** as one of its inputs limiting the output inside the object edges.

We had to apply the **Combined lighting** filter independently to the last two stars because if we duplicated the star, the duplicate would inherit the filter and we wouldn't be able to edit the filters applied to them independently. This means that we can share filters between objects, we can create a filter on one object and apply it to another by enabling it in the **Filter** list when the object is selected, or simply use **Paste Style**.

There's more...

There is an option of **Diffuse Lighting** and **Specular Lighting** primitives that can add even more complexity into the lighting effects, and that is **Light Source**. We can choose between **Distant Light**, **Point Light**, and **Spot Light** as our light sources. All of the light sources come with options that set their location with respect to the object they are shining on.

Distant Light emits parallel rays of light. **Azimuth** controls the direction of where the light is coming from with regards to the canvas plane covering 360 degrees, and the **Elevation** controls how high the light source is above or below the object.

Point Light can be set in space using the usual X, Y, and Z coordinates, shining rays of light in all directions from that location, which are obviously not parallel.

Spot Light is like a **Point Light**, only it doesn't shine in all directions but covers a limited area on the object's surface. **Specular Exponent** and **Cone Angle** are codependent and they control how large the area is and how concentrated it appears to be.

The lighting filters we used in this recipe are the base ones. There are a number of other filters that achieve different 3D effects. You can find most of them under **Bevels** and **Shadows and Glows** filters.

See also

For more information, refer to *Creating a water surface effect* in this chapter, and also *Creating a button to use with the CSS Sliding Doors technique* in *Chapter 10*.

Creating a red wax seal

In this recipe we will apply what we've learned so far about the filters by creating a red wax seal with the help of lighting filters.

The drawing will consist of three objects: the stamp area, the stamp sign, and the remaining wax surrounding the stamp area. Each object will be filtered independently to achieve a realistic look and adjust the filter settings to a particular object size.

How to do it...

The following steps will demonstrate how to create a wax seal:

1. Select the **Ellipse** tool (*F5* or *E*) and create a 250 px wide circle inside the page area. Set its fill to a dark shade of red, such as #D40000, and remove the stroke. This will be the wax stamp area.

2. Apply the **Inner Shadow** filter to the circle by going to **Filters | Shadows and Glows | Inner Shadow**.

3. Select the **Pencil** tool (*F6* or *P*) and create a wavy outline (using the **Freehand line** setting and shape set to **None**) around the circle where you want the wax edge to be. Set its fill to the same shade of red (#D40000) and remove the stroke. This is the spilled wax object.

4. Select the circle behind the object (hold *Alt* and click to select under) and duplicate the circle (*Ctrl + D*). Add the spilled wax object to the selection and go to **Path | Difference** (*Ctrl + -*).

5. Apply the **Combined lighting** filter to the outer wax object by going to **Filters | Bevels | Combined lighting**.

6. Select the circle and make it slightly bigger so the background doesn't shine through at the edges where the circle meets the wax object. Hold *Shift* to scale from the circle center and *Ctrl* to maintain the ratio.

7. Open the `inkscape.logo.svg` file that comes with your Inkscape installation under the `share/clipart` folder and copy the logo into the wax seal document centering it over the stamp area. The Inkscape logo will be our stamp sign.

8. Ungroup the logo (*Shift + Ctrl + G*). Combine the white objects into one (*Ctrl + K*), then add the black mountain/ink into the selection and go to **Path | Difference** (*Ctrl + -*) to get a single path to serve as the stamp sign.

9. Apply the **Combined lighting** filter to the logo path by going to **Filters | Bevels | Combined lighting.** Now set the fill color of the logo to the same shade of red we used previously (#D40000).

What we have now does resemble a wax stamp but we need to do some tweaking to make it more realistic and finish the drawing. We'll edit each object's filter one by one and adjust them so they together form a meaningful drawing.

The outside wax should look plumper so we'll adjust that object and also the **Inset** filter of the stamp area because together they form the 3D illusion of the wax surrounding the stamp area.

The Inkscape logo should have more defined edges so it's more believable that it was created using a stamp. The following steps add fine touches to the stamp:

1. Open the **Filter Editor** by going to **Filters | Filter Editor...**.

2. Select the spilled wax object, choose the first **Gaussian Blur** primitive, and increase its **Standard Deviation:** to 20.

3. Select the **Diffuse Lighting** primitive and set **Surface Scale:** to 20, **Constant:** to 0.9, and **Elevation** to 50. The object should now look a bit plumper.

4. Select the second **Gaussian Blur** primitive and increase its **Standard Deviation:** to 12.

5. Select the **Specular Lighting** primitive and set **Surface Scale:** to 20, **Constant:** to 1.3, **Exponent:** to 40, and **Elevation** to 50.

6. Select the circle (stamp area), in the **Effect** area. Select **Gaussian Blur** and set its **Standard Deviation:** to 8.

7. Select the **Offset** primitive and change both deltas to 8.

8. Select the **Flood** primitive and change the **Flood Color:** to #2E0000 (very dark brown). This will soften the shadow.

9. Select the Inkscape logo path and in the first **Gaussian Blur** primitive change **Standard Deviation:** to 3.

10. Select **Diffuse Lighting** primitive and set **Surface Scale:** to 5, **Constant:** to 0.9, and **Elevation** to 50.

11. Select the second **Gaussian Blur** primitive and set its **Standard Deviation:** to 3.

12. Select the **Specular Lighting** primitive and set **Surface Scale:** to 4, **Constant:** to 1.3, **Exponent:** to 40, and **Elevation** to 50.

Although we tweaked the filters to get the desired 3D effect, it still seems like something's missing. It's hard to avoid shadows in the real world, and that seems to be missing from our drawing. We can see where the light is coming from but there are some shadows missing that should be there. Also the outer wax object surface isn't smooth as a result of the filters we applied, we can fix it with some blurring. The following steps add the finishing touches to our wax stamp:

1. Add the **Drop Shadow** filter to the Inkscape logo by going to **Filters | Shadows and Glows | Drop Shadow...** and set the **Blur radius, px** to 3, **Opacity, %** to 50, and both offsets to 1.

2. Select the outer wax object and add the **Drop Shadow** filter, and set the **Blur radius, px** to 7, **Opacity, %** to 70, and both offsets to 3. We now have our wax seal!

How it works...

Cutting out a hole in the outer wax object ensured we got correct highlights. If we hadn't done that the filter would be applied to the object as if it's a piece of material without indentations and we wouldn't get the highlights in the bottom-right of the object. This example also shows us we can edit the paths after a filter has been applied and the filter will automatically adjust to the new shape.

Both **Diffuse light** and **Specular light** start with the **Gaussian Blur** primitive. The output from that **Gaussian Blur** is used by the lighting primitives and it changes the object's appearance to more or less flat. This is the first step in changing the object "size".

Lighting primitive settings take some experimentation before you can predict their outcome, but it's well worth the effort. The object size also has some effect on the final result. If you apply the same filter to two object of different sizes the outcome won't be scaled. To achieve the same effect on an object of a different size the filter settings need to be adjusted.

There's more...

You probably noticed artifacts on the outer wax surface. They sometimes happen with lighting filters due to limited resolution on the bump map used in those filters. To remove them we can add another **Gaussian Blur** filter primitive to the **Effect** list of that object and apply enough blurring to make the artifacts go away. After that we need to clip the object to its original edges using clipping or another **Composite** filter primitive with the second **in** attribute set to **Source Graphic** and the **Operator:** to **In**.

This workaround doesn't help with specular light through because blurring destroys the effect.

See also

For more information, refer to the *Blurring* and *Using lighting effects* recipes in this chapter.

Creating a brushed steel effect

In this recipe we will modify the **Film grain** filter to resemble brushed steel, a texture that is often used as panel textures for websites and interfaces of operating systems, such as Mac OSX and Enlightenment DR16 for Linux and BSD.

How to do it...

The following steps will demonstrate how to create a brushed steel effect:

1. Select the **Rectangle** tool (*F4* or *R*) and create a 600 x 300 px rectangle. Set its fill to **20% Gray** and remove the stroke.

2. Apply the **Film grain** filter by going to **Filters | Image effects | Film grain**.

3. Open the **Filter Editor** by going to **Filters | Filter Editor...**. The **Film grain** filter and the **Turbulence** primitive will be selected.

4. Under the **Effect parameters** tab, click on the **Link** button to unlink the X and Y **Base Frequency:** setting.

5. Move the **X** slider of the **Base Frequency:** almost all the way to the left. Keep an eye on the drawing and stop when the pattern looks acceptable (0.005 in my case).

6. Select the **Composite** primitive and change the **K1:** attribute to 0.3, **K2:** to 0.7, **K3:** to 0.15, and **K4:** to 0.05. We have our brushed steel texture!

How it works...

When trying to create a new texture from an existing filter the first important step is to choose the most convenient filter to start from. A brushed steel effect is very often created using a noise texture as the starting point, so **Film grain** seemed perfect for the job.

The **Turbulence** primitive has a very convenient option to set a different **Base Frequency:** value for the X and Y directions. That is how we achieved the "stretched" look.

Changing the **Composite** K arithmetic values helped us get the color right. Playing with different value combinations can get us to the desired result. For best results, don't move far away from 0 in any direction. Hovering over the sliders gives us tooltips that describe what each attribute does so, if you're mathematically inclined, try reading them and see if you can predict the outcome of various value combinations—you'll probably find out that drawing is more fun!

We didn't have to change the **Color Matrix** primitive because the settings from the **Film grain** suited us perfectly for the steel gray look. Try changing the saturation **Value(s):** option to 1 and see a nice rainbow effect through our steel.

See also

For more information, refer to the *Creating a water surface effect* recipe in this chapter.

Creating a water surface effect

In this recipe we will create a filter the mimics a water surface using the **3D wood** filter. It might be surprising to use something that has "wood" in its name to create something completely different! There are filters with "liquid" in their names that can be used to achieve similar effect, but this recipe will show us that lateral thinking while searching for the "right" filter can be very beneficial; by being imaginative we can solve a problem in an innovative way.

How to do it...

The following step will demonstrate how to create a water surface effect:

1. Select the **Rectangle** tool (*F4* or *R*) and create a 600x300 px rectangle. Set its fill to a shade of blue, like #0044AA, and remove the stroke.

2. Apply the **3D wood** filter by going to **Filters | Materials | 3D wood**.

3. Open the **Filter Editor**. The **3D wood** filter and the **Gaussian Blur** primitive will be selected.

4. We immediately notice that the wood grooves are too fine to represent water ripples so we adjust the **Turbulence-Base Frequency:** sliders to 0.006 and 0.04 to get "bigger" ripples.

5. **Octaves:** option also brings in too much detail so we reduce it to 2

6. Our "ripples" still don't look realistic, as they are too blurry. This is due to the first **Composite** primitive being set to show the **Source Graphic** inside the area defined by the **Gaussian Blur** primitive. To correct this we composite the **Source Graphic** with the **Turbulence** primitive by clicking on the lower arrow on the **Composite** primitive and dragging it to the right and up until it reaches the arrow or the bottom line of the **Turbulence** primitive.

7. The **Displacement MapScale:** option affects how "disturbed" our water surface is. Any value between 50 and 100 can do, and I went with 80.

8. The **Flood** primitive introduces a beige color for the original wood effect. Replace it with white (#FFFFFF) and notice we now have the light reflections form the ripples.

9. The set of primitives near the bottom of the list consisting of **Gaussian Blur**, **Specular Lighting**, and the two **Composite** primitives that follow, only affect the object edge to create the 3D effect. We can bypass them by making **Convolve Matrix** primitive feed from higher up in the list: click on the **Convolve Matrix** arrow and drag to the right and up until you reach the **Composite** that is above the **Gaussian Blur**.

10. Go back to the **Turbulence** primitive and take a look at what the effect looks like when **Type:** is set to **Turbulence**—it's still a water surface, but maybe rain is making it ripple more.

11. Duplicate the object and move it away. Remove the filter by going to **Filters | Remove Filters**.

12. For comparison, apply the **Shaken liquid** filter by going to **Filters | Textures | Shaken liquid** and set the **Turbulence** primitive **Base Frequency:** to 0.016 and 0.052. We now have three different water surface filters to choose from.

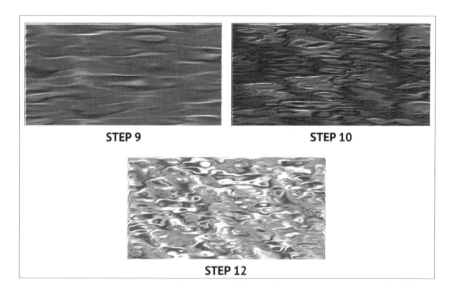

STEP 9   STEP 10

STEP 12

There's more...

The set of primitives we bypassed can be removed completely from the **Effect** list, but we left them in there just in case we change our minds and want to create a 3D plate with a water effect on it. Filter primitives can be removed by right-clicking on them and choosing **Remove**.

Using a different shade of blue or green and adjusting the saturation changes the scene atmosphere from night to day or the type of water (sea, lake, pool). Since we set the **Flood** to white we don't have to adjust the highlight color. It is enough to simply change the fill color of the object.

The possibilities offered by combining primitives are endless. Once you start playing with them you will be inspired to create new combinations and experiment with different settings. You can find more interesting texture filters under the **Bumps**, **Materials**, **Overlays**, and **Texture** categories.

See also

For more information, refer to the *Using lighting effects* and *Creating a brushed steel effect* recipes in this chapter.

Filtering all objects in a layer

A blending filter primitive can be applied to a layer by using the **Layers** dialog and selecting a **Blend** mode. There's a catch however: you can only choose one from a predefined list.

There is a way though to apply a complex filter to a whole layer manually. This method was first invented by the Inkscape forum user kelan (`http://www.inkscapeforum.com`) and expanded by Ivan Loulette. It involves playing some dirty tricks with the XML editor, but the results are quite effective.

This recipe will guide us through that method of adding a filter to all objects in a layer.

How to do it...

The following steps will demonstrate how to use a filter on all the objects in a layer:

1. In a new document open the **Layers** dialog (*Shift + Ctrl + L*) and create a new layer. Name it "Filtered".

2. Select the **Rectangle** tool (*F4* or *R*) and create a rectangle. Set its fill to `#0044AA` and remove the stroke.

3. Apply the **3D mother of pearl** filter by going to **Filters | Materials | 3D mother of pearl**.

4. Open the XML editor (*Shift + Ctrl + X*), expand the `svg:defs` element, and select the `svg:filter` element inside it.

5. In the right-hand pane find the `id` attribute, select it by clicking on it and copy its value from the bottom area. It will be of the form "filter1234".

6. Select the `svg:g` element in the left-hand pane that has `inkscape:label` set to "Filtered".

7. Add a `style` attribute by writing "style" into the field next to the **Set** button, writing "filter:url(#filter1234)" into the text area box at the bottom (where the number 1234 is the number we copied from the filter `id`), and pressing the **Set** button. Our **Filtered** layer now has the **3D mother of pearl** filter applied.

8. Close the XML editor and notice our rectangle now has the filter applied to it twice, once as an object and the second time because it's in the layer where that filter is applied. Go to **Filters | Remove Filters** to remove the "object" filter, so only the one from the layer stays.

9. Select the **Star** tool (*Shift + F9* or ***) and create a star in **Filtered** layer. The **3D mother of pearl** will be automatically applied to it, as will any object we create in that layer.

How it works...

Filters and their settings are kept in `svg:defs` elements along with any gradient or pattern information too. Every such resource from `svg:defs` has a unique ID called the `id` attribute. To apply a filter or some other resource to an object, a reference to the filter we want to use is added inside the object's `style` attribute.

What we did here is reference a filter from a layer instead from an object in a layer. This isn't surprising if we remember that the Inkscape layers are nothing more than SVG group elements with a bit of special "Inkscape sauce" (there are no layers in the SVG specifications).

Maybe in some future versions of Inkscape, this method will be accessible through a graphical interface so it will be easier to apply it.

See also

For more information, refer to the *Designing plate rims using layers*, the section on *XML editor as textual layers dialog* in *Chapter 3*.

Creating your own filter from scratch

If modifying a preset filter seems like too much work we can create a filter from scratch, which we will do in this recipe trying to achieve a "Nebula" effect.

How to do it...

The following steps will demonstrate how to create your own filter:

1. Open the **Filter Editor** by going to **Filters | Filter Editor...**.

2. Press the **New** button. Notice a new filter is created in the **Effect** list without any primitives.

3. Click on the filter name and rename it to "My Filter".

4. Beneath the **Effect** pane there is a widget to add a new primitive to the current filter. Select **Gaussian Blur** from the drop-down list and press the **Add Effect:** button.

5. Change the **Standard Deviation:** in the **Effect parameters** tab to 10.

6. Now select **Turbulence** from the drop-down list and press the **Add Effect:** button. Set **Type:** to **Fractal Noise**, **Base Frequency:** to 0.008, and **Octaves:** to 5.

7. Select **Displacement Map** from the drop-down list and press **Add Effect:** button. Set the **Scale:** slider to 100.

8. Select **Composite** from the drop-down list and press the **Add Effect:** button. Click on the top arrow and drag it to the right and up until it reaches the arrow or the bottom line of the **Turbulence** primitive.

9. Select **Turbulence** from the drop-down list and press the **Add Effect:** button. Set **Type:** to **Turbulence**, **Base Frequency:** to 0.015, and **Octaves:** to 1.

10. Select **Composite** from the drop-down list and press the **Add Effect:** button. Click on the bottom arrow and drag it to the right and up until it reaches the arrow or the bottom line of the first **Composite** primitive.

11. Open the XML editor (*Shift + Ctrl + X*), expand the `svg:defs` element, and select the `svg:filter` element inside it.

12. Add a `color-interpolation-filters` attribute by writing "color-interpolation-filters" into the field next to the **Set** button, writing "sRGB" in the text area box at the bottom, and pressing the **Set** button. Our filter is done.

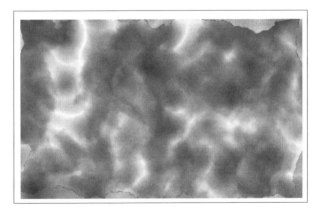

How it works...

As we could see from the example, it's very easy to create new filters and change their structure. The tricky part is to understand the primitives so we know which one to pick next and how to set it up. Studying the structure of the preset filters can help us understand the concept better and gain some experience.

Our "Nebula" example could certainly be improved. Can you think of any suggestions which may improve the picture and make it similiar to those awe-inspiring astronimical pictures taken by observatories and satellites?

In the end we added a special attribute to our filter using the XML editor. This attribute is only necessary if you plan to display your drawing in a SVG renderer other than Inkscape because Inkscape doesn't use the standard SVG color space (**linearRGB**) with filters. This only needs to be done on filters we create from scratch, as the preset ones already have that attribute.

8

Putting it All Together

In this chapter, we will cover:

- ▶ Creating a wallpaper
- ▶ Exporting a wallpaper in different formats
- ▶ Creating a hatching effect over a photo
- ▶ Creating a coloring book using the Paint Bucket tool
- ▶ Creating rail sleepers using Markers
- ▶ Creating a woven straw mat
- ▶ Assembling a modern chair using the 3D Box tool
- ▶ Creating a flow chart using connectors

Introduction

In the previous chapters, we have focused on the basics of object creation and manipulation, improving our understanding of Inkscape's general philosophy. Having learned the nouns, verbs, and adjectives of vector graphics design, we know enough rudiments of the language to express our creativity in more elaborate and fulfilling ways.

A beautiful work of art can be appreciated at different levels: we can admire it for its aesthetic qualities, but we can also look at it as an example of a visual problem that has been solved by an artist. "How did he manage to pull off those amazing shades of color?" "How did she achieve such a realistic sense of perspective?" Then, when asked about it, the artist simply reveals a combination of simple, almost banal, techniques already known to us.

Very often we have at least a general idea of *what* we want to draw; it's *how* to achieve it that's unclear. The challenge is getting there without making too many compromises, or any at all, on the overall quality and completeness of the final drawing; which is also our reward, so to speak.

In this chapter we will approach different real world scenarios and tasks, and solve them employing what we have learned so far.

Creating a wallpaper

Desktop wallpapers have always been an important component of a computing environment, making it feel more personal and tailored to the user's taste. Many digital graphics artists have successfully exploited wallpapers as a showcase for their art. Wallpapers are a very effective vector for artists wanting a greater exposure and their popularity has spawned countless website directories, galleries, and archives.

In this recipe we will create an *abstract art* wallpaper by employing part of the knowledge we have gathered from the previous recipes.

How to do it...

The following steps will demonstrate how to create a wallpaper:

1. Open **Document Properties** (*Shift* + *Ctrl* + *D*) and change the **Page size** to 1024 x 768 px, a very common screen size of the 4:3 aspect ratio.

2. Enable **Snap to the page border** 🔲 by clicking on the button in the snapping bar. Create a rectangle using the **Rectangle** tool (*F4* or *R*) that covers the page area exactly by snapping it to the top-left and bottom-right corners while drawing. Fill it with green (#46ef74) and create an *elliptic radial* gradient inside it, using the **Gradient** tool.

3. Set the end stop to a dark shade of green (such as #19622b). Add some lighter shaded stops of green in between and move them along the gradient path to get a nice transition. Move the gradient near the bottom-right corner and rotate it to the left a bit by dragging the peripheral circular radial handles.

4. Select the **Text** tool (*F8* or *T*) and create a text object by clicking on the canvas and typing "INKSCAPE". Move the text to the bottom right corner at the center of the gradient.

5. Adjust the text properties to your liking. Size 40 seemed ideal for this case, and we only increased the letter-spacing by selecting all while in the **Text** tool (*Ctrl* + *A*) and briefly holding *Alt* + >, or increasing the number in the relative field marked with the 🄰🄰 icon. We made the fill color dark green (#005522) and the stroke a lighter green (#00d455), and also set the stroke width to 0.75 px.

6. Select the **Pencil** tool (*F6* or *P*) in **Spiro spline** mode with **Smoothing:** set to 30 and **Shape:** to **Triangle in**. Create several wavy lines starting near the text and moving away.

7. Select the **Ellipse** tool (*F5* or *E*) and create a very thin horizontal ellipse. Copy it to the clipboard 🔲 (*Ctrl* + *C*).

8. Select the **Pencil** tool again (*F6* or *P*) and change **Shape:** to **From clipboard**. Create several wavy lines along the ones we created in Step 6. Use the **Node** tool (*F2* or *N*) to adjust the shapes.

9. When you're happy with the shapes, select them all (*Ctrl + A*) and convert them to paths (*Shift + Ctrl + C*). Combine them into a single path (*Ctrl + K*) and set their fill color to green (#0bc454), stroke to lighter green (#11e74f), and stroke width to 1.

10. Select the **Rectangle** tool (*F5* or *E*) and create a rectangle large enough to cover the vines object, and snap it to the bottom-right corner. Set it's fill to black, and reduce the opacity a bit so that you can see where the vines are.

11. Create an elliptic gradient with the center where the center of the text is. Set the end stop color to white and adjust the gradient size so the dark area surrounds the text and touches the vine ends. Go back to the **Selector** tool (*Space, F1* or *S*) and change the object opacity back to 100.

12. Use *Alt* to select the vine object below, add the black and white rectangle to the selection and go to **Object | Mask | Set** to make the vines appear like they are fading in.

13. Select the **Ellipse** tool (*F5* or *E*) and create an ellipse that covers the text. Set its fill to a very light shade of green (#aaffb2) and create a centered elliptical gradient. Add more stops and move them to make the center "glow" larger. Send the ellipse back behind the text (*Page Down* twice).

14. Select the vines object and send it behind the ellipse (*Page Down* twice).

15. Select the **Pen** tool (*Shift+F6* or *B*) and create a leaf by drawing a closed path with two cusp nodes. Fill it with a green linear gradient and set its stroke to the same stroke color of the vines (select the **Dropper** tool (*F7* or *D*). Press and hold *Q* to temporarily zoom in the selection, and pick the color from the vine stroke while pressing *Shift*). Also create an open path down the middle of the "leaf", remove its fill, and set stroke to the same color as before. Set both path strokes to 0.75 and group the paths.

16. Stamp the leaf group several times along the vines (*Space*). Flip, rotate, and resize the stamped leaves as necessary.

17. Select the **Star** tool (*Shift + F9* or ***) and create an 8 corner star with **Spoke ratio:** 0.25. Set fill color to orange (#ff6600), stroke color to white, and stroke width to 0.8.

18. Duplicate the star (*Ctrl + D*) and change the **Spoke ratio:** to 0.17. Set the fill color to orange (#ff6600) and **Blur:** to 14. Send it back behind the original star (*Page Down*) and group them together, and keep the group selected.

19. Select the **Spray** tool (*Shift + F3* or *A*), set **Mode:** to clones, **Width:** to 10, **Amount:** to 20, **Rotation:** to 70, **Scale:** to 45, and **Scatter:** to 70. Click and drag around the text to spray clones of varying size and rotation.

20. Switch to the **Selector** tool (*Space, F1* or *S*) and select one of the star groups. Unlink the clone (*Shift + Alt + D*) and scale it down holding *Ctrl* to maintain the ratio.

21. Switch back to the **Spray** tool 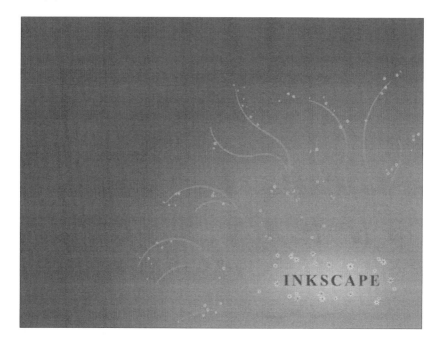 (*Space, Shift + F3* or *A*) and spray the stars over the top parts of the vines and some around the text.

How it works...

While creating our design we had to create our own ellipse to use with the **Pencil** tool because the preset one creates "lines" that are too thick for our wallpaper.

The leaves wouldn't look good if we positioned them randomly so we needed complete control over that part of the drawing process. That is why we used stamping and tweaked them manually instead of using the **Spray** tool or **Tiled clones**.

There's more...

Wallpaper authors generally package and distribute their creations as a set of image files in different resolutions, relative to the 4:3 and 16:9 (Widescreen) aspect ratios, for the end-user's convenience of not having to stretch or crop it to match the native screen resolution.

We will cover this process in the next recipe.

See also

For more information, refer to the *Editing paths with Node tool*, *Creating paths using the Pen (Bezier) tool*, *Creating smooth paths with Spiro Spline*, *Creating and editing text*, and *Masking* recipes in *Chapter 1*. Also see *Recreating HAL 9000 using radial gradients* and *Picking and assigning with the Dropper tool* in *Chapter 2*, and also *Creating a stylized flower using Snapping* in *Chapter 3* and *Drawing a tree with cloned leaves using the Spray tool* in *Chapter 4*.

Exporting a wallpaper in different formats

There are many screen sizes these days that we need to take into account when creating wallpaper designs. The most noticeable issue involves different screen aspect ratios. The 4:3 ratio is inherited from the old CRT monitor era, although it's still widely used. The new standard that wide screens introduced is the 16:9 aspect ratio and its presence is rapidly growing. If we also include the new hand-held devices, such as smartphones and tablet computers, the number of different screen size aspect ratios to take into account is increased further.

In this recipe we will go through the process of exporting a wallpaper design into different sizes and screen-size ratios, trying to cater every possible scenario. We will use the wallpaper design from the previous recipe to see how it should be exported.

How to do it...

The following steps will show how to export a wallpaper:

1. Open the `Wallpaper.svg` file from the previous recipe. As we can see the wallpaper is in a very common size of 1024x768 and a screen aspect ratio of 4:3.

2. Open the **Export bitmap** dialog 🖺 (*Shift + Ctrl + E*) and click on the **Page** button. Under **Bitmap size** the **Width:** box will be set to 1024, **Height:** to 768, and the **dpi** to 90.

3. Set the path and the name of the file in the **Filename** field (or use the **Browse...** button) and press **Export**. You will probably see a pop-up showing the progress bar. After the progress bar disappears the image is ready to be opened and viewed using your favorite image viewer.

4. The **Export Bitmap** dialog will remain open so we can export our wallpaper to another size. Change the **Width:** box under **Bitmap size** to 1280; the **Height:** value will automatically update to 960, and the **dpi** will show 112.5.

5. Change the name of the file under **Filename** and press **Export** to create a wallpaper for a 1280 x 960 screen size.

6. Repeat Steps 4 and 5 for each 4:3 screen size ratio you need.

7. Open the **Inkscape Preferences** (*Shift + Ctrl + P*) and make sure that the **Clones | When duplicating original+clones | Relink duplicated clones** option is unticked and all the options found under the **Transforms** section are on.

8. Open the **Layers** dialog (*Shift + Ctrl + L*) and add a new layer above the current one (*Shift + Ctrl + N*). Name it "16:9".

9. Select **Layer 1**, and select everything inside it (*Ctrl + A*). Clone it (*Alt+ D*) and shift the clones to the layer above (*Shift + Page Up*).

10. Turn off the **Layer 1** visibility by clicking on the eye icon next to its name.

11. Select the clone of the page-size rectangle in layer **16:9** and change its width and height by entering 1600 into **W** box and 900 into **H** box on the Selector toolbar (make sure the lock ratio icon is off). The rectangle will shift because of the resize. We can leave it there. Notice how the gradient radius changed as a result of the rectangle size change because we set the transform options to do that.

12. We now have to adjust the rest of the drawing to the new size. Select everything except the rectangle (*Ctrl + A*, then hold *Shift* and click on the rectangle to remove it from selection).

13. Scale the selection up to 120% by holding *Ctrl* to keep the ratio. Track the scale percentage in the statusbar notification area.

14. Move the selection to an ideal position in the bottom-right corner so it fits nicely along the edges. (Turn off snapping (%) if it gets in the way.)

15. Make **Layer 1** visible and toggle the **16:9** layer visibility to compare the designs. If you're not happy with the changes, undo them and tweak until you're satisfied.

16. Select the rectangle in layer **16:9**, open the **Export Bitmap** dialog (*Shift + Ctrl + E*) and keep the **Selection** button pressed. Under **Bitmap size** the **Width:** box will be set to 1600, **Height:** to 900, and the **dpi** to 90.

17. Set the path and the name of the file in the **Filename** field (or use **Browse...** button) and press **Export**.

18. The **Export Bitmap** dialog will remain open so we can export our wallpaper to another size. Change the **Width:** box under **Bitmap size** to 1920, the **Height:** value will automatically update to 1080, and the **dpi** box will show 108.

19. Change the name of the file under **Filename** and press **Export** to create a wallpaper for a 1920 x 1080 screen size.

20. Repeat Steps 16 and 17 for each 16:9 screen size ratio you need.

21. Repeat Steps 7 through 19 for all the other screen-sized ratios you might need. The following is a comparison of the original 1024 x 768 and the 1600 x 900 exported wallpapers:

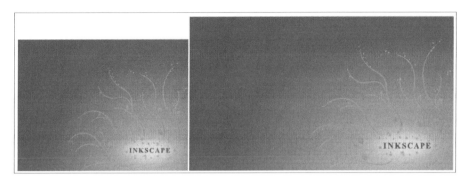

How it works...

If the **dpi** setting in the **Export Bitmap** dialog is set to 90, the **Width:** and **Height:** values will be the same as the page size set in **Document Properties**. This is because 90 dpi is the default resolution of both Inkscape and the SVG specification.

We chose to create another version of the wallpaper for different screen-size ratios because as we saw some size relationships in the drawing are different so we had to make adjustments. The outcome is much better than if we had simply scaled the entire drawing to a new ratio.

Cloning the drawing enables us to quickly update and export the drawing in case of changes. When scaling parts of the drawing for different screen size ratios the clones remain linked, and even if we have to unlink a clone to adjust it there is still a large portion of the drawing that updates automatically keeping the time needed to do the changes to a minimum.

Cloning also enables us to reuse the same file if we're working on a similar design. We copy and rename the file, tweak the original layer quickly, and we have all the other sizes ready to be exported!

There's more...

When scaling wallpapers to smaller screen sizes (iPhone, BlackBerry) you might want to turn off the **Scale stroke width** and **Transform patterns** options because details in the drawing will not be as visible if we scale them down too much. Keeping these options off might help lessen the amount of tweaks. The transform options can also be changed using the buttons on the Selector toolbar.

For dual monitor setups (for example 2560x1024) you'll probably want to clone the drawing twice and align them one next to the other, or even change the design some more by flipping the design and positioning them at the opposite corners of the two screens.

The most common 4:3 aspect ratio screen sizes are listed for convenience: 640x480, 800x600, 1024x768, 1152x864, 1280x960, 1400x1050, 1600x1200, 1920x1440.

Another popular aspect ratio, usually found in netbooks, is 16:10: 1280x800, 1440x900, 1680x1050 and 1920x1200.

 As a general rule, it's best to distribute your wallpaper in the highest possible resolution in each of the aspect ratios.

See also

For more information, refer to the *Creating and editing 2D geometric shapes* and *Creating freehand and straight lines* recipes in *Chapter 1, Creating linear gradients* in *Chapter 2, Creating a stylized flower using Snapping* in *Chapter 3, Drawing clock dial markers using clones* in *Chapter 4*, and *Slicing a web page mockup for website use* in *Chapter 10*.

Hatching over a photo using the Calligraphy tool

Hatching effects can turn a plain looking image into a striking artistic rendition of itself, and be used in comic books, logos, or just about anything you like.

This recipe will show us how the **Calligraphy** tool can speed up the process of creating such an effect. We will create a linen pattern with the number 10 on it using calligraphy hatching on a photo.

How to do it...

The following steps will show how to hatch over a photograph:

1. Choose a photo you like and import it into the current Inkscape document through the **Import** dialog (*Ctrl + I*). For best results, choose a black and white photo with a high contrast. You can also use the one from this recipe (`10er.png`, provided along with the files of this chapter). You will be prompted to choose whether to embed the image into the document or only to link to it. For greater portability choose **embed**.

2. Select the **Calligraphy** tool (*Ctrl + F6* or *C*) and choose the **Tracing** mode as our starting point. Change the **Width:** to 20, **Caps:** to 1.5, and **Mass:** to 6.

3. Zoom and pan the canvas so that you have some space around the photo.

4. Create the first line by crossing the top-left corner with it. Make it slightly curved following the shape from the photo and crossing the photo edges. The line will come out thicker over the photo area.

5. Press *Ctrl* and notice a small circle tracking from the mouse pointer to the line we just created. Moving the mouse away makes the circle larger. Select a distance that will determine the hatching density and create another, holding *Ctrl* key the whole time. As long as you hold *Ctrl*, the distance between the lines will remain the same.

6. Keep hatching until the whole photo is covered in parallel hatchings.

7. Create a new layer (*Shift + Ctrl + N*) and name it "Hatching".

8. Select **Layer 1** from the drop-down list at the bottom of the window. Select all objects (*Ctrl + A*), hold *Shift* and click on the photo to remove it from the selection.

9. Shift the selection to the new layer (*Shift + Page Up*).

10. Hide the **Hatching** layer by clicking on the eye icon and select **Layer 1**.

11. Repeat the hatching only in the vertical direction. Try to set the distance to be the same as in the horizontal direction.

12. Select all objects (*Ctrl + A*), hold *Shift*, and click on the photo to remove it from the selection.

13. Shift the selection to the **Hatching** layer (*Shift + Page Up*).

14. Hide the **Layer 1** layer by clicking on the eye icon and select **Hatching**.

15. Select all objects then select the **Tweak** tool (*Shift + F2* or *W*). Set its **Width:** to 10, **Force:** to 15, and **Mode:** to shrink.

16. Drag over the thin line parts traced outside of the photo area to shrink them even further, effectively erasing them.

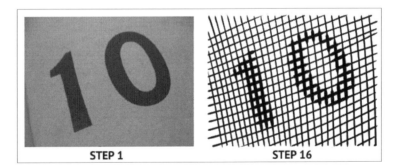

STEP 1   STEP 16

How it works...

Embedding bitmap images into SVG documents will increase the document's file size, but we recommend it if the drawing needs to be distributed or shared with collaborators for additional modifications, as they will receive a full working copy and won't have to worry about something going missing. If you only link to a bitmap file and want to move the file or send it to someone, you have to send both the SVG document and the bitmap file keeping the folder relationships the same.

The contrast in the chosen photo influences how line thickness changes with the background lightness. The most abrupt change is when tracing from white to black. This is why it is sometimes important to edit the picture in a photo-manipulation program (like Photoshop or The Gimp) beforehand, in order to get the best looking hatching effect.

When we created the first batch of hatchings we moved them to another layer and hid them, otherwise the next batch of hatchings would trace over them and create unwanted nodes on the intersections because of the lightness change.

See also

For more information, refer to the recipes on *Creating calligraphic shapes* in *Chapter 1*, *Designing plate rims using Layers* in *Chapter 3*, and *Creating irregular edges using filters* in *Chapter 7*.

Creating a coloring book using the Paint Bucket tool

We have all enjoyed coloring books when we were younger and they still seem to be popular in the contemporary digital age. These books don't lose their appeal even when fully colored. The effect created by the human hand of a child holding a crayon, with its enthusiasm and ingenuity, gives the drawing an aura of innocence, warmth, and vigor.

An artist can imbue his or her drawing with similar qualities by replicating this effect, as we will do in this recipe. Our chosen tool will be the **Paint Bucket**, with which we will bring color into various regions in our drawing, using several old and new tricks.

Getting ready

Using **Paint Bucket** on an empty Canvas won't work because there aren't any closed regions to fill; we have to have objects that define closed or nearly closed regions to spill the paint from the bucket. Open the `ColoringBookPaintBucket.svg` file to find a simple outline of a rainbow we can use to throw bucket colors onto, and zoom in so that the blank rainbow outline fills your screen (3).

Most of the Inkscape tools come with an option to **Show selection cue**. It is disabled by default for **Paint Bucket**, but if having an object selected without a visual cue shown on screen is confusing to you make sure you enable this option in **Inkscape Preferences** (*Shift + Ctrl + P*) under **Tools | Paint Bucket**.

How to do it...

The following steps will demonstrate how to use the Paint Bucket tool to create a coloring book:

1. Select the **Paint Bucket** 🪣 tool (*Shift + F7* or *U*).

2. Click on the **Red (#FF0000)** color chip to set the fill style for the object we are about to create.

3. Right-click on the stroke box in Style indicator and choose **Remove stroke** to make sure the new object doesn't have a stroke.

4. Click inside the first rainbow region (left-most) to color it red. As a result both the first and the second rainbow regions will be red.

5. Hit *Esc* key to deselect the newly created red object.

6. Click on an orange color chip (**#FF6600**) to set the new fill style for the object we are about to create.

7. Move the **Threshold** slider on the **Paint Bucket** toolbar to 100.

8. Click inside the third (from left) rainbow region to color it orange.

9. Hit the *Esc* key to deselect the newly created orange object.

10. Click on the **Yellow (#FFFF00)** color chip to set the new fill style for the object we are about to create.

11. On the **Paint Bucket** toolbar click the **Reset paint bucket parameters to defaults** button to set the **Paint Bucket** options back to default (**Threshold** slider back to 15).

12. Select **px** as units from the drop-down box of **Grow/shrink by:** and enter the number 5.

13. Click inside the fourth (from left) rainbow region to color it yellow.

14. Hit *Esc* to deselect the newly created yellow object.

15. On the **Paint Bucket** toolbar, click the reset to defaults button (**Grow/shrink by:** option goes to 0).

16. Click on the **Lime (#00FF00)** color chip to set the new fill style for the object we are about to create.

17. Zoom out to 12% by entering 12 in the **Z:** box in the right-bottom corner of the window.

18. Click inside the fifth (from left) rainbow region to color it lime.

19. Hit *Esc* to deselect the newly created lime object.

20. Return to the previous zoom amount by hitting the ` key.

21. Click on the **Aqua (#00FFFF)** color chip to set the new fill style for the object we are about to create.

22. Set **Close gaps:** on the **Paint Bucket** toolbar to **Small** (it might take a while).

23. Click inside the sixth (from left) rainbow region to color it aqua. The following is what we end up with:

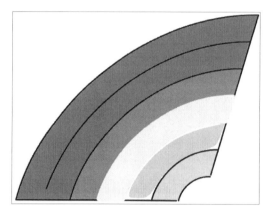

How it works...

When clicking with the **Paint bucket** tool in a region it tries to find similar pixels to encompass them all in a single object, so the result is always a new vector object that doesn't change existing ones in any way. Instead of clicking we can also click and drag to cover a larger area.

The red fill took over two rainbow regions because they aren't separated; there is a visible gap between them where the black line doesn't come all the way to the bottom.

There's more...

If we zoom in on the edges of our red and orange regions we'll see that unlike the orange one, the red object rarely touches the region boundaries:

This is because the settings we used when creating the red region and the zoom amount weren't enough to show enough pixels along the edges for the **Paint Bucket** tool to include them in the new object.

Increasing the **Threshold:** for the orange region ensured that there are no "empty" pixels between the region and its boundary.

Growing and shrinking the region

Another way to make sure the new object fills in the region without cracks is to set the **Grow/ Shrink by:** option to a positive number. It will expand the object by the specified amount so it can compensate for the "missing pixels" that aren't visible because the zoom amount is too low. We used this option to create the yellow region; it partially covers the outline and there are no cracks.

Setting it to a negative number will shrink the object, which can also be useful in some cases. In the following example I created the red star-like shape and used a negative **Grow/Shrink by:** option to create all the other objects on top of it:

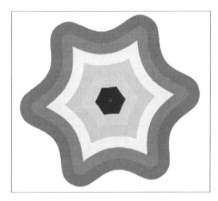

Filling the lime region we saw how the zoom amount has an influence on which pixels will be considered as acceptable neighbors and which ones will be excluded. Zooming out will effectively shrink the new object, while zooming in will ensure a more precise filling.

Filling regions when zoom is large

When zooming in close for precision, some parts of the region we wish to fill might be hidden off screen. Holding _Shift_ while filling will join the newly created object with the previous one. To avoid creating sub-paths (with visible gaps between them), instead of merging them with Union them, set a small amount to the **Grow/shrink by:** option.

The "aqua" region isn't entirely closed. There are gaps on either side where the color can spill out from, but hasn't because we used the **Close gaps:** option which ensured the **Paint Bucket** will ignore small gaps in our line drawing even when they are clearly visible.

The Paint Bucket and strokes

The **Paint Bucket** is often used on line art and comics but this doesn't mean those are the only applications. **Paint Bucket** calculates neighbors even on colored/nontransparent regions.

Paint Bucket objects can also be set with a stroke; this doesn't change the resulting path but it does expand visually so this is another trick that can be used to fill in the cracks.

The Paint Bucket and gradients

It doesn't stop here. The **Paint Bucket** can also be applied to gradients, as in any other case the options and zoom amount influence which neighbor pixels are acceptable to be included in the new object.

Filling noncontiguous regions

If we have a number of regions that need to be filled using the same settings we can save some time by holding the *Alt* key while dragging across those regions.

Constrain fill region

In all our examples we used the default constraint of the **Fill by:** option, namely **Visible Colors**, but more are available. In complex drawings with lots of objects or gradients constraining by a more specific condition can be helpful to achieve a more precise result depending on our needs.

See also

For more information, refer to the *Changing fill and stroke color using a palette* and *Creating linear gradients* recipes in *Chapter 2*.

Rail sleepers using markers

This recipe will show us how to use the marker to arrange objects along the path without distorting them, by creating a set wooden sleepers commonly found in railway tracks.

How to do it...

The following steps will demonstrate the use of markers:

1. Select the **Pencil** tool (*F6* or *P*) and create a wavy line around 650 px wide with **Smoothing:** set to 70. Make sure you don't make the curvature too steep.

2. Add more nodes by using the **Add Nodes** extension. Go to **Extensions | Modify Path | Add Nodes...**, select **By max. segment length** and enter 150 into the **Maximum segment length (px)**.

3. Select the **Rectangle** tool (*F4* or *R*) and create a 70x170 px vertical rectangle. Set its fill to #aa4400, remove stroke, and round the corners with 7 px.

4. Apply the 3D wood filter to it by going to **Filters | Materials | 3D wood**.

5. Change the display mode to **No Filters** (*Ctrl* + *5*) so the screen redraw doesn't lag when working.

6. Convert the rectangle to a marker by going to **Object** > **Objects to Marker**. The rectangle will disappear but will be available as a marker. The style shown will be the color applied to its fill and stroke. The way it looks with the filter applied isn't rendered there.

7. Select the wavy line and open the Fill and Stroke dialogue (*Shift* + *Ctrl* + *F*). On the **Stroke style** tab select the marker we just created for all start, mid, and end markers. It should be on top of the list. (If you can't see it, try closing the drop-down and opening it again.)

8. Change the Display mode to **Normal** (press *Ctrl* + *KP_5* twice) so you can see the end result:

How it works...

If we had made the line curvature too steep the markers would overlap in places if they weren't apart enough. Adding more nodes using the extension ensures the nodes are equidistant.

The 3D effect of the 3D wood filter doesn't work as expected on small sizes, that is why we made the sleepers so wide. We can fix the 3D wood filter to work as expected on smaller sizes by using the **Filter Editor**.

The **No Filters** mode is very useful when we have many filters or if they are too complex. We can still see the colors in the drawing so not having filters rendered isn't too much of an obstacle, and it speeds things up significantly.

There's more...

Along with path interpolation this method can be used to fake bending gradients. The trick is to create a thin vertical rectangle with the gradient we want to "bend" and convert it to a marker. The path we are applying it to has to have a lot of nodes spaced out closely together so when the marker is applied there are no gaps between consecutive markers and they seamlessly blend, as shown in the following image:

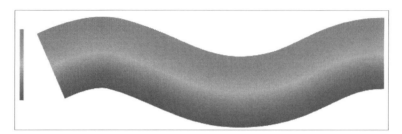

We can also create a clone of the rectangle and convert the clone to a marker. This way we can change the gradient on the rectangle and the markers applied to paths will automatically update.

See also

For more information, refer to *Create freehand and straight lines* in *Chapter 2*, *Using Pattern Along Path* in *Chapter 5*, and *Creating a water surface effect* in *Chapter 7*.

Creating a woven straw mat

In this recipe we will create and apply a special texture to an artistic composition of shapes, in order to produce the image of a woven straw mat. We will generate the texture from a primitive and then apply filter effects to it to change the overall look. Finally we will decorate our map with the artistic rendition of a woven flower.

This is a good example on how Inkscape can produce an elaborate drawing in a relatively small number of steps.

How to do it...

The following steps will show how to create a woven straw mat:

1. Open the **Document Properties** (*Shift + Ctrl + D*) and set the document background color to very dark brown by entering `221e11ff` into the **RGBA:** box on the **Background:** pop-up.

2. Select the **Rectangle** tool (*F4* or *R*) and create a 200 px square by holding *Ctrl*. Fill it with the color #dbc68c. Create a vertical linear gradient and set the end stop color to #aa8a58. Add more stops and move them to create nice shading transitions.

3. Apply the **Film grain** filter to it by going to **Filters | Image effects | Film grain**.

4. Open the **Filter Editor** (**Filters | Filter Editor**), the **Film grain** filter and **Turbulence** primitive will be selected. Under the **Effect parameters** tab unlink the **Base Frequency:** and move the Y (bottom) slider all the way to the left (value 0) and **Octaves:** to the right (value 10).

5. Select the first **Composite** primitive by clicking on it and change the K attributes to 0.3. 0.5, -0.4, 0 (in that order).

6. Apply the **Combined lighting** filter by going to **Filters | Bevels | Combined lighting**.

7. Select the first **Gaussian Blur** primitive and change the **Standard Deviation:** to 1. Do the same for the second one too.

8. Select the **Diffuse Lighting** primitive, set **Surface Scale:** to 0.1 and **Constant:** to 1.1.

9. Select the **Specular Lighting** primitive, set **Surface Scale:** to 0.3, and **Constant:** to 0.5.

10. We now have the basic straw effect so rename the filter to "Straw" by clicking on its name.

11. Open the **Edit | Clone | Create Tiled Clones** dialog from the menu and press the **Reset** button to get all the default values.

12. Set to create 3 rows and 3 columns. On the **Shift** tab set **Shift Y: Per row:** and **Shift X: Per Column:** both to -0.5 % and on the **Rotation** tab. Set both angles to -90°, turn on **Alternate: Per column:** and finally check that the **Symmetry** is set to **P1: Simple translation**.

13. Press the **Create** button. You will see 9 squares rotated so they look like woven straw.

14. Select the **Ellipse** tool (*F5* or *E*) and create a small circle while holding the *Ctrl* key. Set its fill to the same gradient we used for the straw rectangle.

15. Clone the circle several times (*Alt + D*) and arrange the clones at the center of the middle straw rectangle.

16. Select the original circle (*Shift + D* when its clone is selected) and apply the **Straw** filter to it by ticking its box when the circle is selected.

17. Rotate each clone to simulate different lighting reflections and to change the grain direction so it's different from the rectangle grain.

18. Select the **Pen (Bezier)** tool (*Shift + F6* or *B*) and create a leaf-like object.

19. Copy the original rectangle (select under the first clone using *Alt* + mouse click and do *Ctrl + C*). Select the leaf-like object and **Paste Style** (*Shift + Ctrl + V*).

20. Select the **Gradient** tool (*Ctrl + F1* or *G*) and move the start and end gradient handles to the ends of the leaf-like object to adjust it to its position.

21. Clone the leaf-like object several times (*Alt + D*) and arrange the clones around the circles in the middle of the rectangle tiles.

How it works...

We had to shift the tiles a bit to make them overlap, removing the think lines between them where the background shines through. This creates a more realistic effect of woven straw.

The trick to make the filter look like straw is adjusting gradient colors and lighting primitives so they work together, and also adjusting the **Composite** K attributes. It takes a bit of playing with the settings until the right effect is achieved. For best results keep the K attribute values close to 0.

See also

For more information, refer to *Creating and editing 2D geometric shapes* in *Chapter 1*, and the *Blurring, Using lighting effects*, and *Creating a brushed steel effect* recipes in *Chapter 7*.

Assembling a modern chair using the 3D Box tool

We have seen that Inkscape is capable of producing three-dimensional *looking* art. This effect is achieved by arranging 2D shapes to give the resulting object a sense of perspective. Although Inkscape is not (and was never intended to be) a substitute for 3D CAD software, we can build some pretty complex objects with this technique.

In this recipe we will assemble a three-dimensional chair using the **3D Box** tool.

How to do it...

The following steps will demonstrate how to construct a chair in three dimensions:

1. Zoom to fit the page width into the window (*Ctrl + E or 6*). Pan or scroll to the bottom half of the page.

2. Select the **3D Box** tool (*Shift + F4 or X*) and create a box in the bottom-left part of the page. Check that the **Angle X** and the **Angle Z** parameters are locked (grayed out) and the **Angle Y** parameter is selected and set to 90 degrees. Set the fill to **40% Gray**, stroke to **10% Gray**, and stroke width to 2.

3. Resize it along the **Z axis** by holding *Ctrl* and dragging the right-hand corner of the front-right-hand side to the right, then resize along the **Y axis** by dragging the top-left corner upwards while holding *Ctrl*.

4. Resize the box along the **X axis** by dragging the left-most corner downwards while holding *Ctrl*. This will be the back of the chair.

5. Enable snapping to cusp nodes and paths by enabling the buttons **Snap nodes or handles**, **Snap to cusp nodes**, and **Snap to paths** on the snapping toolbar.

6. Duplicate the box (*Ctrl + D*), hold down the *Shift* key, and click on the central "x" handle to move the box along the **Z axis** and towards the right. This will be the left arm of the chair.

7. Drag one of the nodes while holding *Shift* to snap to the bottom-right corner of the original box. Grab the right-hand node and move it to the left while holding *Ctrl* to make the box smaller along the **Z axis**.

8. Send the box back behind the original one (*Page Down* or *End*).

9. Duplicate the second box (*Ctrl + D*) and hold *Shift* while moving it to the left until it is positioned to the side or the original box.

10. Hold *Ctrl* while dragging one of the nodes to snap to the original box.

11. Hold *Shift* and drag the left node of the left-most box to the right to make the box smaller, approximately the same size as the one on the right.

12. Select the middle box and duplicate it (*Ctrl + D*). Move it to the right while holding *Ctrl*, this will be the chair seat.

13. The seat should not be as tall as the back, and also in our case won't be all the way to the floor. To achieve that, hold *Ctrl* while dragging one of the top nodes to the bottom, and one of the bottom nodes upwards.

14. Drag the left-most node of the seat box to the left while holding *Ctrl* until it snaps to the back of the chair box path.

15. Select the left arm (the one farthest from us) and hold *Ctrl* while dragging one of the front nodes to the left until it reaches the seat edge.

16. Select the right arm and stretch it using both *Shift* and *Ctrl*. This will create an optical illusion that the arm is behind the seat when it should be in front of it. To fix this bring the right arm to the front with *Page Up* or *Home*.

17. Again use *Shift + Ctrl* to scale the right arm until it reaches the edge of the seat.

18. Color the chair sides with your favorite colors selecting the side with the **Node** tool (*F2* or *N*) or by using the **Selector** tool and holding down the *Ctrl* key.

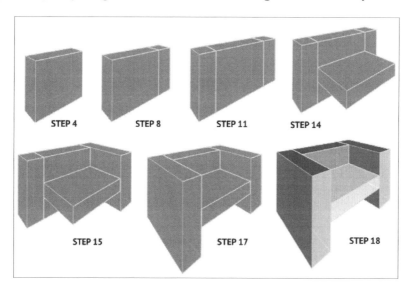

There's more...

Does the chair look a little too hard and uncomfortable for your taste? Inkscape can make it much more appealing with the click of a button. Try selecting the chair group and applying the **Filters | Blurs | Evanescent** filter. Thanks to the shading effect of the blur, it now seems much softer and appealing.

See also

For more information, refer to *Creating and editing 3D boxes* in *Chapter 1* and *Creating a stylized flower using Snapping* in *Chapter 3*.

Creating a flow chart using connectors

A flowchart is a graphical representation of a process, be it an algorithm or a business procedure. Many Office packages offer some sort of application to create them. However, wouldn't it be great to use a powerful program like Inkscape to create some truly spectacular diagrams... or at least make them less boring to read?

This recipe will show us how to create charts in Inkscape using the **Connector** tool and some other useful helpers.

How to do it...

The following steps will demonstrate how to create charts:

1. Open the **Document Properties** (*Shift + Ctrl + D*) and under the **Grids** tab create a new **Rectangular grid**. Set **Spacing X:** and **Spacing Y:** to 10.

2. Select the **Rectangle** tool (*F4* or *R*) and create a wide rectangle. Set its fill to `#fef0d8`, stroke to `#fdca01`, stroke width to 2, and corner radius to 10 px.

3. Select the **Text** tool (*F8* or *T*), choose the desired font family and size on the toolbar. Set the text to bold and center it by pressing the buttons on the toolbar.

4. Create a text object by clicking and typing "Option 1".

5. Center the text over the rectangle by using the **Align and Distribute** dialog (*Shift + Ctrl + A*).

6. Select both objects (*Ctrl + A*), duplicate them (*Ctrl + D*), and position them next to the first rectangle.

7. Change the text of the second text object to "Option 2 long title". Notice how the text leaked out of the rectangle.

8. Select the **Rectangle** tool (*F4* or *R*) and with it widen the rectangle. Select the text and the rectangle and center them using the button in the **Align and Distribute** dialog (*Shift + Ctrl + A*).

9. Select the wider rectangle and its text, duplicate (*Ctrl + D*) and position it below the first two rectangles.

10. Duplicate the first "row" and position it below everything. Change the text so the labels are all unique.

11. Select the **Connector** tool (*Ctrl + F2* or *O*), hover over the top-left rectangle, and take notice of the handle that appears at the center. Click that handle and drag across to the bottom-right rectangle, release the mouse when you reach its center connector handle.

12. Switch to the **Selector** tool (*Space, F1* or *S*), select the middle rectangle, switch back to the **Connector** tool (*Space, Ctrl + F2* or *O*), and press the **Make connectors avoid selected** objects button. Notice how the connector immediately clears the middle rectangle area.

13. Connect the top-right and the bottom-left rectangles. Notice how the connector avoids the middle rectangle even as we move the mouse around before making the connection. This way we can see what the connector layout might look like depending on where it lands.

14. The connectors will now look a bit weird. It's hard to distinguish which rectangles are connected. Select the second connector and open the **Fill and Stroke** dialog (*Shift + Ctrl + F*) under the **Stroke style** tab and change the **Width:** to 2 and **Dashes:** to dashes.

15. Select the middle rectangle and its text and move it to the right. Notice the connectors change shape to adjust to the new layout.

16. With the middle rectangle still selected press the **Make connectors ignore selected objects** button on the **Connector** toolbar. Notice the connectors now pass over the rectangle.

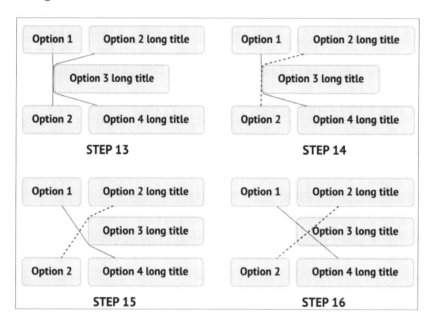

How it works...

Setting the text to center makes it easier later if we duplicate one set of options and change the text, the edited text will also be centered. The grid enables us to change the rectangle size quickly without thinking about alignment.

Using the connectors is easy and the option to avoid certain objects can speed up creating various charts. When used in an appropriate and non-distracting way, different styles can make diagrams more expressive and interesting. Take care not to overdo it: the important thing here is to convey information, not to aggravate it with meaningless embellishment.

There's more...

You can change the connector markers by selecting them, opening the **Fill and Stroke** (*Shift +
Ctrl + F*) dialog and choosing them from the **Stroke Style** dialog **Start Markers**, **Mid Markers**,
and **End Markers**.

See also

For more information, refer to the *Creating and editing 2D geometric shapes*, *Editing paths
with Node tool*, and *Creating and editing text* recipes in *Chapter 1*.

9
Raster and Almost Raster

In this chapter, we will cover:

- ▶ Exporting to PNG with different dpi
- ▶ Importing raster images of different dpi
- ▶ Isolating part of a raster image
- ▶ Using Raster extensions
- ▶ Creating Gradient meshes
- ▶ Painting a mosaic using the Tweak tool
- ▶ Tracing bitmaps
- ▶ Manually tracing a red wax seal
- ▶ Creating a photorealistic mobile phone

Introduction

Even though Inkscape is a vector graphics program it is perfectly capable of working with raster images, combining them with vectors when necessary. This chapter contains recipes that will show us how to use Inkscape as a raster editor, how to create some raster effects using vector objects without using SVG filters, and how to produce photorealistic drawings in Inkscape.

Exporting to PNG with different dpi

The most common way of presenting SVG drawings created using Inkscape is by exporting them to **PNG** (**Portable Network Graphics**) format. This recipe will show us how this is accomplished and what to look out for, in particular when it comes to exporting the same drawing size (width and height in absolute units like inches) into a picture with a different dpi value. We will also use two of the images we export here in the following recipe, in order to practice importing of images with different dpi.

How to do it...

The following steps will demonstrate how to export an image to PNG:

1. Choose the **Rectangle** tool (*F4* or *R*) and create a square. Set its fill to **Blue** (**#0000FF**) and apply a diagonal gradient using the **Gradient** tool (*Ctrl + F1* or *G*). Remove stroke and set it to 450x450 px in size.

2. Switch back to the **Selector** tool (*Space*) and set the units temporarily to inches by choosing **in** instead of **px** in the drop-down on the Selector toolbar. Notice the size of the square corresponds to 5x5 inches.

3. Open the **Export bitmap** dialog (*Shift + Ctrl + E*), and the **Selection** button will be selected and under it the **Width:** and **Height:** boxes will display values of 450 (the set square size). Change the units from **px** to **in** by using the drop-down list.

4. Under **Bitmap size** set 90 in the **dpi** box automatically making the **Width:** and **Height:** 450 px, equal to their set size.

5. Under **Filename** enter the location where you want the file to be exported, name it `rectangle90dpi.png`, and press the **Export** button. The file will be exported but the **Export Bitmap** dialog will remain open.

6. Double the size of the dpi setting by entering 180 into the **dpi** box. Notice how **Width:** and **Height:** automatically change to 900 doubling the resulting image pixel size, but the **Width:** and **Height:** under the **Export** area still remains 5 inches, or if you change the units to 450 px.

7. Under **Filename** enter the location where you want the file to be exported, name it `rectangle180dpi.png`, and press the **Export** button. We now have two PNG raster images of the same absolute size but because of the different dpis they are of different pixel sizes.

8. Open the **Document Properties** (*Shift + Ctrl + D*) and change the background color of the document to fully opaque white by increasing the **A** slider to 225.

9. Repeat the Steps 3 and 4 and under **Filename** enter the location where you want the file to be exported, name it `rectangle90dpiWhite.png`, and press the **Export** button.

10. Open all three exported images in your favorite image viewer and compare them at 100% zoom. The following is a screenshot with checkerboard pattern marking transparency (I used GIMP):

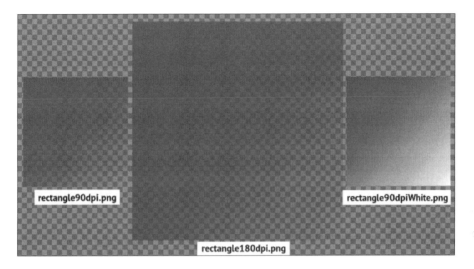

How it works...

Setting the proper document size beforehand is a good practice that can save time in the long run, even in the case of vector graphics where scaling is lossless and doesn't affect the inherent quality of a drawing. So if you plan to export the page area and not only parts of the drawing, set up the correct page size under **Document Properties** (*Shift + Ctrl + D*).

We chose a size of 450px because it corresponds exactly to 5 inches (90 px per inch). This relationship is always valid in Inkscape because Inkscape always uses a fixed dpi of 90 for displaying content. Exporting with 90 dpi means that the exported image size will be the one we set in **Document Properties** (*Shift + Ctrl + D*) and see in the Canvas with **Zoom factor** set to 1:1 (*1* or **View | Zoom | Zoom 1:1**). This is the workflow we use most often; setting the intended page size under Document Properties (if page area is important) and using 90 dpi when exporting.

Changing the dpi during export changes the number of pixels that will be generated. Pixels here can be considered as units of image information, the smallest bits that can't be divided into even smaller parts. So if we want to increase the amount of information in an image, make it more dense to reach print quality. For example, we have to increase the dpi, which will inevitably increase the pixel size of the image, while keeping the absolute image size in inches.

This is what the first two exports show us. The absolute image size was always 5 inches, while doubling the dpi also doubled the pixel dimensions of the image, from 450x450 to 900x900. Notice how the gradient didn't change or move in the second export; it is the same drawing only rendered in a higher definition.

Even though the default document background color in Inkscape is fully transparent (*Opacity* set to 0) it is not indicated with a checkerboard pattern like in some other graphics applications and appears to be white. This means that we don't have to do anything special to get a transparent background; it's already there. To create the third export we changed the document background color to a fully opaque white for demonstration purposes.

Export bitmap versus Save as Cairo PNG

We can save to Cairo PNG format through the **Save as...** dialog. However, it doesn't save transparency; it is an experimental format that shouldn't normally be used in production environment. The correct way to get a PNG format of our drawing is to use the **Export bitmap** dialog (*Shift + Ctrl + E*). A blueprint is in place to move all the non-native formats from the **Save as...** into the **Export bitmap** dialog: `https://blueprints.launchpad.net/inkscape/+spec/save-as-vs-export`

There's more...

There are a few more tricks that extend the utility of Inkscape's export feature. We shall now look into some of them.

Removing the Alpha channel

Inkscape always adds an alpha channel to the exported PNG, even if the image doesn't contain transparency, which adds to the file size. If the images are to be used online it is desirable to make them as small in size as possible. To do this we can use the GIMP or some other raster application to remove the alpha channel and reduce the palette size to only necessary colors. Using this method I was able to reduce the size of the `rectangle90dpiWhite.png` file from 9.2 KB to 3.4 KB (`rectangle90dpiWhiteOptimized.png`). The size reduced by more than half. You can compare the files and see that there is no visible difference between them.

Sharp edges with the PixelSnap extension

When exporting objects with straight edges or even raster graphics we expect the edges to be sharp, and we also expect that the raster graphics we import doesn't lose quality when exported. As already mentioned in *Chapter 2*, we can snap to the pixel grid or use the **PixelSnap** extension (under **Extensions | Modify Path | PixelSnap...**) to solve this problem.

Extracting embedded images

If we have an SVG document with a raster image embedded into it and we want to extract it out of the document so the image is linked instead of embedded, we can use the **Extract Image** extension.

Select the embedded image and go to **Extensions | Images | Extract Image...**, enter the name you want for the extracted image without the extension and press **Apply**. The image will be extracted into the user home directory unless a path to the file is specified (again the file name should be without an extension, as it will be assigned automatically) and a reference to the external image location is created inside the SVG, so the drawing hasn't lost any components. The image is extracted unaffected with the rest of the drawing. If there are objects on top or below the image they will not be included in the extraction.

See also

For more information, refer to the *Making objects partially transparent* and *Creating linear gradients* recipes in *Chapter 2, Geometric illusions using Grid* and *Autosaving documents* in *Chapter 3, Exporting a wallpaper to different formats* in *Chapter 8, Importing raster images of different dpi* in *Chapter 9*, and *Slicing a web page mockup for website use* in *Chapter 10*.

Importing raster images of different dpi

In this recipe we will familiarize ourselves with importing raster images into Inkscape and learn how to handle images of different dpi that we plan to export in the end. We will use two of the images we exported in the last recipe as examples.

How to do it...

The following steps will demonstrate how to import raster images:

1. Open the **File | Import** dialog (*Ctrl + I*), and navigate to the folder with the images extracted in the last recipe. Select the `rectangle90dpi.png` file and press **Open**.

2. Another small dialog will open with the choice to embed or link the image; choose embed and press **OK**.

3. Open the **Import** dialog again(*Ctrl + I*), navigate to the folder with the images extracted in the last recipe, select the `rectangle180dpi.png`, and press **Open**.

4. This time choose to link the image and press **OK**.

5. Open the **XML Editor** (*Shift + Ctrl + X*) and the last image should be selected in the left pane. Select the `xlink:href` attribute from the right pane and notice it only contains the reference to the external image location.

6. Select the image we imported first in Steps 1 and 2 by clicking on it in the Canvas or selecting it in the **XML Editor**. Select the `xlink:href` attribute, expand the bottom area so you can see more of its contents and notice it contains a seemingly random string of letters, beginning with `data:image/png;base64` (the data header of a PNG image containing its MIME type and encoding scheme).

7. Open your file browser in a folder containing some images and drag one of the images into the Inkscape window. Notice how the cursor changes into the one with the "+" sign. You will get the same pop-up window asking if you want to embed or link the image, press **Cancel**.

8. Select the **Selector** tool (*F1* or *S*) and on the toolbar change the units from **px** to **in**. Select the two imported images in turn and notice the first one has the width and height of 5 inches, and the other 10 inches.

9. Select the second image (10 inches), lock the ratio by turning on the lock icon on the Selector toolbar, and enter 5 into either the **W** or **H** box. The other one will update automatically. This image will now have the same pixel size as the one we imported first.

10. Open the **Export Bitmap** dialog (*Shift + Ctrl + E*) and the **Selection** button will be selected. Change the units to **in** and notice that the absolute size is 5 inches. Set the **dpi** under **Bitmap size** to 180, the original image dpi. Under **Filename** enter the location and the name of the image and press **Export**.

11. Open the exported image in an image viewer and notice it has the same pixel size as when we imported it into Inkscape, even though we scaled it down in the meantime.

How it works...

Using the **Import** dialog, only one file can be imported at a time, but if we drag the file to the Canvas instead, many can be imported without opening the dialog more than once. In version 0.48 the option to choose between embedding or linking images is introduced and triggered when importing or dragging files into the Canvas. If any raster information (an image or a part of it, copied from GIMP for example) is pasted into Inkscape it automatically gets embedded.

If we plan to share our documents with others or publish them online it's recommended to embed any raster image if they are used in the document. So there's no need to worry about sending the linked files as well and keeping the tree structure of the document intact so the links don't break.

When working with graphics that will be seen on a digital screen, where pixels are the foundation of the display size, dpi doesn't matter. We can export our drawing to any pixel size and disregard what the **dpi** box says. It's the same with importing images we intend to use on screen—the dpi of the imported image doesn't matter because the image pixel size will always be imported into the same number of pixels in Inkscape.

This situation is different when dealing with absolute units like inches and images that have a dpi other than 90. This can be unintuitive to those who don't have a deeper insight into the different image storage and display techniques (vector and raster, screen and print). Inkscape always respects pixel information and always displays it in 90 dpi. If an image we import has 180 dpi which is double the Inkscape default, the image absolute size will also appear to be twice the original size. That is why we have to scale the image after importing so when we're exporting our work in the end we can end up with the original absolute size and the original dpi. The scale factor is calculated by dividing the original dpi by 90.

In other words if we import a 5 inch image that has 180 dpi we have to scale it down by 50% so when exporting the absolute size would still be 5 inches and we could set the dpi to 180 to get the same absolute size and quality as the original image.

There's more...

If we embedded a 180 dpi image into Inkscape, scaled it down by 50%, and used the **Extract Image** extension, the resulting image would have 180 dpi and it would appear to be double in pixel size than the one we scaled inside Inkscape. Thus we can see that the **Extract Image** extension respects the internal image properties when extracting.

Make a Bitmap Copy

The **Make a Bitmap Copy** command is a shortcut for quickly exporting the selected object as a PNG file and then reimporting it as a raster image. It is found under the **Edit** menu and has an option under **Bitmaps** in **Inkscape Preferences** (*Shift + Ctrl + P*) of which resolution to use when using dpi (the default is 90 dpi).

In contrast with the **Import** option when the **Make a Bitmap Copy** is executed on a raster image it respects the image absolute size and dpi setting from the **Inkscape Preferences** (the dpi of the copied image doesn't matter). This means that the images produced in this way always have the same pixel size as their original, but their dpi (the quality or the quantity of information) depends on the settings from the **Inkscape Preferences**.

See also

For more information, refer to the *Exporting to PNG with different dpi* and *Isolating part of a raster image* recipes in this chapter, and *Slicing a web page mockup for website use* in *Chapter 10*.

Isolating part of a raster image

A common task when manipulating photos is isolating a particular element of the image by removing the background along its edges. Inkscape can serve this need well and provides a lot of functionality for achieving pixel perfect results, as we will see in this recipe.

How to do it...

The following steps will demonstrate how to isolate parts of a raster image:

1. Import (*Ctrl + I*) the `Flower.png` image accompanying this chapter, and choose to embed it.

2. Snap it to the pixel grid using the **PixelSnap** extension by going to **Extensions | Modify Path | PixelSnap...**.

3. Select the **Pen (Bezier)** tool (*Shift + F6* or *B*) and create a closed path that traces around the flower.

4. Set the path fill to **Lime (#00FF00)**, remove the stroke, and decrease opacity to 30% so you can see the photo below the path.

5. Select the **Node** tool (*F2* or *N*) and adjust the path so its edges cover the flower edges exactly.

6. Select both the photo and the path and clip them by going to **Object | Clip | Set** (clipping isn't affected by the path's partial transparency).

7. If there are still unwanted parts of the flower background showing around the flower enable the **Show clipping path(s) of selected object(s)** button 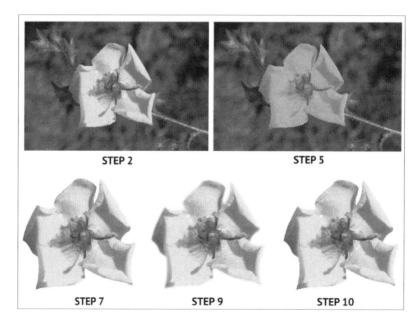 on the Node toolbar and adjust the clipping path.

8. Create a bitmap copy of the clipped photo (*Alt + B*), move it away and **PixelSnap**. Notice we now have only the isolated flower image without the clip.

9. Feather the flower edges by going to **Filters | ABCs | Feather**.

10. Open the **Filter Editor** by going to **Filters | Filter Editor...**. Select the **Gaussian Blur** primitive and change the **Standard Deviation:** under **Effect parameters** to 1.

11. Duplicate the clipped image from Step 7 (*Ctrl + D*) and release the clip by going to **Object | Clip | Release**.

12. Select the path, set the opacity to 100%. Set the fill color to white, stroke to black, stroke width to 1, and blur to 1.

13. Select both the photo and the masking path and go to **Object | Mask | Set**.

STEP 2

STEP 5

STEP 7

STEP 9

STEP 10

How it works...

There are two steps when trying to isolate part of a raster photograph that can help get the best results. The first one is precisely tracing the object edges, so when they are clipped there is no background leaking in. The second one is blurring the edges somehow to compensate for the imprecision of the clipping path. The first trace doesn't have to be done with the **Pen (Bezier)** tool, as the **Pencil** can sometimes be easier to use, but it can sometimes be difficult to find the appropriate **Smoothing:** setting. Too much smoothing will make us lose precision, and not enough will leave us with a huge number of nodes that are hard to adjust afterwards, although *node sculpting* can help.

The **Paint Bucket** can also be used by varying the **Threshold:**, zooming, and holding *Shift* to add all the painted regions to the same path automatically. Still it will probably need adjusting with the **Node** tool afterwards unless we're tracing very distinct regions.

Softening the edges can be done by using a slightly blurred white mask instead of clipping, or we can use the **Feather** filter on a bitmap copy (don't forget to adjust the dpi for the bitmap copy in the **Inkscape Preferences**). If we **Feather** the clipped photo, the photo edges will be feathered and not the clipped part of the photograph; that's why we use the bitmap copy option.

There's more...

If the object we are trying to isolate is on a white background we can modify the **Light eraser** filter found under **Filters | Transparency utilities** to make the white areas transparent for us. After this filter is applied to the bitmap add the **Color Matrix** primitive to it in the **Filter Editor** and modify the last two numbers in the last matrix row to 20 and -1. Try changing the number 20 to see if some other value fits better for that particular image.

See also

For more information, refer to the *Creating freehand and straight lines*, *Editing paths using the Node tool*, *Clipping*, *Masking*, and *Patterns* recipes in *Chapter 1*. Also refer to *Tracing bitmaps* later in this chapter.

Using raster extensions

Inkscape comes with some common raster editing functions in the form of extensions. We will use some of the extensions in this recipe to see what might be possible in raster editing using Inkscape.

How to do it...

The following steps will demonstrate some of the commonly used raster extensions:

1. Import (*Ctrl + I*) the `Flower.png` image accompanying this chapter, and choose to embed it.

2. Duplicate it (*Ctrl + D*) or stamp it (*Space*) seven times so you have eight copies in total.

3. Apply the following raster extensions (all are under **Extensions | Raster**) with the noted settings to the images separately one by one:

   - **Add noise** (**Laplacian Noise**)
   - **Edge** (3)
   - **Oil paint** (7)
   - **Shade** (120, 30)
   - **Solarize** (1)
   - **Swirl** (130)
   - **Unsharp Mask** (30, 20, 50, 0)
   - **Wave** (25, 150)

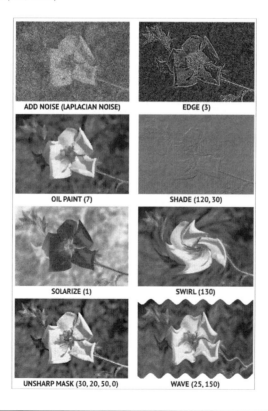

ADD NOISE (LAPLACIAN NOISE)	EDGE (3)
OIL PAINT (7)	SHADE (120, 30)
SOLARIZE (1)	SWIRL (130)
UNSHARP MASK (30, 20, 50, 0)	WAVE (25, 150)

How it works...

Raster extensions use the `ImageMagick` package to apply raster effects. The official installer for Inkscape 0.48 on Windows operating systems comes with all the necessary files to use the extensions, but on other systems `ImageMagick` and `PythonMagick` packages must be installed separately. See the following sites for more details:

`http://www.imagemagick.org`

`http://www.assembla.com/wiki/show/pythonmagickwand`

Calling each extension we get a pop-up window with the particular effect options to apply to the image. There is also the **Live preview** option that can be very useful when trying to find the right option settings without applying the effect and undoing it if we don't like the result.

There's more...

If these raster effects aren't enough we can edit the image in an external editor, but this method only works on linked images. Which editor to use can be configured in **Inkscape Preferences** (*Shift + Ctrl + P*) under **Bitmaps**.

If you right-click on a linked image there is an option **Edit Externally...** that opens the editor we set in the preferences. When the changes to the image in the external editor are saved the image is automatically updated in Inkscape.

See also

For more information, refer to the *Importing raster images of different dpi* recipe in this chapter.

Creating gradient meshes

Gradient meshes are used to enhance the realism of objects with reflective surfaces, such as a ceramic jar or a brass trumpet, and also to create abstract wallpapers that are colorful without being too distracting.

Inkscape doesn't have a gradient mesh tool like some other applications do, but we will work around this limitation in this recipe.

How to do it...

The following steps will demonstrate a workaround to gradient meshes:

1. Select the **Rectangle** tool (*F4* or *R*) and create a rectangle. Set its fill to none, stroke to black, and convert it to a path (*Shift + Ctrl + C*).

2. Select the **Node** tool (*F2* or *N*) and drag each of the four sides to distort them.

3. Duplicate the object (*Ctrl + D*).

4. Select the **Pencil** tool  (*B*), hold *Shift* and create a horizontal subpath intersecting the left and right side of the object; then create a second vertical subpath intersecting the top and bottom sides. The resulting path should be shaped like a cross, dividing the irregular rectangle in four sections.

5. Select the subpaths object and the top distorted rectangle. Do a **Path | Division** (*Ctrl + /*) and the result will be four separate, irregular objects.

6. Select one of the four new objects and do a **Dynamic Offset** (*Ctrl + J*); offset the path by almost a third of the object height. Convert the offset to a path in the end (*Shift + Ctrl + C*).

7. Repeat Step 6 for the remaining three objects.

8. Set the fill of each of the small objects to a different color and remove the stroke.

9. Blur each of the objects so that their edges are smoothly blended together, and then group them (*Ctrl + G*).

10. Select the original distorted rectangle object (use *Alt* to select the layer below) and bring it to the front (*Home* or *Page Up*). Add the group to the selection and go to **Object | Clip | Set**.

11. Enter the clipped group by double-clicking on it and adjust the z-order of the blurred objects to achieve the effect you like.

STEP 5   STEP 8   STEP 11

How it works...

The trick when creating gradient meshes is to figure out beforehand what kind of shapes we need to split our original object and which colors to use on them so that when they are blurred the result is the expected shading.

Overlaying the object with a net of sub-paths in the same object is probably the quickest way to divide the object into pieces.

The object offset should be large enough to compensate for the fading of the blurred edges, but if it's too large the mesh might not look the way we wanted because the object overlap seems to "shift" the edges. If the desired result can't be achieved by adjusting the blur amount and the path offset it's time to gain more control by dividing the original object into a finer grid.

The same method can be used to produce conical gradients. The trick is to use very thin and long triangles and rotate them around the sharpest point.

Path and color interpolation can also be used if we want to get very smooth calculated transitions, as we can observe in this screenshot from the Inkscape website:

```
http://inkscape.org/screenshots/gallery/inkscape-0.45-gradient-mesh-
experimental.png
```

 Although there doesn't seem to be a way to easily create gradient meshes in Inkscape or SVG in general, this area is being being actively developed and future versions of the program will likely contain a more orthodox method for generating them.

See also

For more information, refer to _Creating paths using the Pen (Bezier) tool_ in _Chapter 1_ and _Rail sleepers using Markers_ in _Chapter 8_.

Painting a mosaic using the Tweak tool

In this recipe we will use the **Tweak** tool as a paint brush to paint over a collection of objects that form a mosaic pattern. This is an example of how to come close to brush painting in Inkscape.

How to do it...

The following steps will demonstrate how to create a mosaic pattern:

1. Select the **Rectangle** tool (_F4_ or _R_) and create a 500x500 px rectangle. Set its fill to none, stroke to black, stroke width to 3, and duplicate it (_Ctrl + D_).

2. Apply the **Voronoi pattern** to the duplicate by going to **Extensions | Generate from Path | Voronoi pattern...** Set the **Average size of cell (px)** to 30, **Size of Border (px)** to 50, and press the **Apply** button.

3. Convert the pattern to objects by going to **Object | Pattern | Pattern to Objects** or by using _Shift + Alt +I_. The result will be straight lines as separate objects.

4. Combine the objects into a single path (_Ctrl + K_).

5. Add the rectangle to the selection (click on its border while holding down *Shift*). Do a **Path | Division** (*Ctrl + /*), this will create the mosaic tiles, color the tiles fill with red (**#D40000**), and set stroke width to 3.

6. With all of the tiles still selected select the **Tweak** tool (*Shift+F2* or *W*), the object bounding box selection cue will disappear but the objects will still be selected.

7. Set the **Tweak** tool 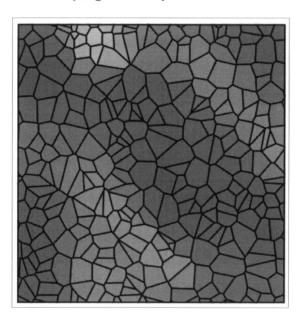 fill color to orange (**#FF6600**) by clicking on the palette chip. Notice that the **Fill:** box in the top-right corner of the window shows this change.

8. Set the **Width:** on the **Tweak** tool toolbar to an amount that covers roughly six mosaic tiles depending on your zoom. Set the **Force:** to 50 and **Mode:** to **Paint the tool's color upon selected objects**.

9. Paint over the mosaic, switch to a different color by clicking on the palette chips and paint over the tiles until you get the look you like.

How it works...

One of the modes of the **Tweak** tool is to paint a set color onto selected objects. This mode can be used for quick color corrections but if we apply it to a lot of small objects that overlap one another or are spaced out tightly we can get the feeling as if we're painting with a raster graphics paint tool. With the **Width:** and **Force:** options we are changing the "brush" properties. The other part of the effect comes from the shape of the objects and the way they are arranged.

In this recipe we used the **Voronoi pattern** to quickly create mosaic tiles where each tile is an independent object, so it can be colored easily. The tiles we used aren't very small but it still felt almost like painting, didn't it?

Our example is very simple with a small number of tiles so we were able to select them all at the same time and paint over particular areas. When working on a large "painting" we can select just objects in certain areas so we don't have to worry about being too precise with the "brush".

Other ways of creating the tiles over which to paint is by using **Edit | Clones | Create Tiled clones**, the **Spray** tool, and even the **Tweak** tool in Duplicate objects mode. The objects can overlap, and be of different shapes and sizes which can produce interesting effects.

See also

For more information, refer to the *Drawing a colorful grid of tiled clones* and *Drawing a tree with cloned leaves using the Spray tool* recipes in *Chapter 4*, and *Tracing bitmaps* in this chapter.

Tracing bitmaps

Tracing bitmaps is a way of getting a vector format for a raster image automatically. Inkscape comes with a tracing functionality, based on the *Potrace™* software utility (http://potrace.sourceforge.net), that scans the image and calculates vector paths that fit the tracing options we have set previously.

In this recipe we will trace an image several times to see what options are available when tracing a bitmap, and compare the results.

How to do it...

The following steps will demonstrate how to trace a bitmap:

1. Import the Flower.png image into the document (*Ctrl + I*), embedding it.

2. Open the **Trace Bitmap** dialog by going to **Path | Trace Bitmap...** or by using *Shift + Alt + B*.

3. Under the **Mode** tab **Single scan: creates a path** set **Brightness cutoff Threshold:** to 0.5 and press the **Update** button in the **Preview** pane. Notice you get a black and white preview of the trace where the background is black and the flower is white.

4. Enable the **Invert image** option and press **Update**, the background of the trace preview will now be white and the flower black. Press **OK** to create the trace; it will appear on top of the image.

5. Move the trace away from the image and select the original image again.

6. In the **Trace Bitmap** dialog change the **Brightness cutoff Threshold:** to 0.35 and press **OK** to create the trace, then move it away from the image.

7. Select the original image and on the **Trace Bitmap** dialog select the **Edge detection** option and press **Update**. Notice the background is now black which we usually don't want when tracing edges. Turn off the **Invert image** option and **Update** again.

8. The edges might seem a bit faint so let's try to find a better setting. Set the **Threshold:** to 0.9 and **Update**, the edges seem even more faint, set the **Threshold:** to 0.1 and **Update**, press **OK** to save that trace.

9. Move the trace away from the image and select the original image again.

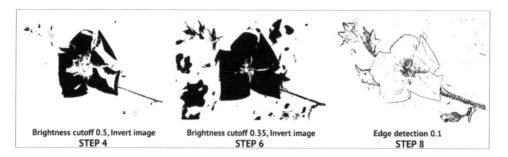

Brightness cutoff 0.5, Invert image
STEP 4

Brightness cutoff 0.35, Invert image
STEP 6

Edge detection 0.1
STEP 8

10. In the **Trace Bitmap** dialog select the **Color quantization** option, set **Colors:** to 8, and press the **Update** button. The flower now looks black with white edges, to change that enable the **Invert image** option and press **OK** button to create the trace.

11. Move the trace away from the image and select the original image again.

12. Select the original image and on the **Trace Bitmap** dialog set **Colors:** to 20, create the trace, move it away, and create another trace but with **Colors:** set to 50. Move it away from the image and select the image again.

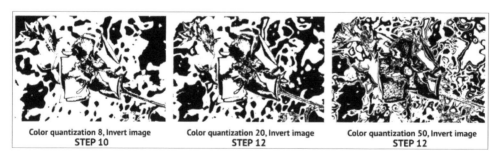

Color quantization 8, Invert image
STEP 10

Color quantization 20, Invert image
STEP 12

Color quantization 50, Invert image
STEP 12

13 Under **Multiple scans: creates a group of paths** select **Brightness steps** and set **Scans:** to 2. Turn off **Invert image**, **Stack scans**, and **Remove background** and press **OK** to create the trace, move it away and create another trace but with **Scans:** set to 8. Move it away from the image and select the image again.

14. Turn on the **Stack scans** option, create another trace, and move it away from the image.

| Brightness steps 2, Smooth | Brightness steps 8, Smooth | Brightness steps 8, Smooth, Stack scans |
| STEP 13 | STEP 13 | STEP 14 |

15. Select the original image again and in the **Trace Bitmap** dialog under **Multiple scans: creates a group of paths** select **Colors** and set **Scans:** to 8. Leave the other options as they were in the previous trace, and create a color trace by pressing the **OK** button. Move the trace away from the image.

16. Select the original image again and change the **Scans:** option to 60 and create another trace. 60 scans might take a bit longer to generate but you can watch the progress information in the Notification area in the statusbar.

17. Create two more scans this time with the **Grays** mode turned on, make one scan 8 times and the other 60 and leave all the other options as they are.

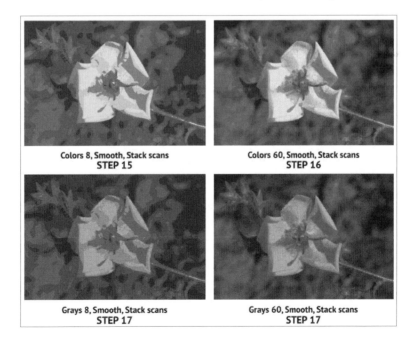

Colors 8, Smooth, Stack scans	Colors 60, Smooth, Stack scans
STEP 15	STEP 16
Grays 8, Smooth, Stack scans	Grays 60, Smooth, Stack scans
STEP 17	STEP 17

How it works....

As we can see there are many different options for tracing a bitmap, thanks to Potrace's powerful algorithms, depending on our need and the image we want to trace. There aren't any universal settings fit for each and every scenario, and values that are "just right" will be different for each image, which is why updating the **Preview** area helps a lot before we can find the settings we like best.

Brightness cutoff is an excellent choice for generating vector pictograms and other simple illustrations with well contrasted edges. The **Edge detection** option can also give us a quick scan of the edges on simple drawings. It becomes less usable if the image is complex and we get a lot of small sub-paths we don't need but the **Eraser** tool can help us there to clean up the path and only keep the important parts.

Color quantization option still produces one scan and one path, but the shape of the path will be determined by the number of colors we set. It's as if the scan is performed that many times based on color changes in the image and the result is gathered into one path in the end.

Multiple scans actually produce multiple paths of different fill colors. They can either be stacked one on top of the other covering some of the areas of other paths, or if the **Stack scans** option is off the paths don't overlap and we can see where the background shines through between the edges. We can hide the visible edge gap by giving the paths a small stroke of the same color as the fill, or by expanding the path by using offset options.

Using the **Colors** option with a large number of scans is the closest we can get to the look of a photograph but it might be resource intensive and unnecessary, it's useful to strike a balance between the number of scans and the raster to vector fidelity.

The **Grays** option is basically the same as the **Colors** only the fill colors are converted to grayscale. If you look closely you'll see that the **Brightness steps** and the **Grays** results with the same number of scans differ. Which of those two to use depends on whether there is more contrast in the image colors or in the brightness information.

> **Trace Bitmap dialog (*Shift + Alt + B*) empty on second call**
>
> The **Trace Bitmap** dialog has a bug that renders it empty when opened the second time in a document. That is why if you plan to do more than one trace keep the **Trace Bitmap** dialog open or reopen the document to get the dialog contents back.

There's more...

The **Trace Bitmap** dialog also has the **Options** tab where we can set the size of the speckles we want suppressed, whether we want to allow the corners to be smooth and how strongly to optimize the paths to reduce the number of nodes or increase the fidelity of the image we are tracing.

SIOX foreground selection

You probably noticed another option available on the **Trace Bitmap** dialog—the **SIOX foreground selection**. **SIOX** stands for **Simple Interactive Object Extraction** and is a way for us to trace over only a part of an image.

To use SIOX create an object that covers only the parts of the image you want traced (make it transparent so you can see better where to position it), the SIOX algorithm will try to extract the object we selected from the background and only trace the object. Both the object and the image must be selected when invoking the command.

Here is an example where only the flower was covered by an ellipse and with the SIOX foreground selection enabled I used **Colors** with 8 **Scans**, and selected the **Smooth** and **Stack scans** options:

If we compare this result with the one where the options are the same only without the SIOX, we can see there are more details in the flower if we use the foreground selection because the color options don't have to adjust to the whole photograph, so the result is more precise.

Autotrace

If you're not satisfied with the results you got using **Trace Bitmap** and Potrace or you need a centerline trace you can try Autotrace:

```
http://autotrace.sourceforge.net/
```

Read more about it on Inkscape Wiki:

```
http://wiki.inkscape.org/wiki/index.php/Tools#Vectorize.2Ftrace
```

See also

For more information, refer to the *Isolating part of a raster image, Manually tracing a red wax seal*, and *Creating a photorealistic mobile phone* recipes in this chapter.

Manually tracing a red wax seal

In *Chapter 7, SVG Filters* we created a red wax seal using filters. In this recipe we will recreate the same kind of lighting found in that drawing, using more objects that will serve as shadows and highlights, and the additional help of our good friend, the **Blur** filter.

How to do it...

The following steps will demonstrate how to recreate the red wax seal lighting:

1. Open the `RedWaxSeal.svg` file from *Chapter 7* and copy the seal into a new document.

2. Make a bitmap copy (*Alt + B*) of the seal that will serve as a reference and move it away.

3. Create three new layers above the current one, name them "insider", "stamp area", and "Inkscape logo".

4. Move the Inkscape logo object to the **Inkscape logo** layer (*Shift + Page Up*). Move the circle stamp area object to the **stamp area** layer (*Shift + Page Up*)

5. Select all of the three wax seal objects and remove all the filters by going to **Filters | Remove Filters**.

6. Hide the **Inkscape logo** and the **stamp area** layers.

7. Select the remaining wax object, duplicate it (*Ctrl + D*). Move the duplicate to the **insider** layer, then hide that layer.

8. Select the remaining object, break the path apart (*Shift + Ctrl + K*) and delete the circle path that comes out as a result of breaking the path.

9. Duplicate the remaining object (*Ctrl + D*), color the fill of the duplicate blue.

10. Select the red object behind the blue one (*Alt* + click to select under), change its fill to **Red (#FF0000)**, and group it (*Ctrl + G*).

11. Add the blue object to the selection and clip it by going to **Object | Clip | Set**.

12. Enter the group by double-clicking, select the red object and duplicate it (*Ctrl + D*). Set the stroke on the duplicate to **Black**, stroke width to 32, and blur it so the shading at the bottom part seems similar to the image reference.

13. Select the **Gradient** tool (*Ctrl + F1* or *G*) and create a linear black to transparent gradient in the object's stroke by clicking near the bottom-right corner of the object and dragging up and to the left so it looks more like the image, add more stops if necessary. Set the end stop to opaque **Red (#FF0000)**.

14. Select the object behind the filtered one (hold *Alt* and click), duplicate it (*Ctrl + D*). Set it's fill to **Black** and cut it (*Ctrl + X*).

15. Double-click outside of the group on the empty Canvas to exit the group and paste the cut object using **Paste In Place** (*Ctrl + Alt + V*).

16. Send the object to the back (*End*). Set the **Blur:** slider on the **Fill and Stroke** dialog to 3, **Opacity:** to 70. Press *Esc* to get the focus back on the Canvas and use arrows keys to move the object to the right and downwards.

17. Enter the group again by double-clicking it and select the object behind the filtered one, duplicate it (*Ctrl + D*), set its fill to **White**. Turn it into a **Dynamic Offset** (*Ctrl + J*) and shrink it so that its outer edges are approximately at the same distance from the edges as the highlights on the reference image.

18. Convert the offset to a path (*Shift + Ctrl + C*), duplicate it (*Ctrl + D*), change its fill color to blue so you can see them apart, turn it into a **Dynamic Offset** (*Ctrl + J*), and shrink so the white object can be seen on the edges.

19. Convert the blue object into a path (*Shift + Ctrl + C*), add the white object to the selection and do a **Difference** (*Ctrl + -*).

20. Select the **Tweak** tool (*Shift + F2* or *W*) and set it to shrink (inset) mode, set **Force:** to 20, and **Width:** to an amount that is around three times larger than the width of the white stripe. Zoom to fit the drawing to the window (*4*) so you can see the reference image while tweaking.

21. Tweak over the white stripe to delete parts of it and only leave the areas that correspond to the highlights along the top edge of the object on the reference image. Change the **Width:** and **Force:** along the way as necessary as well as the mode to push parts if shrink mode distorts them.

22. Set the object **Blur:** to 3, duplicate it (*Ctrl + D*), and reduce the **Blur:** of the duplicate to 1.

23. Exit the group by double-clicking outside of it. Lock **Layer 1** and show the layer **insider**.

24. Select the red object in the inside layer and change its fill to **Red (#FF0000)**. It is now obvious the object has a "hole" in it.

25. Select the **Ellipse** tool (*F5* or *E*) and create a circle that is a bit wider than the hole and center it over it.

26. Add the object with the hole to the selection (holding *Shift*) and perform an **Intersection** (*Ctrl + ***).

27. Duplicate the red stripe object (*Ctrl + D*), set the fill on the duplicate to blue and break it apart (*Shift + Ctrl + K*).

28. Select the larger of the blue circles and make it larger than the wax object by holding *Ctrl* and *Shift*.

29. Add the smaller blue circle to the selection and combine them together (*Ctrl + K*).

30. Select the red stripe object (hold *Alt* and click) and group it (*Ctrl + G*). Add the blue object to the selection and clip them by going to **Object | Clip | Set**.

31. Enter the group, select the **Gradient** tool (*Ctrl + F1* or *G*) and create a linear gradient in the object fill by clicking near the bottom-right object corner and dragging up and to the left. Set the end stop to **Black** and set the blur of the object to 9.

32. Duplicate the object (*Ctrl + D*), set its blur to 0 and fill to **White**.

33. Make it larger by holding *Ctrl* and *Shift* while dragging, the inner edge should reach the place where the bottom highlight starts.

34. Break the object apart (*Shift + Ctrl + K*), select the larger circle and make it smaller (holding *Shift* and *Ctrl* while dragging) to make the white stripe width the same as the bottom highlight in the reference image.

35. Select both white objects and combine them (*Ctrl + K*).

36. Select the **Tweak** tool (*Shift + F2* or *W*) and set it to shrink (inset) mode; delete all of the parts that don't contribute to the bottom highlight.

37. Blur it by the amount of 3.

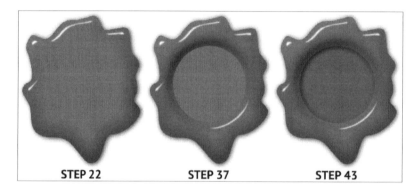

STEP 22   STEP 37   STEP 43

38. Lock the **insider** layer and show the **stamp area** layer; select the circle inside it.

39. Duplicate the circle (*Ctrl + D*) and set its fill to blue.

40. Select the red circle below (hold *Alt* and click) and group it (*Ctrl + G*).

41. Add the blue circle to the selection and clip them by going to **Object | Clip | Set**.

42. Enter the circle group by double-clicking on it and select the circle. Add a **Black** stroke it and make it 15 px wide.

43. Select the **Gradient** tool (*Ctrl + F1* or *G*) and create a linear black to transparent gradient in the circle stroke that goes from top-left to bottom-right to resemble the inner shadow from the reference image.

44. Lock the **stamp area** layer and show the **Inkscape logo** layer.

45. Select the logo object, and duplicate it (*Ctrl + D*). Set the fill color of the duplicate to **Black**, blur it, send it to back (*End*), and move to the right and to the bottom a bit. This shadow helps see the logo on the same color background.

46. Select the red logo object, duplicate it (*Ctrl + D*), and set the fill color of the duplicate to blue.

47. Select the original red logo object again, group it (*Ctrl + G*), add the blue one to the selection. Clip it by going to **Object | Clip | Set**.

48. Enter the group by double-clicking on it and select the logo object.

49. Break apart the object (*Shift + Ctrl + K*), remove the three little ink blots from the selection (hold *Shift* and click), and combine the selection back to get one mountain object and the three little separate ink blots.

50. Select the three little objects and change their fill too **Red (#FF0000)**.

51. Select the **Pen (Bezier)** tool (*Shift + F6 or B*) and create a new object over the bottom part of the left ink blot object that is roughly the shape of the shadow, but the bottom part can leak out of the edges of the object we are shading because the clip will take care of the leaks. Also avoid the large mountain object area so it doesn't mess up the shading there.

52. Set the fill color to black, remove stroke, and blur it to 20.

53 Repeat Steps 51 and 52 for the remaining two ink blot objects recreating the shading from the reference image, adjust the blur amount as needed.

54. Select the **Ellipse** tool (*F5 or E*) and create the highlight objects over the three ink blots; use the reference image to figure out the correct shapes. Set their fill to white and create a white to transparent radial gradient in each; use *Shift* to displace the gradient center if necessary.

55. Select the mountain object and duplicate it (*Ctrl + D*), set its stroke to 6 **Black**, convert the stroke to a path (*Ctrl + Alt + C*), and break it apart (*Shift + Ctrl + K*).

56. Examine the mountain edge on the reference image, notice how certain edge areas have darker and some lighter shadows, and some even aren't shaded but the red color looks brighter because it's directly lit. To recreate this look we will dissect the shadow object into areas and style them differently to achieve a realistic shading effect.

57. Select the **Pencil** tool (*F6 or P*) and create lines over the largest object we created in Step 55; the lines should be perpendicular to the shadow line and cross it in places where the shadow changes style. Make them long enough to extend past the edges that are invisible due to clipping. Hold *Shift* when creating each new line to add them as subpaths into a single object.

58. Add the largest shadow object to the selection and do a **Division** (*Ctrl + /*).

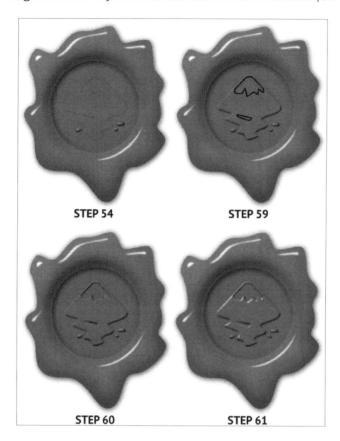

STEP 54   STEP 59

STEP 60   STEP 61

59. Select each of the shadow objects around the mountain object edge one by one and blur it, change its color to **Red (#FF0000)** where necessary, and lower its opacity so it resembles the shading in the image. Use the **Tweak** tool (*Shift + F2* or *W*) if you need to make some paths thinner or more pronounced and use ` (back quote) to quickly zoom in and out of two different zoom levels. A useful combination is the zoom into selection (3) and the other zoom to drawing to see both the vector we are working on and the reference image.

60. Repeat Steps 56 through 59 for the other two subpaths, the mountain snow on the top and the lower hole in the ink. Move the top segment in the snow top area downwards and to the left a bit to make the shadow area thinner and more like in the reference image.

61. Create highlight objects over the mountain object using whatever tool suits you best. Set their fills to **White**, blur to the appropriate amount, and use the **Tweak** tool for additional thinning if necessary.

How it works...

In this recipe we relied a lot on clipping to show only the parts of our blurred shades and highlights we want. Grouping a number of objects before clipping gives us freedom to edit inside the group and thus inside the clip without releasing it. In the **Inkscape Preferences** (*Shift + Ctrl + P*) under **Clippaths and masks** there is an option to **Put all clipped/masked objects into one group**. We could have used this option get the same result without the need to manually group them.

When blurring an object that we clipped with a duplicate of itself to get edge shading, parts of the object near the edge become partially transparent. That is not something we want, so we placed an unfiltered (no blurring) duplicate of the object below the shaded one in Step 12.

When trying to create a realistic effect it's very important to have a keen eye for the various shades and highlights, and then to figure out what shapes to use to recreate the same look. In this recipe to create the outside wax we need two different sets of objects, one on the **Layer 1** and the other on the **insider** layer. This is because the shadows appear on the opposite sides, the outer rim is shaded at the bottom-right corner, and the inside rim is shaded in the top-left corner. We couldn't have created a realistic effect if we used only one object for the outer wax (the object with a hole).

Introducing lighting on an object changes its colors, some areas are tinted and some shaded depending on the light source properties. That is why we changed the base color of some of the objects to a brighter red (from **#D40000** to **Red (#FF0000)**).

Using gradients instead of blurring increases performance significantly, so it's recommended to use them where possible. Blurring is too useful and effective to be ignored completely though, so using the **No Filters** mode (*Ctrl + 5*) is a necessity in order to reduce the time it takes to repaint the screen. In the **Inkscape Preferences** (*Shift + Ctrl + P*) there is now an option under **Filters** to use more than one processor/thread when rendering **Gaussian Blur** on capable machines. As we could see the **Tweak** tool can be faster when touching up objects rather than using the **Node** tool. But the danger is that sometimes the whole path gets modified even though we're working on only a part of an object. It's good to keep an eye on all of the subpaths when tweaking; if they change more than desired (or even vanish) we can undo and tweak more slowly using less clicks or we can change the tweak settings a bit and try again.

Creating a realistic effect can be very tedious and requires patience and attention to detail. The result isn't identical to the one where we used filters but it's close enough. The result can be enhanced further with more objects and more precise tweaks, depending on how much time you are willing or able to spend on it. Experiences such as this recipe make us value SVG filters more and gives us more will to learn more on how to use them.

See also

For more information, refer to the *Creating freehand and straight lines*, *Editing paths using the Node tool*, *Clipping*, and *Path operations* recipes in *Chapter 1*. Also see the *Creating a red wax seal* recipe for a similar lesson using filters in *Chapter 7*.

Creating a photorealistic mobile phone

In this recipe we will recreate a vector picture—a mobile phone—based on its photograph. We will not replicate all the details, but we will nevertheless produce a convincing counterpart of the original.

How to do it...

The following steps will demonstrate how to create a mobile phone vector image:

1. Open the **Import** dialog (*Ctrl + I*) and import the `siemensC75.png` image from the files accompanying this chapter.

2. Examine the image and try to figure out how many objects are needed to recreate the shading on the phone's outer case. The top-right corner seems to be lit the most so this is where we'll use gradients with lighter color stops.

3. Select the **Pen (Bezier)** tool (*F6* or *P*) and trace along the phone edge to create the main shape then move it away.

4. Select the **Dropper** tool (*F7* or *D*) and pick a color from the top right edge of the image. It turned out to be #dbdbdb in my case.

5. Select the **Gradient** tool (*Ctrl + F1* or *G*) and create a radial gradient in the object fill. Use the **Dropper** tool to set the end stop to a color from the bottom edge of the phone. It turned out to be #373737 in my case. Move the gradient to the top center of the object and move the gradient center to the right so that the brightest stop is on the right corner.

6. Duplicate the object (*Ctrl + D*), turn it into a **Dynamic Offset** (*Ctrl + J*), and shrink it a bit. Convert to a path (*Shift + Ctrl + C*) and set its fill to **White**.

7. Select the **Gradient** tool (*Ctrl + F1* or *G*) and create a horizontal linear gradient from one edge to the object center (enable snapping to object center). Set the end point to a color you pick of the image using the **Dropper** tool (#d7d7d7 in my case), create another stop close to the end stop, and pull it close to the edge of the object.

8. Blur the object to 1 to soften the edges. Now the edges look very realistic and we can start working on the surface.

9. Duplicate the blurred object (*Ctrl + D*). Remove the blurring (set it to 0) and shrink it horizontally by holding *Shift* and using one of the horizontal transform arrows.

10. Set its fill to **White** and create a radial white to transparent gradient, then move it to the top-right corner to simulate light falling on it.

11. Select the **Pen (Bezier)** tool (*F6* or *P*) and trace along the metal silver frame around the screen. Set its fill to a multi-stop white to gray gradient, use the **Dropper** tool to pick the colors from the image and rotate the gradient to fit with the light direction.

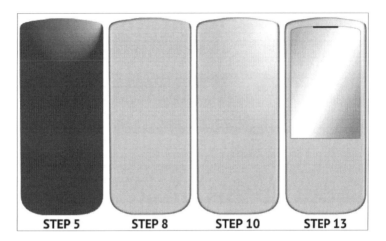

STEP 5   STEP 8   STEP 10   STEP 13

12. Set the object stroke to 0.9 and apply a radial gradient to it. Set color stops to #d5d5d5 and #7f7f7f and move the gradient closer to the top-right corner to make it resemble the image. Blur the object to 0.5.

13. Select the **Pen (Bezier)** tool (*F6* or *P*) and create a straight horizontal line at the top center to represent the phone speaker. Set its stroke to 3, stroke color to **Black**, and under **Stroke style** tab of the **Fill and Stroke** dialog set its **Cap:** to **Round cap**.

14. The black area around the phone screen looks close to a rectangle so select the **Rectangle** tool (*F4* or *R*) and create a rectangle over the image so it's easy to use the rectangle handles to adjust it to appropriate size and also to set the amount of the curved corner radius. Move it to the right place inside the drawing. Center it horizontally using the **Align and Distribute** dialog (*Shift + Ctrl + A*).

15. Set its stroke to **Black** and stroke width to 0.9. Set its fill to #999999, create a radial gradient, and set the end stop to **Black**. Move the gradient to the outside of the top-right corner and rotate a bit counterclockwise to get the lighting effect like in the reference image. Blur the object to 0.4.

16. Select the **Rectangle** tool (*F4* or *R*) and create a sharp corner rectangle over the phone screen. Set its stroke to 2px **Black**, fill to #cbcbcb to black radial gradient, and move the gradient to the outside of the top-right corner.

17. Create another rectangle below the metal screen frame that will represent the control-buttons panel of the phone. Convert it to a path (*Shift + Ctrl + C*), switch to the **Node** tool (*F2* or *N*), and drag the bottom rectangle side downwards a bit grabbing it at the side center.

18. Set the object fill to a multi-stop gray and white radial gradient. Center it inside the fill and make it elliptic by stretching the horizontal gradient path outside of the object while holding *Ctrl* to constrain movement to the horizontal.

19. Set the stroke to a gray radial gradient (#d5d5d5 to #474747), move it closer to the bottom-right corner of the object, and stretch the horizontal gradient path to make it elliptical. Blur the object to 0.4.

20. Create another rectangle at the center of the one we just created that will represent the indentations in the keys. Round the corners to different X and Y values, set the stroke to `#6d6d6d`, and stroke width to 1. Set the fill to a multi-stop gray to white linear gradient to recreate the shading.

21. Select the **Pen (Bezier)** tool (*F6* or *P*) and create a straight horizontal line that splits the control buttons panel into two and is centered over the indentation rectangle. Enable the **Snap nodes or handles** and **Snap to paths** options on the snapping toolbar so the line ends snap to the control panel sides. Set its stroke to 1 and stroke color to `#818181`.

22. Create a rectangle at the center of the control panel area as the case for the center button. Set its stroke to 1px `#555555` and set fill to a white to gray radial gradient. Center the gradient and stretch the handles outside of the object while holding *Ctrl* but make the horizontal one longer. Tweak it until it resembles the image.

23. Create another rectangle at the center of the last one, remove its stroke, round its corners, and set fill to a #dbdbdb to #373737 linear gradient. Stretch the handles outside of the object a bit and rotate the gradient so the darker area is in the top-right corner.

24. Create a square at the center of the last rectangle, and round its corners to 7.7. Set its stroke to 0.7 px width and apply a #9d9d9d to #7e7e7e (that is 58% opaque) linear gradient to it rotating it, so the partially transparent area is at the bottom-left corner. Do the same for the fill only with #9d9d9d to #8e8e8e gradient colors.

25. Create another square centered over the last one, remove its fill, set stroke to **Black** 1.5 px, and create a bottom to top linear gradient. Add a new stop near the start stop and drag it almost to the end stop. Set the end stop to **White**. Under the **Stroke style** tab of the **Fill and Stroke** dialog set its **Join:** to **Round join**.

26. Select the **Pen (Bezier)** tool (*F6* or *P*) and create a small straight horizontal line in the top-left corner of the phone control panel to represent a mark on the button. Set its stroke to 2 px **Black** and **Cap:** to **Round cap**.

27. Clone the line (*Alt + D*) and move it to the top-right corner.

28. Use the tool of your choice to create icons for the other two control keys.

29. The keys on the keypad of the phone on the photo seem a bit small so we will use our Inkscape skills to create different looking ones. First create the keypad background by duplicating (*Ctrl + D*) one of the original large phone shapes. Turn it into a **Dynamic Offset** (*Ctrl + J*), and shrink until it reaches the width of the control panel. Convert to a path in the end (*Shift + Ctrl + C*).

30. Select the control panel object (*Alt* + click to select under) and duplicate it (*Ctrl* + *D*).

31. Add the object from Step 29 to the selection and do a **Difference** (*Ctrl* + /), break apart (*Shift* + *Ctrl* + *K*), and delete the top object (*Del*).

32. Set its stroke to 0.75 px **60% Gray** and fill to a white to transparent linear gradient that stretches vertically only near the top of the object to create faint light reflection.

33. Duplicate keypad background object (*Ctrl* + *D*), move it down a bit so you can see it better, and use the **Node** tool to move the bottom nodes up to make the object shorter because we only need the gradient part.

34. Select the **Gradient** tool (*Ctrl* + *F1* or *G*) and create a vertical top to down gradient in the object stroke that reaches approximately half of the object height so only the top side stroke is visible.

35. Create two clones of the object (*Alt* + *D*), drag them down, and arrange them to be equally distant.

36. Select the clones and their original, and group them (*Ctrl* + *G*).

37. Select the keypad background object (hold *Alt* and click to select under), duplicate it (*Ctrl* + *D*), and set its fill to red. Add the group to the selection (*Shift* + click) and clip by going to **Object | Clip | Set**.

38. Enable **Snap to paths** and **Snap to cusp nodes**. Use the **Pen (Bezier)** tool (*F6* or *P*) to create two vertical lines while holding *Ctrl* from the bottom corners of the center button area to the bottom of the keypad object, and hold *Shift* when creating the second line to add it to the first one into the single object. Set their stroke to 0.75 px and **60% Gray**.

40. Add the text to the keys in a font you like for this phone design. Convert them to paths (*Shift* + *Ctrl* + *C*) and you have a finished vector phone.

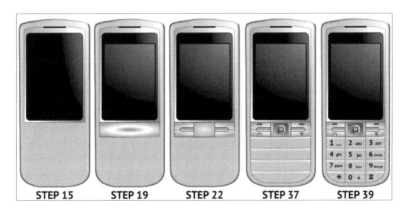

| STEP 15 | STEP 19 | STEP 22 | STEP 37 | STEP 39 |

How it works...

When trying to create a realistic effect the trick is to always look at the photo or the real object first and try to figure which and how many vector objects to use and how to style them in Inkscape. Often the effect is created more easily with layering objects one on top of the other, embedding the original image in the background. Finally, a touch of blur adds to the realistic effect, blending the objects edges and creating the feeling we're looking at a three-dimensional object.

There's more...

Layers come in handy when building complex objects such as this one. When creating many small objects, some of them might get accidentally dragged around or deleted, wasting time.

In this recipe we could have used three separate layers: a bottom one for the body of the phone, a middle one for the screen and the metal frame, and a top one for the keypad.

See also

For more information, refer to the *Creating and editing 2D geometric* shapes and *Creating freehand and straight lines* recipes in *Chapter 1*. Also refer to the *Creating linear gradients*, *Recreating HAL 9000 using radial gradients*, and *Picking and assigning colors with the Dropper tool* recipes in *Chapter 2*.

10
Web Graphics Preparation

In this chapter, we will cover:

- ▶ Creating "Aqua" style buttons
- ▶ Creating a reflection effect
- ▶ Creating curled stickers
- ▶ Creating a golden award with ribbon
- ▶ Creating repeating backgrounds using Tiled clones
- ▶ Creating a button to use with the CSS Sliding Doors technique
- ▶ Creating rollover images
- ▶ Creating small icons and favicons
- ▶ Creating a 960 Grid System template
- ▶ Creating a web page mockup
- ▶ Slicing a web page mockup for website use

Introduction

The recipes from this chapter will show us how to create some common web elements and effects as well as a complete website mockup and slice it for use with an HTML layout. Many of these tips and tricks aren't limited to web design, however, and can be applied to other scenarios and contexts.

Creating "Aqua" style buttons

In this recipe we will recreate a popular style seen in many user interfaces, from operating systems to web pages. It's often used for widgets, such as buttons and scrollbars.

How to do it...

The following steps will demonstrate how to create "Aqua" style buttons:

1. Select the **Rectangle** tool (*F4* or *R*) and create a 450x150 px rectangle as the base for the button. If you hold the *Ctrl* key you can get the correct ratio, then lock the ratio on the Selector toolbar and change the width to 450 and the height will automatically change to 150. You can also type these dimensions directly into the **Rectangle** toolbar.

2. Round the corners by dragging the radius handle while holding *Ctrl* all the way to the middle of the button vertical edge.

3. Set its fill to **Blue (#0000FF)**, stroke to **Navy (#000080)**, and stroke width to 8.

4. Duplicate the rectangle (*Ctrl + D*), remove its stroke, and set fill to **Aqua (#00FFFF)**. Reduce the height to about half of the original one by dragging the top arrow handle downwards, and reduce the width a bit so the object doesn't "leak" outside by dragging one of the side arrow handles while holding *Shift* to keep the object centered.

5. Blur the aqua colored object by 25; don't mind the blur leak, it will be clipped later.

6. Select the blue rectangle again and duplicate it (*Ctrl + D*), set its fill to **White**, and remove its stroke.

7. Scale the white object down to around 92% by dragging a corner arrow handle while holding *Shift* (to keep centered) and *Ctrl* (to maintain the ratio) keys.

8. Move it up a bit until it almost reaches the blue object stroke edge (*Arrow Up*).

9. Convert the white rectangle to a path (*Shift + Ctrl + C*) and use the **Node** tool (*F2* or *N*) to select the bottom two nodes and drag them up while holding *Ctrl* or by using *Arrow Up*.

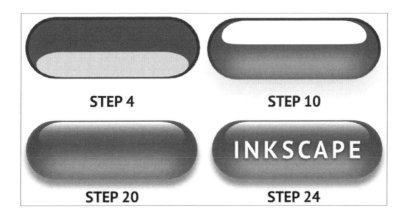

STEP 4   **STEP 10**

STEP 20   **STEP 24**

10. Switch to the **Selector** tool (*Space, F1* or *S*) and reduce its height by dragging the bottom arrow handle upwards.

11. Select the **Gradient** tool (*Ctrl + F1* or *G*) and create a linear vertical gradient in the object fill by dragging from the top to bottom edge.

12. Create a gradient stop by clicking on the center of the gradient path and moving it upwards a bit. Add more stops and move them to smooth out the color transitions if necessary.

13. Select everything (*Ctrl + A*) and group (*Ctrl + G*).

14. Enter the group by double-clicking it, select the blue rectangle (*Alt* to select under), and copy it (*Ctrl + C*).

15. Exit the group by double-clicking on an empty area of the canvas and **Paste In Place** (*Ctrl + Alt + V*).

16. Change the fill to **Red (#FF0000)** and remove stroke to make it obvious it is not part of the drawing—it will be used as a clipping object.

17. Add the group to the selection (*Alt + Shift*) and clip by going to **Object | Clip | Set**.

18. **Paste In Place** again (*Ctrl + Alt + V*), set the new object fill to #006aff (lighter blue), remove its stroke, blur it by 4, and reduce the opacity to 60%.

19. Move the focus back to the Canvas from the **Fill and Stroke** dialog, send the object to the back (*End* or *Page Down*), and move it downwards (*Arrow Down*).

20. Enter the group by double-clicking it, select the blue rectangle and set its blur to 6.

21. Select the **Text** tool (*F8* or *T*), on the toolbar set the alignment to center, and choose a font of your choice. Create a text object by clicking at the center of the blue rectangle and typing "INKSCAPE". Fine tune the blur on the text object to make it look better.

22. Set the text color to **White**, remove the stroke and center the object over the blue rectangle using the **Align and Distribute** dialog (*Shift + Ctrl + A*).

23. Make sure the text is in front of the blurred aqua rectangle but behind the white highlight (*Page Up* and *Page Down*).

24. Duplicate the text (*Ctrl + D*), set its fill to **Navy (#000080)**, blur it to 4. Then send it back behind the white text (*Page Down*) and move down a bit (*Arrow Down*).

25. Exit the group by double-clicking on an empty area of the Canvas.

There's more...

When converting the design into a web template where we don't know the length of the button text we can use the sliding doors technique (which is explained in the CSS sliding doors technique recipe) to make the button "expand" with the text.

Since we don't want any text inside the button image, we will export it after first removing the text object and its shadow. The button text will be generated inside the website HTML and styled with a `text-shadow` CSS property, supported by all modern browsers.

See also

For more information, refer to the *Creating and editing 2D geometric shapes*, *Creating and editing text*, *Clipping*, *Editing paths using the Node tool* recipes in *Chapter 1*. Also refer to *Creating linear gradients* in *Chapter 2* and the *Creating a reflection effect* and *Creating a button to use with the CSS Sliding Doors technique* recipes in this chapter.

Creating a reflection effect

We will now enhance the "Aqua" style button we just created in the previous recipe with a nice reflection effect. You will be surprised by how much more impressive the image will look once we have finished.

How to do it...

The following steps will demonstrate how to give our button a reflection:

1. Open the `Button.svg` document accompanying this chapter and copy the final button version into a new document.

2. Select the shadow rectangle and use the top arrow handle to scale it down vertically, then move it up until it's completely behind the button (*Arrow Up*).

3. Open the **Fill and Stroke** dialog (*Shift + Ctrl + F*) and increase the **Blur** of the shadow to 8.

4. Use the side arrow handle to shrink the shadow horizontally while holding *Shift* to keep it centered so it doesn't stretch beyond the button width.

5. Select all (*Ctrl + A*), group them(*Ctrl + G*), and duplicate the group (*Ctrl + D*).

6. Flip the duplicate vertically (*V*) and move it downwards holding the *Ctrl* key to restrain motion to vertical. Move it until the button bottom edges touch. If rendering becomes slow, change the **Display mode** to **No Filters** (*Ctrl + 5*)

7. Select the **Rectangle** tool (*F4* or *R*) and create a rectangle that is larger than the button. Remove its stroke, set the fill to **White**, opacity to 80, and position it over the duplicated flipped button so it touches the original button edge.

8. Set the opacity of the white rectangle back to 100.

9. Select the **Gradient** tool (*Ctrl + F1* or *G*) and create a vertical linear white to transparent gradient (use *Ctrl* to constrain to vertical orientation). Stretch it from the edge of the button to the bottom edge of the flipped button text.

10. Add another stop by double-clicking on the middle of the gradient path. Select it and move upwards a bit. Repeat three more times for each of the bottom gradient path segments to create a non-linear gradient.

11. Select the group behind the white gradient rectangle (*Alt* to select under). Add the white rectangle to the selection (*Shift*) and perform a mask by going to **Object | Mask | Set**.

How it works...

We adjusted the shadow so the button looks like it is "standing" upright on a surface and not laying down on it. This will probably be unnecessary when creating your own reflections although it's useful to keep the perspective in mind.

We used a mask with a non-linear gradient to achieve a nicer fading transition.

See also

For more information, refer to *Masking* in *Chapter 1*, *Creating linear gradients* in *Chapter 2*, and *Creating "Aqua" style buttons* seen earlier in this chapter.

Creating curled stickers

In this recipe we will draw a curled sticker commonly used for simple website messages such as promos or "special price" tags. We will first create the sticker, and then use clipping to create the illusion of the curled end peeling off.

How to do it...

The following steps will demonstrate how to create a curled sticker:

1. Select the **Star** tool (*Shift* + *F9* or ***) and create a 30 corner star with **Spoke ratio:** set to 0.93. Remove its stroke and set fill to **30% Gray**.

2. Select the **Gradient** tool (*Ctrl* + *F1* or *G*) and create a linear gradient in the object fill by dragging from the top-right corner to the bottom-left corner. Set the opacity of the end stop to 100.

3. Create a new gradient stop by double-clicking on the middle of the gradient path; select the new stop by clicking on it and changing its color to **10% Gray**.

4. Duplicate the object (*Ctrl* + *D*) and change its fill to **White**.

5. Scale it down a bit by holding *Ctrl* (to maintain its ratio) and *Shift* (to keep it centered) while dragging one of the corner arrow handles.

6. Duplicate the object (*Ctrl* + *D*) and change its fill to **Purple (#800080)**.

7. Scale it down a bit by holding *Ctrl* (to maintain its ratio) and *Shift* (to keep it centered) while dragging one of the corner arrow handles.

8. Select the **Gradient** tool (*Ctrl* + *F1* or *G*) and create a linear gradient in the object fill by dragging from the top-right corner to the bottom-left corner. Set the opacity of the end stop to 100.

9. Create a new gradient stop by double-clicking on the middle of the gradient path, and select the new stop by clicking on it.

10. Use *Color Gestures* to change the selected gradient stop to a lighter color. Hold the *Ctrl* key while clicking in the **Fill:** box in the bottom-left corner and dragging towards the Canvas, then left and right to adjust the lightness.

11. Select the silver star and duplicate it (*Ctrl* + *D*), change its fill to **70% Gray**, set its **Blur** to 2, and send to back (*End* or *Page Down*) to create a small shadow.

12. Select everything (*Ctrl* + *A*), group all of it (*Ctrl* + *G*), and duplicate (*Ctrl* + *D*).

13. Select the **Rectangle** tool (*F4* or *R*) and draw a rectangle larger than the sticker. Reduce its opacity to 80%, position it over the sticker, rotate and shift it a bit so that 5 of the sticker spikes stick out.

14. Enable **Snap nodes or handles** and **Snap to cusp nodes** on the **Snapping** toolbar.

15. Duplicate the rectangle (*Ctrl + D*). Switch to the **Selector** tool (*Space*, *F1* or *S*) and move the duplicate so it covers only the five remaining spikes that were sticking out, snapping to the side of the original rectangle.

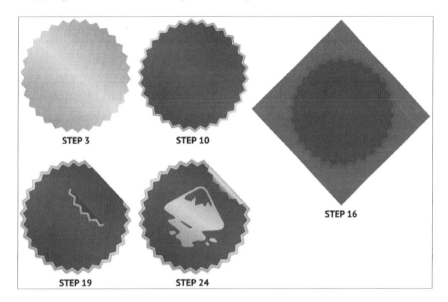

16. Switch back to the **Rectangle** tool (*Space*, *F4* or *R*) and reduce the size of the rectangle by dragging one of the square handles while holding *Ctrl* to drag along the rectangle side.

17. Select one of the sticker groups (*Alt* to select under), add the larger rectangle to the selection (*Shift*) and clip by going to **Object | Clip | Set**.

18. Select the other group (that isn't clipped, check in the notification area in the statusbar). Add the smaller rectangle to the selection (*Shift*) and clip by going to **Object | Clip | Set**.

19. Bring the smaller group to the front (*Home* or *Page Up*) and flip it vertically (*v*) and horizontally (*h*).

20. Zoom in on the edge of the larger sticker group and move the smaller sticker so the edges align perfectly. The easiest is to watch the points where gray meets white and white meets purple. If the rendering becomes slow because of the blurred shadow switch to **No filters** under **Display Mode** (*Ctrl + 5*).

21. Enter the smaller group by double-clicking it and delete (*Del*) the purple and white stars.

22. Select the gray star inside the group (only the five spikes visible from clipping). Select the **Gradient** tool (*Ctrl + F1* or *G*) and notice the gradient path become visible. Drag the end stop closer to the visible unclipped part of the star; adjust the gradient so the color transitions are parallel to the edge where the sticker is curled. Deselect **Enable snapping** if it gets in the way (%). Once you adjust it to be parallel you can hold *Ctrl + Alt* while dragging gradient handles to keep the gradient path orientation.

23. Select the start stop and change its color to a darker gray (**60% Gray**) to get a more realistic curl.

24. Add your favorite logo, position it over the sticker, and apply the same gradient we used in the larger sticker part keeping the gradient orientation. If you want to add the Inkscape logo, copy it from the `inkscape.logo.svg` file found under `inkscape/clipart` folder. Ungroup it (*Shift + Ctrl + G*), and use **Difference** (*Ctrl + -*) to make holes in the main object where the snow is. Enable **Snap from and to centers of objects** to position it over the sticker center. Go back to **Normal** view to see the shadows (*Ctrl + 5*).

See also

For more information, refer to *Creating and editing 2D geometric shapes* in *Chapter 1* and *Adjusting hue, lightness, saturation, and stroke width using Color Gestures* and *Clipping* in *Chapter 2*.

Creating a golden award with a ribbon

This recipe will show us how to draw a golden award with a ribbon using interpolation extension and gradients.

How to do it...

The following steps will demonstrate how to create a golden award:

1. Select the **Star** tool (*Shift + F9* or ***) and create a 300 px upright star with 30 corners. Set **Spoke ratio:** to 0.96 and **Rounded:** to 0.2 by dragging upwards while holding *Ctrl* key.

2. Set its fill to `#e1c446` and remove its stroke.

3. Select the **Gradient** tool (*Ctrl + F1* or *G*) and create a linear gradient in the object fill by dragging from the top-left corner to the bottom-right corner. Set the opacity of the end stop to 100.

4. Create a new gradient stop by double-clicking on the top one-third of the gradient path. Select the new stop by clicking on it and change its color to #f8ecbd (double click on it to pop up the color selector).

5. Duplicate the star (*Ctrl + D*), remove its fill and set stroke to 1 px, **Black**.

6. Convert it to a path (*Shift + Ctrl + C*). Select the **Node** tool (*F2 or N*) and press *Tab* once to select the first node, it should be at the very top.

7. Enable **Snap from and to centers of objects** on the Snapping toolbar.

8. Select the **Ellipse** tool (*F5 or E*) and create a circle by dragging from the star center outwards while holding *Ctrl* (to make a circle) and *Shift* (to draw from the starting point outwards), the starting point will snap to the star center. Make the circle smaller than the star.

9. Convert the circle to a path (*Shift + Ctrl + C*). Select the **Node** tool (*F2 or N*) and press *Tab* once to select the first node; it should be at the right-hand side.

10. Switch to the **Selector** tool (*Space, F1 or S*) and rotate the circle 90° counterclockwise while holding *Ctrl* to snap to certain angles. Keep looking at the Notification area in the statusbar to reach the correct degree.

11. Switch back to the **Node** tool (*Space, F2 or N*) and press the *Tab* key once to select the first node; it should now be at the very top. Select all the nodes (*Ctrl + A*) and press the *Insert* key three times to add more nodes to the path.

12. Add the 1px stroke star to the selection (*Shift*), combine them into one path (*Ctrl + K*). Open the **Path Effect Editor** dialog (*Shift + Ctrl + 7*) and apply the **Interpolate Sub-Paths** effect; notice the new shapes appear between the circle and the star.

13. Make sure that **Equidistant spacing** is ticked and increase the **Steps** to 10 in the **Current effect** area for the **Interpolate Sub-Paths** effect.

14. Convert the effect to a path (*Shift + Ctrl + C*) and set stroke width to 2.

15. Select the **Gradient** tool (*Ctrl + F1* or *G*). On the **Gradient** toolbar choose linear gradient and object stroke and under **Change:** choose the same golden gradient we used for the star. This will apply the golden gradient to the interpolated paths stroke. It should automatically be applied horizontally, which creates enough contrast with the background so we can leave it as it is.

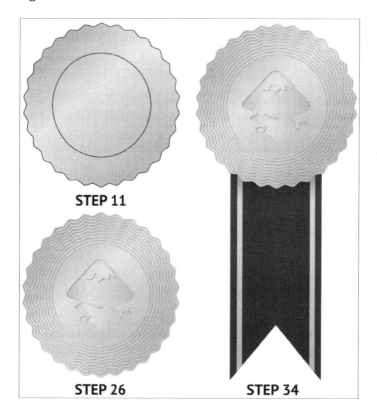

16. Select the start gradient stop and copy its color by right-clicking on the **Fill:** box in the bottom-left corner of the window and choosing **Copy color**.

17. Duplicate the object (*Ctrl + D*). Set the duplicated object's stroke color to the one we just copied by right-clicking on the **Stroke:** box in the bottom-left corner of the window and choosing **Paste color**.

18. Move the object a bit to the right and bottom by using *Alt + Arrow Right* and *Alt + Arrow Bottom*.

19. Send the object behind its original (*Page Down*) so we get a delicate shadow.

20. Import (*Ctrl + I*) the `inkscape.logo.svg` file found under the `inkscape/clipart` folder. Ungroup it (*Shift + Ctrl + G*), select the two white objects, and combine them (*Ctrl + K*). Add the mountain object to the selection (*Shift*) and use **Difference** (*Ctrl + -*) to make holes in the main object.

21. Move the logo over the golden star, its center should snap to the star center. Make the logo smaller so it fits inside the clear area of the star by dragging one of the corner arrow handles while holding *Ctrl + Shift* (to maintain the ratio and to keep it centered).

22. Select the **Gradient** tool (*Ctrl + F1* or *G*). On the Gradient toolbar choose linear gradient and object fill and under **Change:** choose the same golden gradient we used for the star. This will apply the golden gradient to the logo fill. Move the gradient handles to position them from the top-left to the bottom-right corner so it follows the star gradient position.

23. Apply the **Inner Shadow** filter to the logo by going to **Filters | Shadows and Glows | Inner Shadow**.

24. Open the **Filter Editor** by going to **Filters | Filter Editor…**. If no filters are selected in the dialog, deselect then select the logo object again.

25. Remove the **Gaussian Blur** primitive from the **Effect** list by right-clicking on it and selecting **Remove**.

26. Select the **Offset** primitive by clicking on it and change both Deltas under **Effect parameters** tab to 1.5, select the **Flood** primitive and change the **Flood Color:** to the same color we used on the grooves "shadow" (#ccac21).

27. Select the **Rectangle** tool (*F4* or *R*) and create a vertical rectangle that is a bit narrower than the golden star, remove its stroke, and set fill to **Navy (#000080)**.

28. Open the **Align and Distribute** dialog (*Shift + Ctrl + A*) and center the rectangle horizontally over the star and move it vertically, while holding down the *Ctrl* to constrain movement to the Y-axis, to reach the middle of the star with its top edge. Convert the rectangle to a path (*Shift + Ctrl + C*). Select the **Node** tool (*F2* or *N*) and select the bottom two nodes. Press the *Insert* key once to insert one node in between the selected ones.

29. Select the new middle node and move it upwards while holding *Ctrl* to make the ribbon tail.

30. On the **Snapping** toolbar enable **Snap nodes or handles** (it will probably already be enabled) and **Snap to paths**.

31. Select the **Pen (Bezier)** tool (*Shift + F6* or *B*) and create a thin vertical stripe object over the ribbon by snapping to the ribbon path (four nodes) and holding *Ctrl* to make the stripe vertical.

32. Select the **Gradient** tool (*Ctrl + F1* or *G*). On the **Gradient** toolbar choose "Linear gradient" and "Create gradient in the fill", and under **Change:** choose the same golden gradient we used for the star. Change the gradient orientation to vertical (*Ctrl*) and stretch it from the top to the bottom of the stripe. Remove the stroke if present.

33. Duplicate the stripe (*Ctrl + D*), flip it horizontally (*H*). Switch to the **Selector** tool (*Space, F1* or *S*), and move it to the other side of the ribbon while holding *Ctrl* so it only moves horizontally, it will snap into the correct place.

34. Select the blue ribbon object, select the **Gradient** tool (*Ctrl + F1* or *G*), and create a vertical (*Ctrl*) linear gradient in its fill. Set the end stop opacity to 100 and add another stop by double-clicking on the gradient path at approximately the same height as the highlight on the golden stripes.

35. Select the new stop by clicking on it and make it a lighter color by using *Color Gestures*. Click on the **Fill:** box in the bottom-left of the window, hold *Ctrl*, and drag upwards and to the right; move left and right until you reach the desired lightness.

36. Deselect everything (*Esc* twice) and switch to **Selector** tool (*Space, F1* or *S*). Hold *Alt* while dragging over the ribbon to select all the ribbon objects.

37. Group the selection (*Ctrl + G*) and send the group to the back (*End* or *Page Down*).

38. Enter the group by double-clicking on it. Select the blue object, duplicate it (*Ctrl + D*) and set its fill to **Black**.

39. Select the **Gradient** tool (*Ctrl + F1* or *G*). On the **Gradient** toolbar choose radial gradient and object fill, and create a black to transparent radial gradient. Make the handles size a bit larger than the golden star and move the start gradient stop to the center of the star so there is a small shadow over the ribbon top.

How it works...

Holding the *Ctrl* key and dragging upwards while creating the first star made sure the first node of the path will be the one on top. Later we rotated the circle to get its first node to be the one on the top so we get a symmetric pattern while interpolating. If you get uneven interpolation it means the nodes aren't aligned or that the path directions are opposite.

When styling the logo we removed **Gaussian Blur** filter primitive because blurring softens the edges and we were after a sharper look.

See also

For more information, refer to the *Creating and editing 2D geometric shapes*, *Editing paths using the Node tool*, and *Creating paths using the Pen (Bezier) tool* recipes in *Chapter 1*, also the *Creating linear gradients*, *Recreating HAL 9000 using radial gradients*, *Adjusting hue, lightness, saturation, and stroke width using Color Gestures*, and *Creating a stylized flower using Snapping* recipes in *Chapter 2*. Also refer to *Interpolating sub-paths* in *Chapter 5* and *Creating a water surface effect* in *Chapter 7*.

Repeating backgrounds using Tiled Clones

This recipe will show us how to use Inkscape's **Tiled Clones** feature to help us create seamless tiling backgrounds.

How to do it...

The following steps will demonstrate repeating backgrounds:

1. Select **Rectangle** tool (*F4* or *R*) and create a 160x160 px rectangle. Set its stroke to 0.1 **Black**, remove fill, and group it (*Ctrl + G*). This group will be our base tile.

2. Open the **Create Tiled clones** dialog by going to **Edit | Clone | Create Tiled Clones...**.

3. Press the **Reset** button to clear the values to their defaults.

4. Tick the **Use saved size and position of the tile**, set **Rows, columns:** to 5 and press the **Create** button to get 25 clones in total. Leave the original group selected.

5. Open the **Inkscape Preferences** (*Shift + Ctrl + P*), go to the **Clones** section and make sure the **When the original moves, its clones and linked offsets:** is set to **Stay unmoved**, now we can move the original without disturbing the clones.

6. Hold *Alt* and click anywhere on the screen to start moving the selection. Also press *Ctrl* to constrain movement to the horizontal and move the original group to the left next to the clones.

7. Enter the group by double-clicking it and draw the objects you want in your base tile, place them inside the rectangle at approximately the position where you want them to appear

8. Select the rectangle by clicking on its stroke and remove the stroke so it becomes invisible.

9. Zoom out and pan the Canvas by holding the middle mouse wheel/button or *Shift* and the right mouse button so you can see both the original and the clones. It will probably be obvious where the rectangles are because we instinctively positioned the objects away from the rectangle edges.

10. Move the objects in the original group one by one using the arrow keys while looking at the clones to better see how to arrange them so they all look equally distant from one another (disregarding which tile they belong to) and the rectangle base isn't so obvious.

11. Switch to the **Outline** display mode (*Ctrl + 5*) so you can see the rectangles and how they're positioned with respect to other objects inside the tile.

12. Select all the objects inside the original group (*Ctrl + A*) except the rectangle (*Shift* to remove from the selection) and move them together so they fit into the rectangle as much as they can in case some of them "leaked out"—but it doesn't matter if they do. The respective clones will automatically move as well but the positions between them will be preserved.

13. Now we have the desired arrangement, we're ready for exporting into PNG format for use as a website background. Select the cloned tile that is in the middle of the tiled clones area, and unlink the clone (*Shift + Alt + D*). Enter the group by double-clicking it and select the rectangle (use **Outline** mode to select it (*Ctrl + 5*))

14. Open the **Export Bitmap** 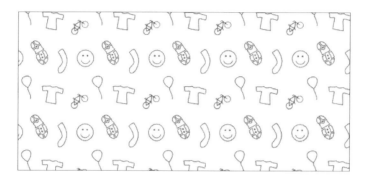 (*Shift + Ctrl + E*) dialog, the **Selection** tab should already be selected and the **dpi** box should be set to 90. Enter the path and the name of the file in the **Filename** field and press **Export**. Here is a cut out of the tiles I created in this recipe:

How it works...

We made the rectangle from the base tile invisible by removing both its fill and stroke. This was necessary in case some of the objects in the group leak outside of the rectangle area; if the rectangle is visible the cloned rectangles will overlap the parts of the objects that leak out. If a background color is needed for the pattern and not all objects are within the base rectangle area we can create a special object, place it behind the pattern and color it with the color we want as background for the pattern.

If the repeating background tiles are used inside Inkscape and not as a repeatable PNG image in a website, the additional benefit of using one large object for the background instead of coloring the base tile is that there are no visible edges between the tiles. Moreover, the background can be styled unevenly.

Getting the objects into the right position is very important to achieve the illusion that the base tile isn't a rectangle. To do that we had to turn off the stroke so that we could focus on positioning without the rectangle edges throwing us off.

If all our objects are within the base rectangle area we can export the base tile and use it as a website background, but if that's not the case we have to export the rectangle area from one of the cloned tiles that is surrounded with other clones from all sides. If we exported the whole tile and not only the rectangle the pattern tiles wouldn't align properly because of the parts that leak out.

To see our exported tile in action open the `RepeatingBackground.html` file accompanying this chapter in your favorite browser.

There's more...

If we want to use the repeatable background within Inkscape it might be convenient to convert the base rectangle area into a pattern (**Object | Pattern | Objects to Pattern** or *Alt + I*). If no parts leak out of the base rectangle we can convert the whole group into a pattern and use the pattern without any modifications. But if there are leaks the pattern size settings are wrong and must be corrected through the **XML editor** (*Shift + Ctrl + X*).

See also

For more information, refer to the *Drawing a colorful grid of tiled clones* recipe in *Chapter 4*.

Creating a button to use with the CSS Sliding Doors technique

In this recipe we will create an image of a button that can be used with the popular CSS "*Sliding Doors*" technique, so that it automatically resizes with the text. The button will have a partially transparent shadow so the usual solution of using a very wide button image won't help because the elements styled with the image overlap and the shadow is visibly stronger in that area. This is solved by making the image twice as wide as we expect our widest button text will occupy, and making half of it completely transparent. We will also see how to export images with sharp edges suppressing the antialiasing with snapping to pixel grid.

How to do it...

The following steps will demonstrate the creation of a button to be used with the CSS Sliding Doors technique:

1. Turn on the **Grid** (#) and make sure the **Snap nodes or handles** button on the snapping toolbar is on.

2. Select the **Rectangle** tool (*F4* or *R*) and create a 600x40 rectangle snapping its corners to the grid. Set it's fill to `#ffe9dc`, round the corners by 5 px by using the **Rx:** and **Ry:** boxes on the **Rectangle** toolbar or by moving the round handles while holding *Ctrl* and snapping them to the grid.

3. Turn off the **Grid** (#).

4. Select the **Gradient** tool (*Ctrl + F1* or *G*) and create a vertical linear gradient in the rectangle fill starting just above the middle and dragging downwards.

5. The end gradient stop will be selected; change its color to `#ffccaa`, then click elsewhere on the rectangle to deselect the end stop (*Esc*).

6. On the **Gradient** toolbar change the selection to the stroke button (instead of the fill) and under the **Change:** drop-down select the gradient applied to the fill, it will create the object stroke with a horizontal gradient, set the stroke width to 2.

7. Make the stroke gradient vertical but opposite in direction to that of the fill gradient by dragging the start stop to the bottom edge and the end stop to the top edge of the rectangle while holding *Ctrl* to make it vertical. Zoom in for better precision, and if the stops snap together, hold down the *Shift* key to separate them.

8. Duplicate the rectangle (*Ctrl + D*); remove its stroke by clicking on the **none** chip on the color palette while holding *Shift*.

9. Select the end stop by clicking on it (still in the **Gradient** tool) and copy its color (*Ctrl + C*). Switch to the **Selector** tool (*Space* or *F1* or *S*) and paste the color (*Ctrl + V*); the fill color will be changed.

10. Move the object behind the original rectangle (*End* or *Page Down*), open the **Fill and Stroke** dialog under **HSL** tab and change the **S** and **L** values to 100 and set the **Blur:** slider to 1.

11. Select both objects (*Ctrl + A*); group them (*Ctrl + G*). Then turn on the **Grid** (#).

12. Select the **Rectangle** tool (*F4* or *R*) and create a rectangle that is 300 px wide and tall enough to cover the group. Make the corners sharp by using the button on the **Rectangle** toolbar, set its opacity to 50% so you can see behind it and position the rectangle over the left part of the group completely covering it including the shadow. The rectangle corners should snap to grid when creating or dragging it, it is important that its right edge is snapped to the pixel grid.

13. Duplicate the rectangle (*Ctrl + D*) and move it over the right edge of the group so it covers only the 6 px wide part of rounded corners. Make it narrower because we only want it to cover the rounded corners, again snapping to grid will make it easier to position it precisely.

14. Select both rectangles (hold *Shift* and click to add to the selection) and combine them into one path (*Ctrl + K*).

15. Add the group to the selection (hold *Shift* and click) and clip them by going to **Object | Clip | Set**. The area of the groups that wasn't covered with the rectangles will become invisible.

16. Zoom in on the top-left corner of the group, notice the rectangle stroke is nicely aligned to the grid, but it's hard to see where the shadow ends. Select the shadow object, its bounding box is close to 3 pixels away from the edge of the rectangle so it's safe to take 3 px around the rectangle as our export area.

17. Select the **Rectangle** tool (*F4* or *R*) and create a 608x48 px rectangle and snap it to the grid so it surrounds the rectangle approximately 3px from all of the edges. Remove the rectangle's fill and stroke to make it invisible, but keep it selected.

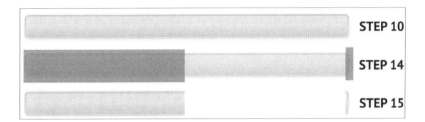

 Remember to change the display mode to **Outline** (*Ctrl* + *5*) to easily select objects without fill or stroke.

18. Open the **Export Bitmap** dialog (*Shift* + *Ctrl* + *E*); the **Selection** tab should be selected and set the **dpi** to the default 90, the **Width:** and **Height:** values should be set to 608 and 68. Enter the desired path and the file name into the **Filename** field and press the **Export** button.

19. Send the image to the person in charge of the website CSS along with the image width, height, and the width of the right edge of the button, measured from where it's cut off to the edge of the whole image (in our case it's 9 px) as those measures are useful in the CSS coding.

How it works...

When working with a web design mockup or even a part of it the grid is very important if we need our images to have sharp edges without antialiasing that Inkscape usually introduces. For best results all stroke widths should be integers, even numbered width strokes should be snapped to the default pixel grid, and odd numbered to the pixel grid that is offset in both directions by 0.5 px and the export should be done at the Inkscape default of 90 dpi. In this example we used objects with even number stroke width and those without a stroke so setting up an additional grid that is 0.5 offset wasn't necessary.

Since the idea of this method is to make the left and the right of the image meet precisely without overlapping to form a button it was important to make those edges very sharp. We were able to do it by snapping the clipping path to the grid.

The **Grid** is also important in the overall image size. Shadows usually aren't perfectly pixel aligned so we couldn't rely on the bounding box of the shadow (or the whole group) for our export. If we had used the shadow object or an object that isn't aligned to the grid when exporting Inkscape, we would have to approximate the image size and round the numbers which doesn't give predictable results required for web design.

That is why we created a rectangle around the shadow, snapped it to the grid evenly around the object and used it to set our exporting area. Here is an example of our finished button on a website compared to the case when the edges aren't sharp; the website background was changed to black to make it more obvious:

Open the `CSSslidingDoors.html` in your favorite browser to see the image in action. To see why the button width is important try increasing only the text size without zooming (*Ctrl + +*) and notice how the "PRODUCTS AND SERVICES" button starts showing the gap on the right side and the left part of the image starts to show on the left side (*Ctrl + 0* to reset the size):

The reason why we couldn't use an image of a full wide button is because the image is applied to two HTML elements and they overlap, so using a full button image we would get stronger shadow in the areas where the two elements overlap, and depending on the actual CSS code we might see sharp corners behind the rounded ones, like in the following:

There's more...

This same example could also be created using two images, one for the left and the other for the right button part, eliminating the transparent area and making the total download size smaller, but at the same time slowing it down because of an additional server request. That is why combining many individual website images into one large is a popular method of speeding up website rendering time; commonly known as **CSS sprites**.

When CSS 3 is more widely supported it will be possible to create some of the button designs using only CSS without any images, but still those can't cover all complex designs so there will be cases when CSS sliding doors will come in handy.

If you need to support Internet Explorer 6, you may want to take a look at the various JavaScript "hacks" available to make transparent PNGs work on this deprecated and aging web browser:

> ▶ **IEpngfix**:
>   `http://www.twinhelix.com/css/iepngfix/`

▶ **JQuery plugin**:
`http://docs.jquery.com/Tutorials:PNG_Opacity_Fix_for_IE6`

See also

For more information, refer to the *Creating and editing 2D geometric shapes* and *Clipping* recipes in *Chapter 1*, *Creating linear gradients* and *Changing Fill and Stroke Color using a Palette* in *Chapter 2*, *Stylized flower using Snapping* and *Creating small icons and favicons* (another example why to look out for antialiased edges) in this chapter.

Creating rollover images

In this recipe we will create an image to use in a rollover effect when hovering over a button. We will use the button design from the previous recipe and create two more design variations to serve as *hover* and *active* button states.

How to do it...

The following steps will demonstrate the creation of rollover images:

1. Open the `CSSslidingDoorsShadow.svg` file accompanying this chapter.

2. Change the **Display mode** to **Outline** (*Ctrl* + 5), select the button and the rectangle from Step 17 in the previous recipe, and copy them (*Ctrl* + C). Create a new document (*Ctrl* + N), turn on the **Grid** (#), place the mouse cursor near the top center of the page and paste (*Ctrl* + V). The objects will be pasted snapping to the grid so we don't need to adjust their position. Save the file (*Ctrl* + S).

3. Change the **Display mode** to **Normal** (*Ctrl* + 5).

4. Zoom in on the left button part. Select the group that holds the button, duplicate it (*Ctrl* + D) and move down while holding *Ctrl*, and let it snap to grid just below the original button but making sure the shadows don't touch.

5. Repeat Step 4 to get another button below the second one.

6. Select the second button group and modify the colors by going to **Extensions | Color | RGB Barrel**. All colors on the button will change to their green counterparts. Repeat the **RGB Barrel** to get the purple version.

7. Select the third button group and use the **RGB Barrel** once to change its colors to green shades.

8. Enter the third button group by double-clicking on it, select the shadow object (hold *Alt* and click to select under) and change its blur from 1 to 0.5 to make it look as if it has been pressed.

9. Change the **Display mode** to **Outline** (*Ctrl* + 5).

10. Select the rectangle around the first button and double-click it to make the **Rectangle** tool active. Drag the bottom-right handle downwards while holding *Ctrl* and snap it to the point that passes the bottom edge of the bottom button by 3 px to make it symmetrical.

11. Open the **Export Bitmap** dialog (*Shift + Ctrl + E*). The **Selection** button should be active, set **dpi** to 90. Enter the desired path and file name into the **Filename** field and press the **Export** button.

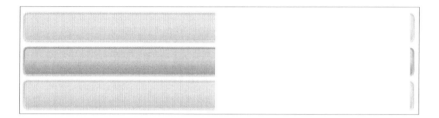

How it works...

As in the previous recipe, it is important to snap to the grid and export at 90 dpi. We used the Sliding Doors example to create the rollover effect but it could have been done with any image we want to create the rollover effect for.

The **RGB Barrel** extension was used to quickly change the colors of the whole group while keeping the shading consistent, but any editing can be made to the duplicated groups to achieve desired "on hover" and "on action" looks.

All three states are collected in one CSS sprite to reduce the server requests and make the website more responsive. Another advantage of such an approach is that the images appear immediately on the change of state without the need to wait for the image of a particular state to be downloaded.

Open the `RolloverHover.html` in your favorite browser to see it in action; the purple button is used when hovering over the buttons and the green one is used when the button is active or in focus (pressed or selected using the *Tab* key):

See also

For more information, refer to *Different color icon sets using RGB Barrel* (another example of a quick color change of a group of objects) in *Chapter 2* and *Creating a button to use with the CSS Sliding Doors technique* seen earlier in this chapter.

Creating small icons and favicons

Desktop application icons have to come in different sizes because of different contexts they are used in and often the website logo is shrunk to the 16x16 pixels size to be used as the site favicon. It would be easy if we could just create the full size icon and scale it or export it to different sizes, but full size usually has a lot of details that get lost when scaled to very small sizes and we may get just a small blur that doesn't resemble the original.

That is why we have to create a different version of an icon to be used in small sizes by removing the details that can't be visible in small scale, accenting certain features and increasing contrast if necessary. This recipe will show us how to transform an icon of a simple clock into its 16x16 version to be used as a favicon. This is a good example on how to work with very small icons.

How to do it...

The following steps demonstrate how to create small icons and favicons:

1. Select the **Ellipse** tool (*F5* or *E*) and create a circle, set its fill to **White**, and stroke to **Black**.

2. Select the **Selector** tool (*Space*, *F1* or *S*) and turn off the button "scale the stroke width by the same proportion" on the **Selector** toolbar, in the **Affect:**section.

3. Lock the ratio by turning on the lock icon and enter 400 into the **W** box to make the circle 400 px in diameter.

4. Duplicate the circle (*Ctrl + D*). Remove its fill, set stroke to **Lime (#00FF00)**, and stroke width to 20.

5. On the **Snapping** toolbar enable **Snap nodes or handles** and **Snap from and to centers of objects**.

6. Create a guide by dragging from the left ruler to Canvas and snap it to the circle center.

7. Select **Pen (Bezier)** tool (*Shift + F6* or *B*) and create the clock hands by creating a four-node closed path where two nodes are close to the clock center on the guide and the other two are the hands tips.

8. Apply the **Bright metal** filter to the clock hands by going to **Filters | Bevels | Bright Metal**.

9. Select the circle with the lime stroke and apply the **Warped rainbow** filter to it by going to **Filters | Textures | Warped rainbow** and then add the **Combined lighting** filter by going to **Filters | Bevels | Combined lighting**.

10. Now we have a finished clock icon we can start creating the 16x16 px favicon. Open the **Icon Preview** dialog by going to **View | Icon Preview...**, select the circle with the black stroke (hold *Alt* and click to select under), and tick **Selection** on the dialog.

11. Examine the different sizes under **Actual Size:** section and notice how the smaller icons lose details and it becomes harder to recognize what they represent.

12. If the screen rendering is too slow switch to the **No filters** display mode (*Ctrl + 5*)

13. Turn on the **Grid** (#), zoom in so you can see both the major and minor grid lines. Select the **Rectangle** tool (*F4 or R*) and create a 16 px square by snapping to the grid, set it's stroke to 0.1 **Black**, and remove fill.

14. On the **Selector** toolbar make sure the button to scale stroke as the object is scaled is enabled.

15. Zoom out and select the clock objects (don't forget the bounding box of the filtered circle is much larger that the one of the black stroke circle), duplicate them (*Ctrl + D*), and group them so they are easier to manipulate (*Ctrl + G*).

16. On the **Selector** toolbar enter 16 into the **W** box to scale the icon and center it over the rectangle.

17. Select the clock hands and the filtered circle and go to **Filters | Remove Filters**.

18. At the very small size of 16x16 px the hands will be barely visible. Make them stand out more by moving the center hands nodes with the **Node** tool (*F2 or N*).

19. Turn off the button to scale stroke as the object is scaled is enabled on the **Selector** toolbar.

20. The clock rim seems too thin, to make it thicker select the black stroke circle and increase the stroke from 2.4 to 3. Then enter 16 in the **W** box on the **Selector** toolbar.

21. The circle is now not centered so open the **Align and Distribute** dialog (*Shift + Ctrl + A*) and center is with respect to the rectangle.

22. Select the lime stroke circle and change its stroke width to 1.5 then enter 14.5 in the **W** box on the **Selector** toolbar and center using the **Align and Distribute** dialog.

23. Change the lime stroke color to a darker one using the color gesture on the bottom left stroke box while holding *Ctrl* to affect lightness.

24. Select the rectangle, remove its stroke and export the selection through the **Export Bitmap** dialog (*Shift + Ctrl + E*). The following image shows a comparison of the original icon with the blown up favicon version and the favicon in real size:

For more information, refer to the *Creating and editing 2D geometric shapes* and *Creating paths using the Pen (Bezier) tool* recipes in *Chapter 1*.

Creating a 960 Grid System template

The 960 Grid System is a well-known and frequently used layout for web pages. It provides a blueprint that helps the developer in building a layout that is optimized for most commonly used screen resolutions. '960' refers to the width in pixels of the outer page wrapper.

In this recipe we will create a template set up for such a design, based on the 12-column layout, so it can be easily reused.

How to do it...

The following steps will demonstrate the creation of a 960 Grid System tempate:

1. Open the **Document Properties** (*Shift + Ctrl + D*) dialog and under **Page** tab set **Width:** to 960 px and **Height:** to 1000.

2. On the **Grids** tab create a new **Rectangular grid**, set **Spacing X:** and **Spacing Y:** to 10 and **Major grid line every:** to 8. In the 12-column system column width is 60 px and each column has a 10 px margin on the left and right so major grid lines will fall down the gutter centers.

3. Select the **Pen (Bezier)** tool (*Shift + F6* or *B*) and create a line 10 px from the vertical page edges and the vertical major grid lines, snap to grid, line lengths aren't important. These lines mark the possible content edges:

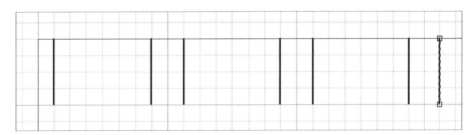

4. Select all lines (*Ctrl + A*) and convert them to guides (*Shift + G*).

5. The grid we created in Step 2 has 10 px spacing, but in web design pixels are the smallest units and it is useful to also create a pixel grid. Open the **Document Properties** (*Shift + Ctrl + D*) dialog and on the **Grids** tab create a new **Rectangular grid**, set **Grid line color:** to #808080 by reducing the **S** value to 0, set **Major grid line every:** to 0 and disable **Visible** and **Snap to visible grid lines only** options.

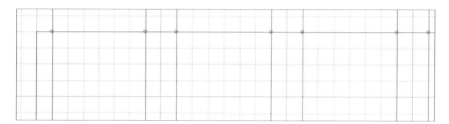

How it works...

The guides we created mark the possible content edges so combined with grids they provide a quick and easy way of creating a coherentand optimized web page layout. Keeping only the 10 px grid visible makes the space less cluttered so we can focus on designing the page and not worry about micro-managing the placement of each element. Although the 1 px grid is made invisible snapping is still sensitive to it, so we get a feeling like we're working with a raster application. If there is a need to make the 1px grid visible at some point we can open the Document Properties (*Shift + Ctrl + D*) and turn on the **Visibility** option.

See also

For more information, refer to the *Geometric illusions using Grid* (more information on how to set up a grid), *Creating a simple flashlight using Guides* (more on guides), and *Creating a stylized flower using Snapping* (how to use snapping for fast and precise drawing) recipes in *Chapter 3*.

Creating a web page mockup

In this recipe we will create a simple a web page mockup using the 960 Grid System with the help of the template we created in the previous recipe and the button design from the CSS sliding doors recipe.

How to do it...

The following steps will demonstrate a web page mockup:

1. Open the 960GridTemplate.svg accompanying this chapter and save it under a different name (*Shift + Ctrl + S*). Grids and guides should already be enabled.

2. Select the **Rectangle** tool (*F4* or *R*) and create a 960x5 px rectangle at the top of the page. Zoom in on the right edge so it's easier to snap to the invisible grid, check the **H:** box on the toolbar to make sure you have the correct height. Set its fill to `#8b5c3d` and remove stroke.

3. Create another rectangle just below the first one but make it 960x115 px, set its fill to `#f0e4dd`. Select the **Gradient** tool (*Ctrl + F1* or *G*) and create a vertical linear gradient in the rectangle fill, and position the end stop just below the rectangle middle.

4. Select the **Text** tool (*F8* or *T*) and create a text object for the website logo. Set its fill to `#5a3c28` and align the object with the third guide from the left and center it vertically with respect to the gradient rectangle using the **Align and Distribute** dialog (*Shift + Ctrl + A*).

5. Select the **Star** tool (*Shift + F9* or ∗) and create a seven corner 60 px star with rounded corners to serve as the logo icon, move the handles until you get a pattern you're happy with. Set the star fill to `#5a3c28` and remove stroke.

6. Center the star vertically with respect to the logo text and place it inside the first content column (between the guides).

7. Open the `CSSslidingDoorsShadow.svg` file accompanying this chapter, copy the two objects under Step 10 that form a wide button (*Ctrl + D*) and paste them into the document (*Ctrl + V*).

8. Select the **Text** tool (*F8* or *T*) and create a center aligned text object for one of the navigation buttons, set its fill to `#5e2500` and position it over the wide button so it's vertically centered and around 15 pixels away from the left button edge.

9. Duplicate the text (*Ctrl + D*), set its fill to **White**, move down a bit (*Alt + Arrow Down*), and send to back (*Page Down*).

10. Select the **Rectangle** tool (*F4* or *R*), select the button rectangle, and drag the bottom right handle towards left while holding *Ctrl* to constrain movement to horizontal until the button looks symmetrical with respect to the text.

11. Select the button shadow and adjust its width in the same way, snapping the bottom right corner to the bottom right corner of the button rectangle so the shadow remains symmetric.

12. Group all the button objects to make the button easier to move around (*Ctrl + G*) and duplicate it (*Ctrl + D*).

13. Enter the duplicated group by double-clicking it and also double-click the text to select it with the **Text** tool; change the text to some other navigation item text.

14. Select the **Selector** tool (*F1*) and select the duplicate white text below (hold *Alt* and click to select under), select all (*Ctrl + A*) and replace it with the new text.

15. Select the **Rectangle** tool (*F4* or *R*) and adjust the button rectangle and shadow to the new text width using the rectangle handles like in Steps 11 and 12.

16. Center the two text objects horizontally after the button width adjustment using the **Align and Distribute** dialog (*Shift + Ctrl + A*).

17. Exit the group by clicking on an object outside of the group, center the two buttons vertically with respect to the gradient rectangle and snap them on either sides of a gap on the right side of the header.

18. Select **Rectangle** tool (*F4* or *R*) and create a 960x180 px rectangle below the gradient one, set its fill to `#f8f2ee`.

19. Create another rectangle, set its size to 310x180 px and snap it to the top-left corner of the one we created in the previous step (enable the **Snap to paths** feature in the **Snapping** toolbar for additional help). Open the **Fill and Stroke** dialog (*Shift + Ctrl + F*) and set the rectangle fill to a pattern by clicking on the **Pattern** icon, and then selecting **Wavy white** from the **Pattern fill** list.

20. Select the **Node** tool (*F2* or *N*) and notice the pattern handles at the top left corner of the page appear. Drag the **x** handle downwards and snap it to the top-left corner of the pattern rectangle.

21. Move the square pattern handle to adjust the pattern size, snap it to the grid so we can later slice it more easily.

22. Create two 60 px squares and snap them on top of the pattern rectangle inside the first content column to serve as small image placeholders.

23. Create two flowed text objects next to the small rectangles by clicking and dragging with the text tool across the pattern rectangle columns.

24. Render some placeholder text by going to **Extensions | Text | Loremipsum...**. Set the **Number of paragraphs** to 2, **Sentences per paragraph** to 4, and press **Apply**. Adjust the text size and set its color to `#5a3c28`.

25. Create another flowed text object that stretches from fifth to ninth content column, set its fill to `#5a3c28` and make the font size a bit larger than on the previous two text objects.

26. Create another text object above the flowed text, copy several words from the flowed text into it, increase its font size, and set fill to `#d25400`.

27. Select the **Rectangle** tool (*F4* or *R*) and create a 220x140 px rectangle. Set its fill to **10% Gray** and position it across the last three content columns on the right hand side from the text to serve as the placeholder for a map.

28. Create a 220x200 px rectangle, position it below the pattern rectangle, snap it across the first three content columns, and set its fill to **White**.

29. Create a flowed text object across the newly created rectangle and render **Loremipsum** text into it.

30. Create a title text object, copy some text from the flowed text object, increase its size, and set fill to `#946342`.

31. Select the white rectangle and text objects over it, group them (*Ctrl + G*), create three clones of the group (*Alt + D*), and snap them to cover the rest of the content columns in one row. Hold *Ctrl* to constrain movement to horizontal.

32. Select the **Ellipse** tool (*F5* or *E*), create a vertical 1x160 px ellipse (if the snapping makes it difficult to make the ellipse 1 px wide use the **W** box on the Selector toolbar). Set its fill to **30% Gray** and snap it down the center of the gutter between the first two text groups.

33. Clone the ellipse twice (*Alt + D*) and snap the clones in the middle of the remaining two gutters between text groups; hold *Ctrl* to constrain movement to horizontal.

34. Select the gradient rectangle from the header, duplicate it (*Ctrl + D*) and move down below the text groups to serve as the footer. Double-click it to activate the **Rectangle** tool and reduce its height by dragging the bottom right handle upwards.

35. Select the top brown rectangle, duplicate it (*Ctrl + D*), and move down below the footer rectangle.

36. Select the **Text** tool (*F8* or *T*), create the footer copyright text. Set its fill to #5a3c28 and center it over the footer rectangle using the **Align and Distribute** dialog (*Shift + Ctrl + A*).

See also

For more information, refer to *Create and edit 2D geometric shapes* and *Create and edit text* in *Chapter 1*, *Create linear gradients and Patterns* in *Chapter 2*, and *Geometric illusions using Grid*, *Creating a simple flashlight using Guides*, *Creating a stylized flower using Snapping*, and *Leaflet design using Align and Distribute* in *Chapter 3*.

Slicing a web page mockup for website use

A web page mockup is sliced into particular images when the mockup is ready to be converted into an HTML and CSS template for a typical website use. In Inkscape 0.48, there is an extension that helps with the slicing process and we will use it in this recipe to slice up the mockup we created in the previous recipe.

Getting ready

Not all mockup elements need to be sliced or exported into images to be used on a website. CSS can take care of a lot of the styling and positioning and is the preferred way because of the performance gains and ease of maintenance. The parts that are usually sliced out of a mockup are those that can't be easily recreated with CSS like gradients (CSS 3 specification includes gradients) and complex graphics elements.

Before we start with the slicing process we should first take a look at the mockup and decide which parts will be sliced out.

Since we still can't fully rely on CSS gradients (yet!) we will use the most common approach: bitmap images. In our previously created Web mockup, we can see that we have a gradient in the header and footer rectangles, but the footer is styled with the exact same gradient and it hasn't been scaled; we can use one slice for both those elements.

The wavy pattern is also a slicing candidate and the thin ellipse separator between the text groups also needs to be an image.

Since we took the navigation buttons from one of our previous recipes we already have the exported images ready so we don't have to slice them out or create new "sliding doors" and rollover images.

Another slice we have to do is the logo, and it would be useful to export it with a transparent background so it doesn't matter where it's positioned over the background gradient and can be used elsewhere.

Full alpha transparency isn't supported in Internet Explorer, but there are ways to overcome the problem by the use of JavaScript. See the CSS Sliding Doors recipe for more information.

The exported images should be named meaningfully to make coding CSS easier so we'll enter the names we want them to have on export in the Slicer extension dialog.

How to do it...

The following steps will demonstrate how to slice up a web page mockup:

1. Open the `WebpageMockup.svg` file accompanying this chapter.

2. Go to **Extensions | Web | Slicer | Create a slicer rectangle...**, in the **Name:** field enter "logo", leave everything else as default and press **Apply**. Notice a new transparent red rectangle appears on the page.

3. Position the rectangle over the logo and resize it to tightly fit around it.

4. Go to **Extensions | Web | Slicer | Create a slicer rectangle...**, in the **Name:** field enter "mainBG", and press **Apply**.

5. Position the new rectangle over the header gradient, set its size to 3 px wide and tall enough to cover all the color blends in the header rectangle, use the **Dropper** (*F7* or *D*) tool to find out where the blends stop by hovering with it over the gradient area and looking at the statusbar **Notification** area.

6. Go to **Extensions | Web | Slicer | Create a slicer rectangle...**, in the **Name:** field enter "wavy", and press **Apply**.

7. Position the new rectangle over the wavy pattern, snap it to the top-left corner of the pattern object, and snap the bottom-right handle to the point where the square pattern handle is located (select the pattern rectangle to see where the handle is and remember it or mark the spot with guides).

8. Go to **Extensions | Web | Slicer | Create a slicer rectangle...**, in the **Name:** field enter "separator", and press **Apply**.

9. Set the size of the new rectangle to 1x160 px and center it over the ellipse separator using the **Align and Distribute** dialog (*Shift + Ctrl + A*).

10. Go to **Extensions | Web | Slicer | Export layout pieces and and HTML+CSS code....** In the **Directory path to export:** enter the path to the directory where you want the exported slices to be created, use the **Create directory, if it does not exist** if you entered a non-existing folder into the path, and press **Apply**.

11. Open the directory using your favorite File browser and examine the exported images.

There's more...

We didn't use the **HTML+CSS** option because this option is only as a helper tool that enables you to see all of the exported images on one page absolutely positioned to mirror their pixel positions inside the mockup.

The logo and the wavy pattern were exported along with their backgrounds, but often we'll want to export the design elements without the background they're on. In such cases we have to copy the items (and not the background objects) outside of the mockup edges and position the slices over them.

You do have to be careful when exporting to the same location twice because the files with the same names will be overwritten.

If you'd like to see the exported slices in action open the `WebpageMockupSlicing.html` in your favorite browser.

See also

For more information, refer to the *Creating a 960 Grid System template, Creating a web page mockup for website use,* and *Creating a button to use with the CSS Sliding Doors technique* recipes seen earlier in this chapter.

11
SVG in Websites

In this chapter, we will cover:

- ▶ Creating an interactive map for a web game
- ▶ Creating an editable business chart
- ▶ Creating a navigation menu
- ▶ Creating an interactive physics simulation
- ▶ Creating a slideshow presentation with JessyInk

Introduction

The SVG format is well suited for web graphics technology. It is based on XML and can be easily manipulated (for example, using JavaScript) and efficiently compressed, and it can be scaled and resized without losing image quality. It is a **W3C** (**World Wide Web Consortium**) recommendation and an open standard. So why isn't it supported by web browsers?

At this time of writing, SVG is officially supported by nearly all major web browsing technologies, including the Trident engine in Internet Explorer 9 (which will probably be released in 2011). Mobile device support is lagging behind, but will eventually catch up (especially on Apple and Android devices).

Therefore, it makes sense to start learning how to use SVG in our web projects, especially in games, where HTML5 and SVG is seen as a strong competitor to Adobe Flash and Silverlight technologies.

 Be aware, however, that SVG element's support and rendering are implemented differently in each browser, or might not be complete. These recipes have been tested on the latest stable version (3.6.13) of *Mozilla Firefox* (`http://www.mozilla.com/firefox/`) available at the time of writing, but some might not work as expected in other browsers.

In this chapter we will explore what might be the future of Web browsing thanks to SVG technology, providing a richer, more dynamic, and better optimized user experience.

Creating an interactive map for a web game

This recipe will show us how to combine vector graphics and JavaScript together, assigning `hover` and `onClick` events to SVG elements. We will create a simple introductory page for an imaginary online game, where the player must choose/select one of three kingdoms to start the game. A kingdom can be chosen by clicking on it on the map, or by clicking its coat of arms. `Hover` effects give the user visual feedback about which kingdom will be selected if the mouse button is clicked.

The drawing will be created in Inkscape, saved in the Plain SVG format, embedded into an HTML page, and animated with JavaScript. This recipe will show us how easy it is to create an attractive presentation to an interactive web game.

Getting ready

In order to easily bring JavaScript powered interactivity across all browser platforms, we will use the popular **JQuery** framework.

JQuery can be downloaded from the official Web site: `http://www.jquery.com`.

We will also use an additional library to interact with our SVG drawing, called JQuery SVG. This plugin can be downloaded from:

`http://plugins.jquery.com/project/svg`

Finally, we will need some recipe-specific JavaScript code. This can be downloaded from Packt Publishing's website, as part of the code bundle made available as a companion to this book:

`http://www.packtpub.com/support`

All the necessary files can be found in the code bundle archive, inside the folder relative to this chapter, so be sure to download and extract it to a local directory.

How to do it...

The following steps will demonstrate the creation of our web game:

1. Open the **Document Properties** (*Shift + Ctrl + D*), select the **Landscape** orientation, and change the **Background:** to light blue by entering "bfedffff" into the **RGBA:** box.

2. Press *5* to fit the page in the Canvas window. Select the **Pencil** tool (*F6* or *P*), set **Smoothing:** on the Pencil toolbar to 20, and create a closed irregular path that will serve as the main continent where the various kingdoms are located.

3. Create a line that crosses the continent object and visually divides it in two; the smaller part will be one of the kingdoms. Create the second line that crosses over the larger continent section and also crosses the first line, so now we have the continent visually divided into three parts.

4. Select all (*Ctrl + A*) and jitter the path edges by going to **Extensions | Modify Path | Jitter nodes...**, setting both of the displacements to 10, deselecting the **Shift nodes**, selecting the **Shift node handles** option, and pressing **Apply**. If the paths look a little irregular, don't worry. We'll smooth them out in the next step.

5. Select all objects again (*Ctrl + A*), select the **Node** tool (*F2* or *N*), select all of the nodes (*Ctrl + A*), and convert them all to smooth nodes by clicking on the **Make selected nodes smooth** ☑ icon on the Node toolbar or using *Shift + S*.

6. Select the first line and the continent object and use **Path | Division** (*Ctrl + /*). This will divide the continent into two parts and the first line will disappear.

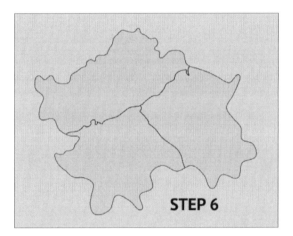

STEP 6

7. Select the second line and the continent part object behind it and use **Path | Division** (*Ctrl + /*) again. We now have the continent precisely divided into three kingdoms.

8. Open the Object Properties (*Shift + Ctrl + O*), select one of the kingdom objects, and give it a name by typing it in the **Id** field, and press **Set**. Do the same for the other two kingdom objects and close the Object Properties dialogue. We chose north, east, and west to easily distinguish them.

9. Decorate the kingdoms with your desired game icons; we can create them from scratch or import some clipart from http://openclipart.org/. If some objects cross over more than one kingdom (rivers for example) cut them into parts by duplicating the kingdom with the border that crosses the object and do a Division on the object (*Ctrl + /*). In some cases it will be necessary to use cutting or clipping depending on the style.

10. Group all objects related to one kingdom (*Ctrl + G*) and repeat this for the other two kingdoms, so you get three groups in total.

11. Open the Object Properties (*Shift + Ctrl + O*), select one of the kingdom groups, give it a name in the **Id** field, and then press **Set**. Repeat for the other two groups and close the Object Properties window when done. Using `northGroup`, `westGroup`, and `eastGroup` made sense in our case.

12. Select the **Rectangle** tool (*F4* or *R*) and create a wide rectangle to serve as the top part of our coat of arms. Copy it (*Ctrl + C*), switch to the **Selector** tool (*Space, F1* or *S*), and lock the ratio by enabling the icon on the toolbar.

13. Select the **Ellipse** tool (*F5* or *E*) and create a circle while holding *Ctrl* to lock the ratio.

14. Paste size to the circle by going to **Edit | Paste Size | Paste size** and convert it to a path (*Shift + Ctrl + C*).

15. On the Snapping toolbar enable **Snap nodes or handles** and **Snap to cusp nodes** and snap the circle along the bottom.

16. Add the rectangle to the selection (*Shift* + click) and use **Path | Union** on them (*Ctrl + +*).

17. Duplicate this object (*Ctrl + D*) two times and decorate each differently to serve as the coat of arms for the three kingdoms.

18. Group each coat of arms section separately (*Ctrl + G*).

19. Open the Object Properties (*Shift + Ctrl + O*), select one of the coat of arms groups, type a meaningful name for it in the **Id** field, and press **Set**. Repeat for the other two coat of arms groups. Using `northCoat`, `eastCoat`, and `westCoat` to keep the names coherent.

20. Select the **Text** tool (*F8* or *T*) and click on the Canvas to create a text object, type "Choose kingdom", and decorate it using whatever style suits you.

21. Add a new layer (*Shift + Ctrl + N*) above the current one and name it `hover`. This layer will hold any extra elements that appear only on hover state.

22. Select the three coat of arms groups, clone them (*Alt + D*), and shift the clones to the newly-created **hover** layer (*Shift + Page Up*).

23. Scale down the clones by the same amount by using the scale corner arrow handles on the selection. The ratio will be kept because we already enabled it earlier on the Selector toolbar.

24. Move each coat of arms clone over to its respective kingdom. They will appear at the place we set them in this step when a kingdom has been selected by clicking on it.

25. Select all (*Ctrl + A*), open Document Properties (*Shift + Ctrl + D*) on the **Page** tab, under **Custom size** click on the **Resize page to content...** to reveal more options, and press **Resize page to drawing or selection**.

26. Save a copy of the file by going to **File | Save a Copy...** (*Shift + Ctrl + Alt + S*), enter the name of the new file, choose **Plain SVG (*.svg)** from the drop-down in the bottom right corner of the window, and press **Save**.

> The difference between Inkscape SVG and the standard (plain) SVG consists of various Inkscape specific document preferences that the program saves for user convenience. For example, layers, window geometry, document background color, and so on. Although the Inkscape SVG elements should not interfere with a SVG capable Web browser or renderer, we played it safe and embedded the drawing using the Plain SVG format instead. This format also typically generates a smaller file size.

27. Use you favorite text editor to create an empty HTML file named `ChooseKingdom.html` and inside the `body` element create a `div` element with an `id` of `gamemap`:

```
<!DOCTYPE html>
<html>
  <head>
    <meta charset="utf-8" />
    <title>Choose your kingdom - The 3 Kingdoms Game</title>
  </head>
  <body>
    <div id="gamemap">
    </div>
  </body>
</html>
```

28. Add CSS styles in the `style` element that style the page to your liking. Make sure the `background-color` property is set to the same color as the map we created in Inkscape so they blend seamlessly:

```
...
<head>
  ...
  <style>body {background-color: #bfedff;}></style>
</head>
...
```

29. Include the `jquery-1.4.3.js`, `jquery.svg.js` and `jquery.svgdom.js` files accompanying this chapter into the document head using the `script` element. These files should all be placed in a subdirectory called `js`:

```
...
<head>
  ...
  <script src="js/jquery-1.4.3.js"></script>
  <script src="js/jquery.svg.js"></script>
  <script src="js/jquery.svgdom.js"></script>
</head>
...
```

30. Move the `SVGMaps.js` JavaScript file inside the `js` directory, and a link to the `SVGMaps.js` script inside our HTML file using the `script` element. This is the file containing the interactivity code for our drawing:

```
<head>
    ...
    <script src="js/SVGMaps.js"></script>
    ...
</head>
```

31. Open `ChooseKingdom.html` file in your favorite SVG supporting browser and hover over the kingdoms. Notice how the appearance changes as a result. Click on the coat of arms and the kingdoms and see how the kingdoms get selected, losing the previous selection. Here is a screenshot of Mozilla Firefox 3 rendering the drawing; right after the user has clicked on the top coat of arms. This action selected the north kingdom which made the ground a little darker and its coat of arms visible above it:

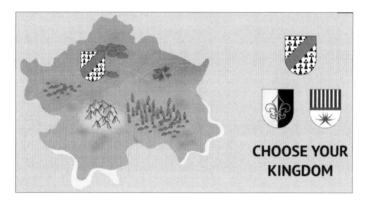

How it works...

Even though Plain SVG format doesn't support layers, we still created one and moved some objects there to make it easier to maintain the drawing. Saving to Plain SVG turns layers into ordinary groups and it doesn't mess up the `id` attributes we depend on for scripting.

The key to connecting the drawing elements with interactive events is in marking them up with unique `id` attributes, so they can be easily recognized by the script. We gave `id`s to group elements so we can change the looks of the map without the need to change the script every time the map is updated. All we have to be careful about is to add the map elements inside the kingdom groups. We can also change the coat of arms looks by entering their group and editing the objects inside; the group will still keep its `id`.

 If an object doesn't have a fill, you can only click on its stroke. This is something to keep in mind when adding `onclick` and `hover` events in JavaScript.

The script `SVGMaps.js` dynamically loads our SVG map file into the `div` element with the `id` of `gamemap` inside the `ChooseKingdom.html` using the `svg.load` jQuery function. The function `bind` connects events with the elements in our drawing, making them respond to mouse events by changing their style attributes. The style attributes we change in this example affect the element's colors and visibility.

The darker green color of the ground on `hover` and `onclick` is set in the `SVGMaps.js` script, and can be changed at the beginning of that script, in three places. The variable is called `this.select_color`.

There's more...

We have used JQuery in this recipe, but there are other JavaScript libraries and techniques for rendering SVG on the Web, available even to browsers that don't natively support it.

The Dojo Toolkit (`http://dojotoolkit.org`), another JavaScript framework, can convert SVG in VML (Vector Markup Language), a now deprecated XML-based format for vector graphics which Internet Explorer supports from version 5.0 onwards.

There is also an ActionScript (Flash) implementation of a SVG renderer available, and a tool for converting simple SVG files into ShockWave Flash, visible in any Flash-enabled browser. For more information, see: `http://code.google.com/p/as3svgrendererlib/`

See also

For more information, refer to the *Creating freehand and straight lines*, *Path operations*, and *Creating and editing text* recipes in *Chapter 1, Importing drawings from OpenClipArt. org* in *Chapter 3, Creating irregular edges* (using Jitter nodes) in *Chapter 6*, and *Creating an interactive physics simulation* in *Chapter 11*.

Creating an editable business chart

In this recipe we will create a basic business chart with editable fields. The user will be able to input a value in percentage and the vertical bars will rise or fall accordingly.

In a real world application, these numbers could be dynamically fed from an XML (RSS) or JSON feedthat streams live information from a database.

How to do it...

The following steps will demonstrate the creation of a business chart:

1. Select the **3D box** tool (*Shift + F4* or *X*) and create a box at the center of the page. On the 3D box toolbar press the "Parallel" icons ‖ relative to the **Angle X:** and **Angle Y:** options and set them to 180° and 90° respectively to create a 1-point perspective, move the Z vanishing point to approximately the center of the box.

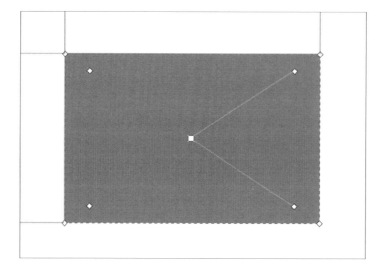

2. Switch to the **Selector** tool (*Space, F1* or *S*) and remove the stroke by holding *Shift* while clicking on the **none** icon ⊠ in the palette and make the box 350px wide and 250px tall by entering those numbers on the Selector toolbar.

3. Turn on the Grid by using **View | Grid** ⊞ (*#*) and snap the box to the grid.

4. Press the *Ctrl* key and select the front side of the box. You will notice a dashed rectangle around the selected side. Delete it (*Del*) and you should now be looking at the inside of the box.

5. Press the *Ctrl* key, select the top box side, and delete it (*Del*).

6. Repeat step 6 for the left and right box sides.

7. Switch back to the **3D box** tool (*Space, Shift + F4* or *X*) and move the vanishing point handle to the top-middle of the box. Use the Grid lines to find the exact point.

 We need to do this because 3D box handle snapping is not available yet. It will be officially introduced in the next version of Inkscape.

Using the XML Editor (*Shift + Ctrl + X*) **for precise positioning**

In rare cases where snapping doesn't work, we can position the handles using the XML Editor. To position the Z vanishing point of a 3D box, we first take note of the `inkscape:PerspectiveID` attribute value which will be in the form `#perspective12345`, then look up that element inside the `svg:defs` element, and adjust the numbers under the `inkscape:vp_z` attribute to the correct coordinates.

8. Zoom in on the left-bottom corner of the box and move the top-left handle of the trapeze (the bottom box side) to make the trapeze 20 px tall. The handle should snap almost precisely to the grid.

9. Select the **Node** tool (*F2* or *N*), select the back box side, and set its fill to **5% Gray** by clicking on the chip in the palette. Also, select the bottom box side and set its fill to **10% Gray**.

10. Select the **Pen (Bezier)** tool (*F6* or *P*) and create a horizontal line across the rectangle area by clicking on the left rectangle edge 20 px from the rectangle bottom edge, then clicking on the right rectangle edge while holding *Ctrl* to keep the line perfectly horizontal, and then right-clicking to finish the line.

STEP 5   STEP 15   STEP 20

11. Set the line stroke to 2px and color to **10% Gray**.

12. Switch to the **Selector** tool (*Space, F1* or *S*) and clone the line (*Alt + D*).

13. Move the cloned line upwards while holding *Ctrl* to keep the movement vertical and snap it 20px away from its original.

14. Stamp the clone (*Space*) and move it 20px upwards snapping to the rectangle edge; repeat until you reach the top of the rectangle.

15. Select the **Ellipse** tool (*F5* or *E*) and create a 60x20 px ellipse. Set its fill to **Green (#008000)**, remove its stroke, and position it precisely over the bottom box side.

16. Select the **Gradient** tool (*Ctrl + F1* or *G*) and create a horizontal gradient inside the ellipse, starting from the left ellipse edge to somewhere on the right-hand side of the ellipse. Edit the gradient so it suits your taste.

17. Open the **Fill and Stroke** dialogue (*Shift + Ctrl + F*), the settings for the end gradient stop will be displayed because the end stop remained selected after the gradient was made. Increase the opacity of the stop to 100 by moving the **Opacity, %** slider to the right and increase the lightness by changing the **L** slider to 148.

18. Remove focus from the slider and the **Fill and Stroke** dialogue and the end stop by pressing *Esc* twice. The ellipse should now be selected and the **Fill and Stroke** dialogue should reflect that by showing the linear gradient applied to it.

19. Under **Repeat:** drop-down choose **reflected** to make the gradient repeat smoothly.

20. Select the **Rectangle** tool (*F4* or *R*) and create a 60x200 px rectangle. The handles will snap to the grid so you can be precise when drawing by looking at the Notification region in the status bar while dragging.

21. Switch to the **Selector** tool (*Space, F1,* or *S*) and move the rectangle so that its bottom side is positioned across the middle of the ellipse by snapping the bottom corners to ellipse edges with the help of the grid.

22. Select the **Gradient** tool (*Ctrl + F1* or *G*) and under **Change:** drop down, select the already existing green gradient we applied to the ellipse.

23. On the **Fill and Stroke** dialogue, set the **Repeat:** drop down to **reflected**.

24. Move the end stop of the gradient horizontally until it reaches the same position as in the ellipse, so the two objects blend seamlessly; snapping to the grid will help keep it horizontal and at the correct spot.

25. Switch to the **Selector** tool (*Space, F1,* or *S*), select the ellipse, duplicate it (*Ctrl + D*), and move to the top of the rectangle snapping the ellipse's left and right edges to the top rectangle corners.

26. Switch back to the **Gradient** tool (*Space, Ctrl + F1,* or *G*) and move the ellipse gradient handles so the gradient path isn't in the same direction as in the rectangle, but make sure the gradient light areas join at the edge of the ellipse creating a 3D cylinder effect.

27. Switch back to the **Selector** tool (*Space, F1,* or *S*), select the ellipses and the rectangle, and group them (*Ctrl + G*).

28. Duplicate the group (*Ctrl + D*) and move it to the right while holding *Ctrl* to keep the movement horizontal.

29. Change the color of the entire duplicated group while keeping the lightness by going to **Extensions | Color | RGB Barrel**. The cylinder will change its colors to a blue gradient.

30. Duplicate the blue group (*Ctrl + D*) and move it to the right while holding *Ctrl* to keep the movement horizontal.

31. Change the color of the entire duplicated group by going to **Extensions | Color | RGB Barrel**. The cylinder will change its colors to a red gradient.

32. Select the **Node** tool (*F2* or *N*) and select the green rectangle with it (the **Node** tool lets us bypass entering the group to select objects within it, just like the **Selector** tool with the *Ctrl* key pressed).

33. Open the Object Properties dialogue (*Shift + Ctrl + O*), change the **Id** field to greenBar, and press the **Set** button:

34. Select the top green ellipse, change its **Id** to greenTop, and press **Set**. Repeat for the blue and red rectangles and top ellipses using their respective colors in the **Id** value, and close the dialogue when you finish.

35. Select the **Text** tool (*F8* or *T*), enable the bold weight, and center it by enabling the corresponding icons on the text toolbar.

36. Create a new text object by clicking on the Canvas and type 100%, adjust the text size using the drop down on the Text toolbar; 24 seemed to work in our case.

37. Switch to the **Selector** tool (*F1*) and move the text object snapping its baseline to the center of the ellipse with the help of the grid.

38. Set the text fill to **White**, the stroke color to **Black**, and the stroke width to 1.

39. Open the Object Properties (*Shift + Ctrl + O*), change the **Id** to greenNr, and press the **Set** button.

40. Duplicate the text (*Ctrl + D*) and move it over the blue cylinder snapping the text baseline to the middle of the ellipse.

41. Change the **Id** to blueNr in the Object properties and press **Set**.

42. Duplicate the text again (*Ctrl + D*) and move it over the red cylinder snapping the text baseline to the middle of the ellipse.

43. Change the **Id** to redNr in the Object properties, press **Set**, and then close the Object Properties dialogue.

44. Save a copy of the file by going to **File | Save a Copy...** (*Shift + Ctrl + Alt + S*), enter the name of the new file, choose **Plain SVG (*.svg)** from the drop down in the bottom-right corner of the window, and press **Save**.

45. Use you favorite text editor to create an empty HTML file named Charts.html. and inside the body element create a div element with an id of charts:

```
<meta charset="utf-8" />
<title>SVG Charts Demo</title>
```

```
      </head>
      <body>
        <div id="charts"></div>
      </body>
    </html>
```

46. Add CSS styles in the `style` element that style the page to your liking.

47. Include the `jquery-1.4.3.js`, `jquery.svg.js`, and `jquery.svgdom.js` files accompanying this chapter into the document head using the `script` element. Place these files in a subdirectory called `js`:

```
    ...
    <head>
      ...
      <script src="js/jquery-1.4.3.js"></script>
      <script src="js/jquery.svg.js"></script>
      <script src="js/jquery.svgdom.js"></script>
    </head>
    ...
```

48. Link to the `Charts.js` script from your HTML file using the `script` element. This is the file containing the interactivity for our drawing:

```
    ...
    <head>
      ...
      <script src="js/Charts.js"></script>
    </head>
    ...
```

49. Open `Charts.html` file in your favorite SVG-friendly browser, click on any of the text objects to make the input form appear, enter a number in it, and press **Enter**. The cylinder will change in height accordingly:

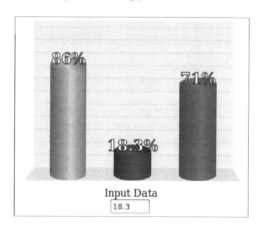

How it works...

The cylinders are made to appear as 3D objects and set on a 1-point perspective 3D box backdrop. As the cylinders change in height, the perspective should change the shape of the top ellipse too, but for simplicity we didn't make any such adjustments. The drawing is still attractive and understandable without the perspective adjustment.

Since the cylinders are positioned close to the background in a 1-point perspective, it's easy to read the scale without worrying about the parallax effect.

As in the previous recipe, we assigned unique `id` attributes to the objects we intend to change with a script so they can be easily selected and manipulated.

Each cylinder consists of a bottom ellipse, the middle rectangle, and the top ellipse. We used a single reflected gradient on all of them and positioned it so that the bottom ellipse blends with the rectangle and the top one completes the 3D effect. To change the cylinder height according to the input data, the script changes the rectangle height accordingly and the ellipse is translated by the same amount to keep the same appearance. The text object updates with each data change and it is also translated by the same amount as the top ellipse.

There's more...

We used a very simple example in this recipe with clever styling to make the scripting part easier. Using more complex designs is also possible but with more scripting to control all of the size and position attributes. Pie charts, using ellipse arcs, and data columns, using 3D boxes, are other examples of chart representations.

SVG JavaScript chart libraries

The `JQuery` SVG plugin has graphing and plotting extensions that create SVG charts in predefined styles. Although using those libraries makes Inkscape redundant it can save time if the control over the chart appearance isn't very important.

See also

For more in formation, refer to the *Creating and editing 2D geometric shapes*, *Creating freehand and straight lines*, *Creating paths using the Pen (Bezier) tool*, *Creating and editing 3D boxes*, and *Creating and editing text* recipes in *Chapter 1*. Also refer to *Changing fill and stroke color using a Palette*, *Creating linear gradients*, and *Different color icon sets using RGB Barrel* recipes in *Chapter 2*, *Geometric illusions using Grids* and *Creating a stylized flower using Snapping* in *Chapter 3*, and *Creating an interactive map for a web game* seen earlier in this chapter.

Creating a navigation menu

In this recipe, we will recycle some of the examples from this chapter to build a page with navigation and content made up of SVG files. We will create the navigation elements in one SVG file, and use the other examples from this chapter to serve as page content. We will also see how the rectangle element box limitation we are used to in HTML doesn't exist in SVG, and we can happily have irregularly shaped clicking areas corresponding exactly to our SVG objects.

How to do it...

The following steps will demonstrate the creation of a navigation menu:

1. Open the **Document Properties** (*Shift + Ctrl + D*) dialog and change the **Background:** to opaque black by moving the **L** slider to the left and **A** to the right. The document background will turn black.

2. Select the **Calligraphy** tool (*Ctrl + F6* or *C*), set the fill of the future object to **White** by clicking on the chip on the color palette, and remove the stroke by clicking on the **none** chip while holding *Shift*. Check that the style is set correctly at the right-hand side of the Calligraphy toolbar.

3. Select **Dip pen** preset on the Calligraphy toolbar, deactivate the option for using the tilt of the input device for the pen's nib [icon] and the **Angle:** field will become available. Enter 30 as the new value and draw the letter G using these settings of the **Calligraphy** tool.

4. **Simplify** (*Ctrl + L*) the path and use the **Node** tool (*F2* or *N*) to modify nodes that create unevenness if necessary.

5. Select the **Text** tool (*F8* or *T*), create a text object by clicking somewhere on the Canvas, and type "AME INTRO". Set the font family to your liking and change the font size so it matches nicely with the "G" we created with the **Calligraphy** tool.

6. Select the **Selector** tool (*F1*) and position the text object close to the "G" so they read "Game intro", convert the text to a path (*Shift + Ctrl + C*), ungroup the letters (*Shift + Ctrl + G*), they will remain selected, add the "G" to the selection (*Shift + click*), and combine the selection into a single path (*Ctrl + K*).

7. Open the `InteractiveMapGame.svg` file accompanying this chapter, copy one of the coat of arms (*Ctrl + C*), paste it over the "Game intro" (*Ctrl + V*), and scale it down if necessary while keeping the ratio (*Ctrl*):

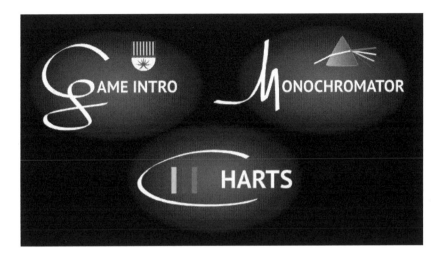

8. Select the coat of arms and the "Game intro" and group them (*Ctrl + G*).

9. Select the **Ellipse** tool (*F5* or *E*) and create an ellipse over the "Game intro" so it covers it and set its fill to #646464. This ellipse will serve as our spot light on hover.

10. Select the **Gradient** tool (*Ctrl + F1* or *G*). On the toolbar select the icon for radial gradient and the fill area, and create a gradient in the ellipse by clicking near the center of the ellipse and dragging to the right while holding *Ctrl* to keep the movement horizontal.

11. Increase the opacity of the end stop to 100 by entering it into the **O:** field in the bottom-left corner of the window, and decrease the lightness of that stop to 0 so you get pure black by clicking in the **Fill:** box in the bottom-left corner while holding *Ctrl* and dragging on the Canvas to the right and down.

12. On the Snapping toolbar enable **Snap from and to centers of objects, Snap bounding box corners**, and **Snap to edges of a bounding box**. Center the gradient by snapping the start (square) gradient handle to the ellipse center, and adjust the gradient paths if necessary so they extend precisely to the ellipse bounding box.

13. Repeat steps 2 to 6 but this time drawing the stylized letter "M" and typing "ONOCHROMATOR" into the text object.

14. Select the **Star** tool (*Shift + F9* or ***), select the **Polygon** mode, set **Corners:** to 3, **Rounded:** to 0.04, and create an upright triangle by dragging upwards while holding *Ctrl* to create the prism icon.

15. Set both the fill and stroke to **White** by clicking and *Shift*-clicking the chip in the color palette. Set stroke width to 1.

16. Select the **Gradient** tool (*Ctrl + F1* or *G*), change the gradient from radial to linear on the Gradient toolbar, and create a horizontal white to transparent gradient inside the prism. Extend the gradient handles outside of the prism.

17. Open the **Fill and Stroke** dialogue (*Shift + Ctrl + F*) on the **Stroke paint** tab and set the **A** slider to middle (127) to make the stroke half transparent.

18. On the Snapping toolbar enable **Snap to paths**.

19. Select the **Pen (Bezier)** tool (*F6* or *P*) and create a three node line that will represent the incident light beam and the refracted part inside the prism. Do that by clicking on the outside of the left-bottom side of the prism, then clicking on the left prism side (it will snap to it), clicking on the right-side of the prism, and finishing the path with a right-click or by pressing *Enter*.

20. Set the stroke to **White** by holding *Shift* while clicking on the color chip in the palette, set its width to 3, and under the **Stroke style** tab of the Fill and Stroke window set **Join:** to **Round join** and **Cap:** to **Round cap**.

21. On the Snapping toolbar disable **Snap to paths** and enable **Snap to cusp nodes**.

22. Press *Esc* twice to remove focus from the Fill and Stroke dialogue and deselect the newly created line.

23. Create another line by clicking on the end node of the previous line (on the right prism edge), then clicking somewhere in the area to the right of the prism, and finish the line by right-clicking or pressing *Enter*.

24. Set its stroke width to 3 and set **Join:** to **Round join** and **Cap:** to **Round cap**.

25. Press *Esc* once to remove focus from the Fill and Stroke dialogue and gain focus on the newly-created line.

26. Switch to the **Selector** tool (*Space*, *F1*, or *S*) and click on the line to get the rotating handles. Move the center of rotation cross handle to the first line node (on the right prism edge) and snap it to the node.

27. Duplicate the line (*Ctrl + D*), and rotate it 15°, holding *Ctrl* while dragging one of the rotate arrow handles.

28. Repeat step 26 two more times to get four lines in total.

29. Set the stroke color of the lines from the top one to the bottom to **Red (#FF0000)**, **Yellow (#FFFF00)**, **Lime (#00FF00)**, and **Blue (#0000FF)**.

30. Select all of the prism icon objects together with the "Monochromator" and group them (*Ctrl + G*).

31. Select the ellipse behind the "Game intro", duplicate it (*Ctrl + D*), move over the "Monochromator", and send it to the back (*End* or *Page Down*).

32. Repeat steps 2 to 6 but this time drawing the stylized letter "C" and typing "HARTS" into the text object.

33. Enable the Grid (*#*), select the **Rectangle** tool (*F4* or *R*) and create a vertical rectangle inside the letter "C", duplicate it twice (*Ctrl + D*), and move to the right so they are equally distant. Use grid to help you position them.

34. Set the rectangle fills to **Lime (#00FF00)**, **Blue (#0000FF)**, and **Red (#FF0000)**.

35. Select the rectangles and the "Charts" object and group them (*Ctrl* + *G*).

36. Select the ellipse behind the "Game intro", duplicate it (*Ctrl* + *D*), move over the "Charts", and send to back (*End* or *PgDn*).

37. Open the Object Properties dialogue (*Shift* + *Ctrl* + *O*), select the group that contains the "Game intro", change the **Id** field to "game", and press **Set**.

38. Select the ellipse behind the "Game intro" (hold *Alt* and click to select under), change the **Id** field to "`gameSpot`", and press **Set**.

39. Select the group that contains the "Monochromator", change the **Id** field to "`monochromator`", and press **Set**.

40. Select the ellipse behind the "Monochromator" (*Alt* + click to select under), change the **Id** field to "`monochromatorSpot`", and press **Set**.

41. Select the group that contains the "Charts", change the **Id** field to "charts", and press **Set**.

42. Select the ellipse behind the "Charts" (*Alt* + click to select under), change the **Id** field to "`chartsSpot`", and press **Set**. Close the Object Properties dialogue.

43. Select all (*Ctrl* + *A*), open Document Properties (*Shift* + *Ctrl* + *D*) on the **Page** tab, under **Custom size** click on the **Resize page to content...** to reveal more options, and press **Resize page to drawing or selection**.

44. Save a copy of the file by going to **File | Save a Copy...** (*Shift* + *Ctrl* + *Alt* + *S*), enter `SVGnavigationPlain.svg` as the name of the new file, choose **Plain SVG (*.svg)** from the drop down in the bottom right corner of the window, and press **Save**.

45. Open your favorite text editor and create an empty HTML file named `SVGnavigation.html` and, inside the `body` element, create two `div` elements with ids of `navigation` and `content`:

```
<!DOCTYPE html>
<html>
  <head>
    <meta charset="utf-8" />
    <title>SVG Navigation</title>
  </head>
  <body>
    <div id="navigation"></div>
    <div id="content"></div>
  </body>
</html>
```

46. Add CSS styles in the `style` element to give the page an attractive look (don't forget the black background because Plain SVG comes without it):

```
    ...
    <head>
      ...
```

```
<style>body {background-color: black;}></style>
</head>
. . .
```

47. Include the `jquery-1.4.3.js`, `jquery.svg.js`, and `jquery.svgdom.js` files accompanying this chapter into the document head using the `script` element. The files should be placed in the `js` directory:

```
. . .
<head>
  . . .
  <script src="js/jquery-1.4.3.js"></script>
  <script src="js/jquery.svg.js"></script>
  <script src="js/jquery.svgdom.js"></script>
</head>
. . .
```

48. Place the `Navigation.js` script in the `js` directory and link it from your HTML file using the `script` element. This file will contain the interactivity code for our drawing:

```
. . .
<head>
  . . .
  <script src="js/Navigation.js"></script>
</head>
. . .
```

49. Open the `SVGnavigation.html` file in your favorite SVG supporting browser, click on the elements, and see the content appear below the navigation. Notice how unlike in HTML the clickable area corresponds precisely to the object's edges, and not to the object's bounding box. The hover effect that reveals the spot light behind the navigation buttons makes it even more clear.

> Making the navigation "buttons" hard to click or using an area that users don't expect lowers the usability and user friendliness of your web application. The example in this recipe is provided only to illustrate the difference between HTML and SVG element handling. In a real-world example the clickable area would probably be enlarged in some way to facilitate clicking.

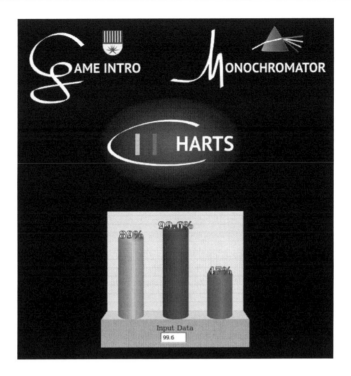

How it works...

The Document background color is an Inkscape-specific property. It's not part of the SVG specification, so this information is lost when saving into Plain SVG format. That's why we had to declare a black background in our CSS styles. Having it declared in the original Inkscape file helped us create the drawing without having to imagine the final outcome.

You may have noticed we simplified the letters created with the Calligraphy tool but not the text objects after converting to paths. This is because (quality) fonts already have the optimum number of nodes after conversion, so simplifying them would distort the letters too much.

The spot light object might seem like a strongly blurred white ellipse, and this is one of the ways to achieve this look, but in this case it was possible to create the same effect using a gradient and we gained a lot in the performance area. Using the blur filter would make the drawing much less responsive in both Inkscape and browsers.

As in the previous recipe we assigned unique id attributes to the navigation objects we want to load the page content when clicked on. Spot lights are hidden using the script and only shown when we hover over the corresponding navigation object. That is why we needed special ids on them.

The content we load into the content area is pulled from the Plain SVG files created in other recipes in this chapter.

See also

For more information, refer to the *Creating and editing 2D geometric shapes, Creating freehand and straight lines, Editing paths using the Node tool, Creating paths using the Pen (Bezier) tool, Creating calligraphic shapes*, and *Creating and editing text* in *Chapter 1*. Also refer to *Changing fill and stroke color using a Palette, Creating linear gradients, Recreating HAL 9000 using radial gradients*, and *Adjusting hue, lightness, saturation, and stroke width using Color Gestures* in *Chapter 2* and *Creating a stylized flower using Snapping* in *Chapter 3*.

Creating an interactive physics simulation

This recipe will show us how powerful SVG can be as an educational tool. We will create a drawing of a simple *Monochromator* optical device, consisting of a light source and a prism, and use a script to generate SVG light beams that simulate the light refraction according to the laws of physics. The drawing will contain widgets that change various physics parameters that influence the "experiment" results, and the script will ensure that the behavior will be realistic.

Although most of the work for this recipe is contained in the script, it is still a useful example of how Inkscape and SVG can be very flexible tools in various simulations and interactive illustrations.

How to do it...

The following steps demonstrate the creation of an interactive physics simulation:

1. Open **Document Properties** (*Shift + Ctrl + D*) and change the **Background:** to opaque black by moving the **L** slider to the left and **A** to the right. The document background will turn black.

2. Select the **Star** tool (*Shift + F9* or ***). On the Star toolbar select the Polygon mode, set **Corners:** to 3, **Rounded:** to 0, and create an upright triangle by dragging upwards while holding *Ctrl* to create the prism.

3. Set its fill and stroke color to **White** by clicking and *Shift*-clicking on the color chip in the palette. Set its stroke width to 3 by right-clicking the stroke size area in the bottom-left corner of the window.

4. Select the **Gradient** tool (*Ctrl + F1* or *G*), select linear gradient and the fill area on the Gradient toolbar, and create a horizontal white to transparent gradient inside the prism. Extend the gradient handles outside of the prism.

5. Open the Fill and Stroke dialogue (*Shift + Ctrl + F*) on the **Stroke paint** tab and set the **A** slider to middle (127) to make the stroke half transparent.

6. On the Snapping toolbar enable Snap nodes or handles and **Snap to paths**.

7. Select the **Pen (Bezier)** tool (*F6* or *P*) and create a line positioned to the left and slightly below the prism by clicking on the Canvas to create the first node, and then clicking on the left prism side to create the second node (it will snap to the prism edge). Finish the line by right-clicking or pressing *Enter*.

8. Select the **Node** tool (*F2* or *N*) and drag the second node off the prism edge closer towards the first node while holding *Ctrl* and *Alt* to keep the node movement along the segment. This path will serve as our light source.

9. In the Fill and Stroke dialogue under **Stroke style** tab, set the stroke width to 6, **Join:** to **Round join**, and **Cap:** to **Round cap**.

10. Select the **Text** tool (*F8* or *T*), click somewhere on the Canvas, and type "Light refraction". On the Text toolbar set the alignment to center and set the desired font family and size and set fill color to **Lime (#00FF00)**.

11. Open the **Align and Distribute** dialogue (*Shift + Ctrl + A*).

12. Switch to the **Selector** tool (*F1*), select the text and the prism, and center them horizontally using the icon on the dialogue. Make sure the text moves with respect to the prism.

13. Move the text vertically below the prism while holding *Ctrl* to keep the movement vertical.

14. Duplicate the text (*Ctrl + D*), but keep it in place. Select the **Text** tool (*F8* or *T*), select all letters (*Ctrl + A*), and type "Total reflection". The new text will replace the old. Set its fill to **Red (#FF0000)**.

15. Duplicate the text (*Ctrl + D*) but keep it in place, select all letters (*Ctrl + A*), and type "No refraction". The new text will replace the old. Set its fill to **20% Gray**.

16. Create the new text object "Prism material" and make it bold using the icon on the Text toolbar.

17. Select the **Ellipse** tool (*F5* or *E*) and create a circle by dragging over the Canvas while holding *Ctrl* to maintain the aspect-ratio of 1:1. Set its fill to **Black**, stroke to **10% Gray**, and stroke width to 3.

18. Duplicate it three times (*Ctrl + D*) and switch to the Selector tool (*Space, F1, or S*).

19. Drag one of the duplicates downwards while holding *Ctrl* to keep the motion vertical, select all the circles, and arrange them vertically equidistant by using the **Make vertical gaps between objects equal** icon on the Align and Distribute dialogue.

20. Select the **Text** tool (*F8* or *T*) and create a text object for each of the circle bullets, and then use the Align and Distribute dialogue to align them next to their bullets. First align the top and the bottom text to their bullets vertically, then select the text objects and make gaps between them equal, just like we did with circle bullets, so the relations will be the same.

21. Repeat Steps 15 to 19 for all the other widget categories (three more).

22. Select all circle bullets in each category that you want to be enabled by default and change their fill to **Blue (#0000FF)**. The script will pick up this information to calculate the simulation when the page is first loaded.

23. Select the **Text** tool (*F8* or *T*) and create a text object with explanations about the experiment. Create new lines when they become too long because they will not wrap.

24. Select the **Rectangle** tool (*F4* or *R*) and create a rectangle that covers the explanation text. Send it to the back of the text (*End* or *PgDn*), and round its corners to 15px using the fields on the Rectangle toolbar.

25. Center the text vertically and horizontally with respect to the rectangle and position it at the bottom-left corner of the document.

26. Open the Object Properties dialogue (*Shift + Ctrl + O*), select the light source line object, change the **Id** field to "beam", and press **Set**.

27. Select the prism, change the **Id** field to "prism", and press **Set**.

28. Select the "No refraction" text object, change the **Id** field to "norefraction", and press **Set**.

29. Select the "Total reflection" text object (*Alt* + click to select under), change the **Id** field to "total_reflection", and press **Set**.

30. Select the "Light refraction" text object (*Alt* + click to select under), change the **Id** field to "refraction", and press **Set**.

31. Select the first circle bullet, change the **Id** field to "glass", and press **Set**. Repeat for each bullet naming the **Id** something meaningful.

32. Save a copy of the file by going to **File | Save a Copy...** (*Shift + Ctrl + Alt + S*), enter `MonochromatorPlain.svg` as the name of the new file, choose **Plain SVG (*.svg)** from the drop down in the bottom-right corner of the window, and press **Save**.

33. Open your favorite text editor and create an empty HTML file named `Monochromator.html`. Inside the `body` element create a `div` element with `svgbasics` as the `id`:

```
<!DOCTYPE html>
<html>
  <head>
    <meta charset="utf-8" />
    <title>Monochromator physics simulation</title>
  </head>
  <body>
    <div id="svgbasics"></div>
  </body>
</html>
```

34. Add CSS styles in the `style` element that style the page to your liking (don't forget the black background because Plain SVG comes without it):

```
. . .
<head>
  . . .
  <style>body {background-color: black;}></style>
</head>
. . .
```

35. Include the `jquery-1.4.3.js`, `jquery.svg.js`, and `jquery.svgdom.js` files accompanying this chapter into the document head using the `script` element:

```
. . .
<head>
  . . .
  <script src="js/jquery-1.4.3.js"></script>
  <script src="js/jquery.svg.js"></script>
  <script src="js/jquery.svgdom.js"></script>
</head>
. . .
```

36. Link to the `Simulation.js` script from your HTML file using the `script` element. This is the file containing the interactivity for our drawing:

```
. . .
<head>
  . . .
  <script src="js/Simulation.js"></script>
</head>
. . .
```

37. Open `Monochromator.html` file in your favorite SVG supporting browser, change the widget options by clicking on the circle bullets to see how they affect the light refraction, and try to find the combination of options that produces special cases of **Total reflection** and **No reflection**:

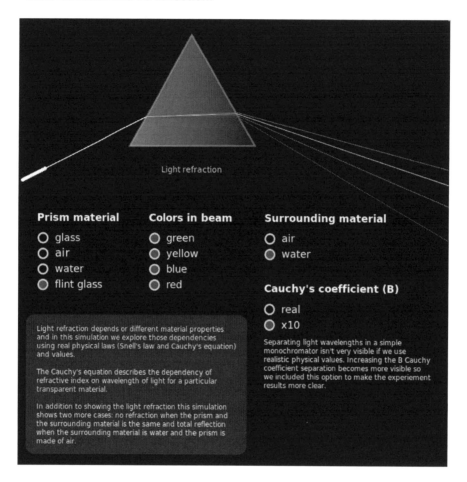

How it works...

As in previous recipes we assigned `id` attributes to various elements so the script can interact with them. The angle of the light beam depends on the orientation of the light source "device". If we change the angle of the line that represents the light source, the beam angle and the whole refraction experiment is recalculated. This means we can open the `MonochromatorPlain.svg`, modify the light source line angle, save and open the `Monochromator.html` in a browser, and the light beam angles will be updated to the new incident angle. The same applies to the prism; its position and shape also influence the light beams and their refraction.

In the Interactive SVG chart recipe the input element we used to interact with the drawing is created in HTML. In this recipe the radio button widgets are exclusively SVG elements. This shows we can choose either way to script the interaction with SVG.

In the case where the prism material is flint glass, surrounding material is air, and Cauchy's coefficient is tenfold, the total reflection happens inside the prism. The calculation for this case is more complicated than the rest of this experiment and it's out of the scope of this book, so the resulting beam positions aren't displayed.

See also

For more information, refer to the *Creating and editing 2D geometric shapes*, *Creating freehand and straight lines*, *Editing paths using the Node tool*, *Creating paths using the Pen (Bezier) tool*, and *Creating and editing text* in *Chapter 1*. Also refer to *Changing fill and stroke color using a Palette* and *Creating linear gradients* in *Chapter 2* and *Leaflet design using Align and Distribute* in *Chapter 3*.

Creating a slideshow presentation with JessyInk

JessyInk is a suite of extensions that use JavaScript code to turn Inkscape layers into presentation slides, viewable in any SVG-enabled browser. You can consider it an alternative to business presentation packages like *Microsoft PowerPoint* and *OpenOffice.org Impress*, and it can also be used for highly customized image galleries.

In this recipe we will create a simple presentation using Inkscape and JessyInk.

Getting ready

First of all we need to install the necessary JessyInk extensions, which are not packaged with Inkscape and must be downloaded separately. Fortunately, Inkscape provides an extension that works like an automated installer; you can find it in the menu, **Extensions | JessyInk | Install/update**.

How to do it...

The following steps will demonstrate how to create a slide show with JessyInk:

1. Open the **Document Properties** (*Shift + Ctrl + D*) dialog and change the **Background:** to opaque black by moving the **L** slider to the left and **A** to the right. The document background will turn black.

2. Under **Custom size** set **Width:** and **Height:** to 800 and 600 respectively, or use any other size you think you might need to project your ideas on.

3. Open the **Layers** dialogue (*Shift + Ctrl + L*) and change the **Layer 1** name to "Master slide" by double-clicking on it or right-clicking and choosing **Rename Layer...** .

4. Go to **Extensions | JessyInk | Master slide...** and type "Master slide" into the **Name of layer:** field and press **Apply**.

5. Go to **Extensions | JessyInk | Transitions**, enter "Master slide" in the **Name of layer:** field, set both **Duration in seconds:** options to 1 and **Type:** to **Fade** and press **Apply**.

6. On the Snapping toolbar enable Snap nodes or handles and **Snap to page border**.

7. Select the **Rectangle** tool (*F4* or *R*) and create a rectangle from corner to corner of the page; it will snap precisely. Set the rectangle fill to **90% Gray** and remove its stroke.

8. Select the **Gradient** tool (*Ctrl + F1* or *G*). On the toolbar make sure that the linear gradient and fill area options are enabled and create a gradient in the bottom-right corner by clicking near the corner (it will snap) and dragging upwards and to the left.

9. Open the **Fill and Stroke** dialogue (*Shift + Ctrl + F*), press *Esc* two times to remove the focus from the gradient so the entire rectangle is selected, and under **Repeat:** select reflected, so some of the gray color also shows in the top-left page corner.

10. Select the **Text** tool (*F8* or *T*), create a text object by clicking on the Canvas, and type " Title text"; set its alignment to right using the icon on the Text toolbar, make it bold, and choose the font family and size that suits you and set fill color to **White**.

11. Switch to the **Selector** tool (*F1*) and position the text in the top-right corner at some distance from the page edges. Enable the Grid (#) to help with positioning.

12. With the text still selected go to **Extensions | JessyInk | Auto-texts...**, choose **Slide title**, and press **Apply**.

13. Select the **Rectangle** tool (*F4* or *R*) and create a rectangle at the bottom of the page snapping to the page corners to serve as the footer.

14. Remove its stroke and set fill to **90% Gray**.

15. Select the **Text** tool (*F8* or *T*), create a text object by clicking on the Canvas, and type " 1"; set its alignment to right using the icon on the Text toolbar, make it bold, and choose the font family and size that suits you and set fill color to **Black**.

16. Switch to the **Selector** tool (*F1*) and position it in the right-bottom corner over the footer rectangle.

17. Use the **Align and Distribute** dialogue (*Shift + Ctrl + A*) to center the number vertically over the footer rectangle.

18. With the text still selected go to **Extensions | JessyInk | Auto-texts...**, choose **Slide number**, and press **Apply**.

19. Create a new layer (*Shift + Ctrl + N*) named "Title" above the current one.

20. Select the **Rectangle** tool (*F4* or *R*) and create a rectangle from one corner to the other corner of the page. It will snap precisely, set the rectangle fill to **Black**, and remove its stroke.

21. Select the **Text** tool (*F8* or *T*) and create a text object by clicking on the Canvas and typing "Monochromator Light refraction". Make the font bold by using the icon on the Text toolbar, center the text alignment, and adjust the font family and size to your liking.

22. Switch to the **Selector** tool (*F1*) and on the Align and Distribute dialogue, choose **Page** from the **Relative to:** drop down, and then center the object both vertically and horizontally.

23. Make the **Title** layer invisible by toggling the eye icon on the dialogue.

24. Create a new layer (*Shift + Ctrl + N*) named "Physics background" above the **Title** one.

25. Select the **Ellipse** tool (*F5* or *E*) and create a circle to serve as a bullet, set its fill to **Blue (#0000FF)**, stroke to **10% Gray**, and stroke width to 6.

26. Clone the circle (*Alt + D*) and move it downwards while holding *Ctrl* to constrain the motion to vertical.

27. Select the **Text** tool (*F8* or *T*) and create a left-aligned object for each bullet. Enter "Snell's law" and "Cauchy's coefficient".

28. Use the **Align and Distribute** dialogue (*Shift + Ctrl + A*) to center the text vertically with respect to their bullets and align their left sides.

29. Select the bullets and their text and copy them (*Ctrl + C*).

30. Make the **Physics background** layer invisible by toggling the eye icon on the dialogue.

31. Create a new layer (*Shift + Ctrl + N*) named "Simulation description" above the **Physics background** one.

32. With that layer selected, do a **Paste In Place** (*Ctrl + Alt +V*).

33. Double click on the top text object to get the **Text** tool and change the text to "SVG is used to represent experimental physical setup"; break into a new line after "represent".

34. Select the **Selector** tool (*F1*), select the bottom bullet and its text, and move them downwards.

35. Double click on the bottom text object to get the **Text** tool and change the text to "JavaScript is used for physics laws simulation through analytical geometry", breaking into a new line when necessary so the text doesn't leak out of the slide.

36. Group each bullet with its corresponding text (*Ctrl + G*).

37. Select the first group and go to **Extensions | JessyInk | Effects....** Under **Build-in effect**, set **Order:** to 1, **Duration in seconds:** to 0.8, **Type:** to **Fade**, and press **Apply**.

38. Select the second (bottom) group and go to **Extensions | JessyInk | Effects....** Under **Build-in effect** set **Order:** to 2, **Duration in seconds:** to 0.8, **Type:** to **Fade**, and press **Apply**.

39. Make the **Simulation description** layer invisible by toggling the eye icon on the dialogue.

40. Create a new layer (*Shift + Ctrl + N*) named "Conclusion" above the **Simulation description** one.

41. Select the **Text** tool (*F8* or *T*) and create a center aligned object typing "SVG and Inkscape rock!", set the fill color to **White**, and increase the font size.

42. Use the **Align and Distribute** dialogue (*Shift + Ctrl + A*) to center the text both vertically and horizontally with respect to the **Page**.

43 Save the file and open it in your favorite SVG-enabled browser. Use *Page Down* and *Page Up*, the arrow keys ,or your mouse wheel to flip through the slides. Here is a screenshot of the first two slides in transition:

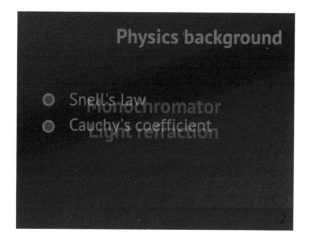

How it works...

As we can see the Master slide should be at the bottom of the layers stack, so the Title slide or any other slide can override the Master looks if necessary. This is what we did with our Title slide.

If we apply the Transitions to the slide that is set as the master slide, we will also apply them to each slide in the presentation. This is a quick way to make the transitions smooth quickly even when dealing with a great number of slides.

The text from the Master slide we set to Auto-text option of Slide title is being replaced on each slide with the name of the layer. This is an automated way to style the titles in one place and have each title text loaded from the layer name. It's the same with Slide numbers: we can style them on master slide, assign the Slide number Auto-text option, and JessyInk will do the rest.

In the case where we need the bullets or any other object to appear separately from the slide, we can use Effects to get more control over the timing of when each bullet or any other object will appear. To set which object should appear first or second we set the **Order:** option.

There's more...

JessyInk comes with a very convenient option to see all the slides on the screen called Index sheet; just press the *i* key. The current slide will be highlighted and we will be able to move from one slide to the next using the arrow keys or the mouse. Clicking on a slide or using *Enter* will make the slide active and expand it to its natural size.

 The default key for entering Index mode might conflict with other key bindings. You can change the bindings for JessyInk extensions in the **Extensions | JessyInk | Key Bindings...** dialogue.

Using + or – keys while in the Index sheet mode rearranges the slides grid by fitting more or less slides into rows. It is also possible to customize all of the key bindings.

Inkscape book slideshow

Find the file `InkscapeBookSlideshow.svg` and open it in your favorite SVG-enabled browser. It is a JessyInk slideshow containing almost all of the examples created in this book. It serves as a reference not only to this book but Inkscape in general.

See also

For more information, refer to the *Creating and editing 2D geometric* shapes, *Creating and editing text*, and *Creating linear gradients* recipes in *Chapter 1*, and the *Designing plate rims using Layers* and *Leaflet design using Align and Distribute* recipes in *Chapter 3*.

12

Draw Freely

In this chapter, we will cover:

- ▶ Compiling the document metadata
- ▶ Command line interface (CLI)
- ▶ Compiling development builds on Linux
- ▶ Modifying an existing extension – Darker extended
- ▶ Creating an extension – Object Guides

Introduction

We named this last chapter after the official motto of Inkscape: to "draw freely" is to create art without limitations of expression, functionality, and freedom. Although version 0.48 is the latest and greatest release of Inkscape currently available (with 0.49 coming very soon), there are still areas where it can be improved and expanded; both from a developer's and user's point of view. Being open source and libre, you'll be happy to know that anybody can do that, by reading the source code and start hacking right away! Creating an extension for something you find useful will probably be useful to others too, and testing Inkscape development builds and reporting bugs is an excellent way of contributing back to the community. Moreover, to "draw freely" means to be unrestricted by physical and digital barriers, as you will want to share and distribute your work for others to enjoy and appreciate. It is therefore important to apply the correct information to it, so it can be found in the maelstrom of information available on the Internet.

Compiling the document metadata

Before distributing your work, you should take care in compiling the document metadata, including the license information. This data is usually extracted by content management systems, search engines, and file managers in some operating systems.

How to do it...

The following steps will demonstrate how to compile the document metadata:

1. Save a new file (*Shift* + *Ctrl* + S) under the name `DocumentMetadata.svg`.

2. Open the **Document Metadata** dialog by going to **File | Document Metadata**.

3. Under the **Metadata** tab are the **Dublin Core Entities** fields. Enter the title of your drawing into the **Title:** field; in this case it's "Empty Space".

 Hover over the fields to get a tooltip with a longer field description.

4. Insert the current date or the date when the document is to be released into the **Date:** field in the ISO 8601 format, one of the forms is YYYY-MM-DD, such as 2011-01-01.

5. Into the **Creator:** field insert the name of the person or organization responsible for creating the content.

6. Into the **Rights:** field enter the link to the Terms and Conditions statement that describes the rights over the document content or a simple Copyright notice.

7. Into the **Publisher:** field enter the name of the organization, a person or a service making the document available. When publishing the document on your website consider entering your website name.

8. Into the **Identifier:** field enter the unique identifier for the document within its publishing context. If you're making the document available on your website to download enter the URI of the document.

9. If you plan to use some other drawing as a base to start your own, like using a drawing from `openclipart.org`, enter a unique identifier of the source in the **Source:** field; this may be the file title, URI or some other identifier.

10. If your document is in some way connected to another use the **Relation:** field to enter the reference to the related document.

11. In the **Language:** field enter the language of the document using two or three letter RFC 3066 language code forms. For English enter "en", "eng", or "en-GB" for British English.

12. In the **Keywords:** field enter a comma-separated list of expressions related to this document.

13. If the contents of the document scope over some geographical region or a time period enter that information into **Coverage:** field.

14. Into the **Description:** field enter the description of the document contents. It can be in a form of an abstract, table of contents, or a reference to such a description.

15. Into the **Contributors:** field enter names of organizations or people who contributed to the content.

16. Switch to the **License** tab and choose the license you wish to apply to the document by clicking on one of the choices from the list or enter an URI to a license not listed here. For files you wish to upload to `openclipart.org` choose **Public Domain**.

17. Save the document (*Ctrl + S*).

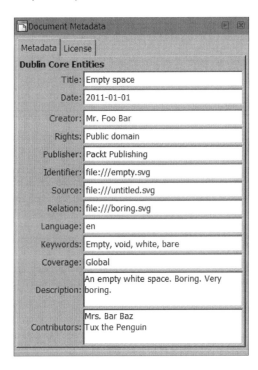

How it works...

The information we entered into the **Document Metadata** dialog is inserted into SVG code inside an `svg:metadata` element and each field is marked with its respective `dc:` element. License information is also inserted under the `svg:metadata` element and is marked up with `cc:License`. You can inspect this using the **XML editor** (*Shift + Ctrl + X*).

Dublin Core metadata entities are a common, small set of resource descriptors that aid cataloging and retrieval of multimedia documents, such as essays, books, sound, video and, of course, images.

You can read more on the official website:

`http://dublincore.org/documents/dces/`

Command-line interface (CLI)

In this recipe we will learn how to use the command line interface to perform various operations on an SVG document we created in one of the previous chapters.

This recipe is intended for users of Mac OSX, Linux, and BSD based distributions. The Inkscape executable officially distributed for Windows is not compiled as a console application. This means that the commands shown here will still work, but no output will be shown on the terminal.

More information, including several ways to get around this limitation, is available on the Inkscape FAQ:

`http://wiki.inkscape.org/wiki/index.php/FAQ`

Getting ready

Download the zipped source files for this book from Packt Publishing's website and extract them to a folder.

How to do it...

The following steps will demonstrate some common commands:

1. Open your favorite terminal; there's no need to open Inkscape this time.

2. Type `inkscape --help` or `inkscape -?` and press *Enter*. You will see a list of options available.

3. One of the first options is **-V, --version** so try it out by typing `inkscape --version` and press *Enter*:

   ```
   $ inkscape -V
   Inkscape 0.48.0 r9654 (Sep  1 2010)
   ```

Use the *Up arrow* to get the last command performed and edit it to save time if the new command is similar to the previous one.

4. To see the usage tips use the `inkscape --usage` command:

   ```
   $ inkscape --usage
   Usage: inkscape [-VzgDCjtTXYWHSx?] [-V|--version] [-z|--without-gui]
               [-g|--with-gui] [-f|--file=FILENAME] [-p|--print=FILENAME]
               [-e|--export-png=FILENAME] [-d|--export-dpi=DPI]
               [-a|--export-area=x0:y0:x1:y1] [-D|--export-area-drawing]
   ```

```
            [-C|--export-area-page]  [--export-area-snap]
            [-w|--export-width=WIDTH]  [-h|--export-height=HEIGHT]
            [-i|--export-id=ID]  [-j|--export-id-only]  [-t|--export-
use-hints]
            [-b|--export-background=COLOR]  [-y|--export-background-
opacity=VALUE]
            [-l|--export-plain-svg=FILENAME]  [-P|--export-ps=FILENAME]
            [-E|--export-eps=FILENAME]  [-A|--export-pdf=FILENAME]
            [--export-latex]  [-T|--export-text-to-path]  [--export-
ignore-filters]
            [-X|--query-x]  [-Y|--query-y]  [-W|--query-width]  [-H|--
query-height]
            [-S|--query-all]  [-I|--query-id=ID]  [-x|--extension-
directory]
            [--vacuum-defs]  [--verb-list]  [--verb=VERB-ID]
[--select=OBJECT-ID]
            [--shell]  [-?|--help]  [--usage]
            [OPTIONS...]  [FILE...]

Available options:
```

5. Change the directory to the location where the *Chapter 12* files of this book are located by typing cd [path to the chapter 12 folder] and pressing *Enter*. Check that the InteractiveMapGame.svg is there by typing ls and pressing *Enter*.

6. Export only the eastern kingdom without displaying any other objects with the background set to black by using the following command and pressing *Enter*:

    ```
    $ inkscape --file=InteractiveMapGame.svg --export-id=eastGroup
    --export-id-only --export-background=#000000 --export-png=east.png
    ```

7. Open the east.png in your favorite image viewer to check that the export went fine. Notice the background around the kingdom is black:

8. Sometimes (when scripting) it is useful to get a list of all objects inside a file along with their position and dimension information. This can be done using query options; try one using the following code:

```
$ inkscape --file InteractiveMapGame.svg --query-all | more
```

9. A lot of the commands we are used to executing through GUI are also available for CLI use through verbs. To get the list of all verbs available use the following command:

```
$ inkscape --verb-list | more
```

10. We'll use the `InteractiveMapGameVerbs.svg` file to demonstrate how verbs are used through CLI. Use the following code to delete the coat of arms and text on the right side of the drawing and redefine the Page size to the new drawing size—notice how the Inkscape window shows up for a second and then closes:

```
$ inkscape --file=InteractiveMapGameVerbs.svg --select=northCoat
--verb=EditDelete --select=eastCoat --verb=EditDelete
--select=westCoat --verb=EditDelete --select=text3346
--verb=EditDelete --verb=FitCanvasToDrawing --verb=FileSave
--verb=FileClose
```

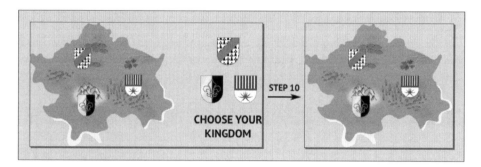

How it works...

Almost all of the commands have both the short one-letter and the longer more descriptive version. We used the longer versions in this recipe for clarity but you'll probably use the short ones for the tasks you do often once you memorize them. This is what the Step 6 command would look like with shorter option versions:

```
$ inkscape -f InteractiveMapGame.svg -i eastGroup -j -b #000000 -e east.
png
```

To start a command that would call Inkscape we first type `inkscape`, then add all the options separated by spaces and press *Enter* to execute the command.

The first option in Step 6 `--file` indicated which file we want to operate on; Inkscape opens this file by loading it into memory. The `--export-id` selects which object to export (we can only export one object with this option at a time). The `--export-id-only` option makes sure no other objects or their parts make it into the export if they are visually inside the bounding box of the object we selected with the `--export-id` option. It is also clear that the `--export-id-only` only works with the `--export-id` defined. The `--export-background` option changes the background color of the area surrounding the exported object if there is any.

If we hadn't specified a background color for our PNG export the default one would have been used. We didn't want the default light blue color to be exported because it would indicate that the kingdom is an island surrounded by water. Using the neutral black took care of this and also made the colors stand out more.

With the `--export-png` option we give the name to the file we want to create. When using this option the command is executed without starting Inkscape GUI, as is also the case with printing, exporting to plain SVG and vacuuming default options.

The query options pull out object information and list them in output. In Step 8 we used one of those options `--query-all` to get the information about all of the objects inside `InteractiveMapGame.svg`. Since we expected a long list we used piping to direct the output from the first command to the command `more` that lets us inspect the list one screen at a time.

When using verbs to edit objects inside files we have to use the `--select` option to select the objects to change; each object must be selected separately and followed by the verb option that makes changes to it.

Verbs can't be used without GUI successfully; that is why we see the Inkscape window for a second while the CLI command is executed. If we didn't use the `--verb=FileClose` option the window would remain open.

There's more...

To expand the capabilities of Inkscape CLI commands we can use shell scripts to edit the files in batches.

Shell mode

Each command from this recipe was started with `inkscape`, which means that we started a new Inkscape instance each time. Inkscape CLI comes with the option `--shell` which enables us to start Inkscape once, execute the commands we want, and then `quit`. This way Inkscape is only loaded once for many commands. The downside is you can't use the *Up Arrow* to get the last commands, you have to type them in full.

See also

For more information refer to the *Creating an extension – Object Guides* recipe later in this chapter.

Compiling development builds on Linux

Testing development builds and reporting bugs before a major version is released is a huge help in the development process. It allows for more bugs to be found because each person uses Inkscape differently so the more testers there are the more bugs are found. It also alleviates testing for programmers so they can spend more time fixing the bugs and implementing new features.

This recipe will show us how to build a development version of Inkscape on Linux.

Getting ready

Inkscape development is done through the **launchpad.net** service which uses the Bazaar distributed version control system. To be able to pull the development source check that you have Bazaar packages installed on your system.

To be able to run Inkscape with all of its features it's necessary to have all the dependencies installed too. Find the list on the Inkscape website and use your favorite package installer to install them.

If you're on Ubuntu you can use this command:

```
$ sudo apt-get install build-essential autoconf automake intltool
libglib2.0-dev libpng12-dev libgc-dev libfreetype6-dev liblcms1-dev
libgtkmm-2.4-dev libxslt1-dev libboost-dev libpopt-dev libgsl0-dev
libpoppler-dev libpoppler-glib-dev poppler-data libpoppler-dev libgnome-
vfsmm-2.6-dev libssl-dev libmagick++9-dev libwpg-dev
```

We also need to find out which revision is the latest so we can download its source. Go to `https://code.launchpad.net/inkscape` and note the number under the first row in the **Last Commit** column.

How to do it...

The following steps will demonstrate how to compile development builds:

1. Open your favorite terminal and create a new directory inside your home directory:

   ```
   $ mkdir inkscapeDev
   ```

2. Change to the newly created directory:

```
$ cd inkscapeDev/
```

3. Checkout the source of the latest revision, replace the [revision number] text in the command with the actual number, and wait for the download to finish; you will see a new folder created inside inkscapeDev named inkscape-[revision number]:

```
$ bzr checkout lp:inkscape inkscape-[revision number]
```

4. Move everything from the inkscape-[revision number] into the inkscapeDev folder because that is where we want to keep the source code:

```
$ mv inkscape-[revision number]/* .
```

5. Run the autogen.sh script, it should be done within seconds:

```
$ ./autogen.sh
```

6. Run the configure script but with the option to install into the directory named after the revision number. It usually takes a bit longer than autogen.sh:

```
$ ./configure --prefix=`pwd`/inkscape-[revision number]/install
```

7. Run the make command with the install option. This one can take a long time to execute and it can consume 100% of your CPU:

```
$ make install
```

 If you have a multicore CPU or multiple CPUs you can use the -j option to select how many cores to use when compiling to shorten the time it takes to execute. For example if you have two cores you can use $ make -j2 install.

8. After the compiling is complete you can start your development Inkscape version by calling /home/[username]/inkscapeDev/inkscape-[revision-number]/install/bin/inkscape. It is useful to create a custom launcher for it's easier to start without the need to remember the revision numbers; just enter the path into the **Command** field.

9. If at a later time you want to compile a newer build and keep the old one intact so you can test the differences you can execute the `bzr update` command from the `InkscapeDev` folder to update the source. Create a new folder for the new revision and configure the make script with a different option for the `install` folder. Here is the example code:

```
$ cd inkscapeDev
$ bzr update
$ mkdir inkscape-[new revision-number]
$ ./autogen.sh
$ ./configure --prefix=`pwd`/inkscape-[new revision-number]/
install
$ make install
```

10. Create a new custom launcher for the updated development build using the path `/home/[username]/inkscapeDev/inkscape-[new revision-number]/install/bin/inkscape`.

How it works...

We moved the source from the `revision-numbered` folder into the neutral `inkscapeDev` so we can later update the source with recent changes without having to download the whole source again. We used the `revision-numbered` folder to store our installation, so we can have many at the same time and test the different development builds at the same time on a single machine.

There's more...

Development builds can also be tested on Windows and Mac OS by using precompiled nightly builds, although those aren't refreshed as often as the source is updated. The information about those builds can be found at `http://inkscape.org/download/`.

Windows precompiled snapshots

Download the nightly builds for Windows from this page: `http://inkscape.modevia.com/win32/?M=D`. Simply unpack the file onto your machine and run `inkscape.exe`. To make choosing the correct file easier sort the **Last Modified** column.

Mac OS X Snapshots

Download the nightly builds for Mac OS from this page: `http://inkscape.modevia.com/macosx-snap/?C=M;O=D`. Read the instructions on how to choose the correct version for your system.

Modifying an existing extension – Darker extended

This recipe will use an existing extension to introduce us into the field of expanding Inkscape functionality with your own code. The extension we will modify is **Darker** found under **Extensions | Color** by adding the interface to input the percentage of darkening we want to apply to selected object colors.

Inkscape extensions are generally written in **Python**, a free and open source scripting language which is flexible, elegant, and powerful.

Getting ready

Since the logic of the extension is written in Python, we need to have it installed on our machine. Mac OS X and Linux distributions generally include it in the base installation of the operating system. Windows users can download and install it from the official website: `http://www.python.org`.

To test it, open your favourite terminal application and write the following:

```
$ python -V
Python 2.6.6
```

This means that the 2.6.6 version of the language is installed.

We also need the `lxml` module for our installed Python version. Linux package managers such as RPM or APT should have it available under the package name `python-lxml`. It is also possible to install it using the *setuptools* "easyinstall", *pip*, or *distribute* module managers. Windows users can benefit from an install wizard available from the Cheese Shop: `http://pypi.python.org/pypi/lxml/`.

Be sure to download a version of the module that is compatible with your installed Python version.

How to do it...

The following steps will demonstrate how to modify the Darker extension:

1. Open your favorite file browser and navigate to the `extensions` folder inside your Inkscape installation.

2. Copy the files `color_darker.inx` and `color_darker.py`.

3. Navigate to the `extensions` folder inside your personal configuration folder and paste the copied files there. In Linux you could use the following command:

```
cp /usr/share/inkscape/extensions/color_darker.* ~/.config/
inkscape/extensions/
```

> On Linux and Mac OS X the folder is located at `~/.config/inkscape/extensions`. Folders and files that start with a "." (dot) are hidden, you may have to reveal them first (*Ctrl + H*). On Windows the folder is under `%APPDATA%\inkscape\extensions`.

4. Rename the files to `color_darker_extend.inx` and `color_darker_extend.py`.

5. Open the `color_darker_extend.inx` in your favorite text editor. You will notice that it is an XML file.

6. Inside the `<_name>` tag change the text from `Darker` to "Darker Extended".

7. Inside the `<id>` tag change the text from `org.inkscape.color.darker` to "org.inkscape.color.darker_extend".

8. Under the `<dependency>` tag that contains `color_darker.py` change the text to "color_darker_extend.py".

9. After the last `<dependency>` tag add the following code:

```
<param name="percentage" type="int" min="0" max="100" _gui-
text="Percentage of darkening">90</param>
```

10. Near the bottom of the file change the text inside the `<command>` tag from `color_darker.py` to "color_darker_extend.py".

11. Save the file.

12. Open the `color_darker_extend.py` file in your favorite text editor. This is a Python script.

13. Type in the code marked in bold , taking care in applying the exact amount of indentation before each line as shown, so the file now reads as follows:

```
import coloreffect

class C(coloreffect.ColorEffect):

    def __init__(self):
        coloreffect.ColorEffect.__init__(self)
        # Add the user defined 'percentage parameter
        # to the list of options
        self.OptionParser.add_option(
            "-p",
            "--percentage",
            action="store",
            type="int",
```

```
            dest="percen",
            default=90,
            help="Percentage of Darkening",
        )
    def colmod(self,r,g,b):
        # Retrieve the Percentage (percen) value from the options
        percen = self.options.percen
        # Modify the FACTOR formula
        FACTOR=(100-float(percen))/100
        r=int(round(max(r*FACTOR,0)))
        g=int(round(max(g*FACTOR,0)))
        b=int(round(max(b*FACTOR,0)))
        return '%02x%02x%02x' % (r,g,b)
c = C()
c.affect()
```

14. Save the file and close it.

15. Open Inkscape, create a rectangle with **Red (#FF0000)** fill, **Lime (#00FF00)** stroke, and stroke width of 32.

16. Stamp the rectangle (*Space*) five times so you get six in total.

17. Select the second rectangle and darken it by 20 percent by going to **Extensions | Color | Darker Extended...**. Enter 20 into the **Percentage of darkening** field and press **Apply**.

18. Select the third rectangle, change the **Percentage of darkening** field value to 40, and press **Apply**.

19. Repeat Step 19 for the rest of the rectangles always increasing the field value by 20 and close the **Darker Extended** dialog. Notice how the 100% case is completely black.

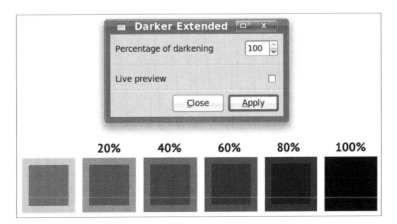

How it works...

Inkscape extensions usually come in two files: an XML (.inx) file that defines the extension interface and its location on the menus, and a Python script (.py) that contains the operational code of our extension. In this recipe we forked the original **Darken** extension by copying and modifying the two relative files in the extensions folder.

The `<param>` tag is where parameters that the users will insert the values of, is defined. Various types can be used (enum, text, float, options), you can find the full list on the Inkscape website. The `<param>` tag we added to the `color_darker_extend.inx` is the input field where the percentage of darkening is entered.

The `color_darker_extend.py` script is invoked when we click on the **Apply** button in the **Darken** pop up panel in the Inkscape interface. It works by *subclassing* the Inkscape `coloreffect.ColorEffect` class and overriding its `__init__()` method to declare the additional option `"-percentage"`; this will define a variable that will store the value input by the user in the GUI. Then, the `colmod` method is a special hook we can tap into to provide the logic of our extension; in this case we process the RGB values of the object according the series of formulas defined in the method. Finally, the method returns the new RGB value to Inkscape, which updates the object color attributes accordingly and renders the result on the Canvas: a "darkened" version of the same object.

See also

For more information, refer to the *Creating an extension – object guides* recipe in this chapter.

Creating an extension – object guides

In this recipe we will go through the creation of a new extension that split an object into sections of equal width using guides. The number of sections will be chosen by the user in a pop up panel.

How to do it...

The following steps will demonstrate how to create a new extension:

1. Open your favorite file browser and navigate to the `inkscape/extensions` folder inside your personal configuration folder.

2. Create two new text files named `object_guides.inx` and `object_guides.py`.

3. Open the `object_guides.inx` file. Add the usual XML header, the `<_name>` tag with the title of the extension, and the `<id>` tag with the definition `org.ekips.filter.object_guides`:

```
<?xml version="1.0" encoding="UTF-8"?>
```

```
<inkscape-extension
xmlns="http://www.inkscape.org/namespace/inkscape/extension">
  <_name>Object Guides</_name>
  <id>org.ekips.filter.object_guides</id>
```

4. Add two dependencies: `object_guides.py` and `inkex.py`:

```
<dependency type="executable" location="extensions">object_guides.
py</dependency>
<dependency type="executable" location="extensions">inkex.py</
dependency>
```

5. The extension will take one parameter, so we need to add a `<param>` tag: an Integer type that controls how many guides should be created. We should also set some sensible defaults, such as the minimum and maximum number of guides:

```
<param name="guides" type="int" min="2" max="100"
_gui-text="Number of guides">2</param>
```

6. The extension should appear under **Render** sub-menu so mark it up with the `<submenu _name="Render"/>` under the `<effects-menu>` tag:

```
<effect>
    <object-type>all</object-type>
      <effects-menu>
      <submenu _name="Render"/>
    </effects-menu>
  </effect>
```

7. The `<command>` tag determines which function should be called when the extension is executed; it should be included inside the `<script>` tag:

```
<script>
  <command reldir="extensions"
interpreter="python">object_guides.py</command>
</script>
```

8. Open the `object_guides.py` file in your favorite text editor.

9. We need to import a few Python modules and classes first: `sys`, `gettext` (the translation machinery), and `subprocess` (for launching external programs), in this way:

```
import sys
import inkex
from gettext import gettext as _
from subprocess import Popen, PIPE
```

10. The next step is to create a function that will be responsible for creating the guides, namely, `create_guide` function that uses the sodipodi document type definition:

```python
def create_guide(position, orientation, parent):
    """ Creates a Guide with a defined position, orientation
    and parent in the DOM.
    """
    inkex.etree.SubElement(
        parent,
        '{http://sodipodi.sourceforge.net/DTD/sodipodi-0.dtd}guide',
        {
            'position': position,
            'orientation': orientation,
        }
    )
```

11. Next we create a class `GuideLineEffect` that inherits the `inkex.Effect` object with its functions and properties:

```python
class GuideLineEffect(inkex.Effect):
```

12. Inside the class we define the `__init__` function where we define the input options of the extension and the way the `GuideLineEffect` object is created:

```python
def __init__(self):
    inkex.Effect.__init__(self)
    # Add the 'sections' option.
    self.OptionParser.add_option(
        "-s",
        "--sections",
        action="store",
        type="int",
        dest="sections",
        default=2,
        help="Number of sections",
    )
```

 Remember that indentation in Python is extremely important, as it defines the block structures of the program.

13. Next we override the `effect` method in the `inkex.Effect` class. This method will be called when executing the extension:

```python
def effect(self):
```

14. Now we need to get the input parameter that tells the script how many guides are to be created:

```
guides = self.options.guides
```

15. We need Inkscape to tell us the position and the dimension of the object (X coordinate and the width), so we will use the function `Popen` of the `subprocess` module, and the Inkscape CLI query functionality, in order to feed this data into our script:

```
q = {'x':0, 'width':0}
# We will now query Inkscape for this information
for query in q.keys():
    p = Popen(
        'inkscape --query-%s --query-id=%s "%s"' % (
            query,
            self.options.ids[0],
            self.args[-1],
        ),
        shell=True,
        stdout=PIPE,
        stderr=PIPE,
    )
    # Wait for the child process to finish
    p.wait()
    q[query] = p.stdout.read()
```

16. With the dimension and position data saved in our dictionary, we can now start to calculate where the guides will need to be positioned:

```
width = float(q['width'])
x = float(q['x'])
if guides > 1
    step = float(width / (guides-1))
else:
    step = 1
```

17. Now it's time to create the guides by calling our `create_guide()` function:

```
while (guides > 0):
    create_guide(str(x), '0', nv)
    x += step
    guides -= 1
```

18. Finally, we need to actually execute our code. We do that by creating an instance of our `GuideLineEffect` class and calling the `affect()` method of its superclass (`inkex.Effect`). Add these final lines:

```
c = GuideLineEffect()
c.affect()
```

19. Open Inkscape and create an object, one star object with nine corners and one free-form **Pencil** path.

20. Select one object and go to **Extensions | Render | Object Guides....** Divide the object into five sections by selecting six guides and clicking on the **Apply** button.

21. Repeat Step 19 for the object object.

How it works...

In most extensions it is important to create a class that inherits from the `inkex.Effect`. Through it we access both the SVG document using the keyword `self` and function `document.getroot()` and methods that create SVG and non-SVG objects inside the document. We also get access to the GUI selection through that class. These are the basic data we need to create various extensions and effects.

This is the final code, complete with some additional checks and safeguards:

```
import sys
import inkex
from gettext import gettext as _

try:
    from subprocess import Popen, PIPE
except ImportError:
    inkex.errormsg(_(
        "Failed to import the subprocess module."
```

```python
    ))
    inkex.errormsg(
        "Python version is : " + str(inkex.sys.version_info)
    )
    exit(1)
def create_guide(position, orientation, parent):
    """ Creates a Guide with a defined position, orientation
    and parent in the DOM.
    """
    inkex.etree.SubElement(
        parent,
        '{http://sodipodi.sourceforge.net/DTD/sodipodi-0.dtd}guide',
        {
            'position': position,
            'orientation': orientation,
        }
    )
class GuideLineEffect(inkex.Effect):

    def __init__(self):
        inkex.Effect.__init__(self)
        # Add the 'guides' option.
        self.OptionParser.add_option(
            "-s",
            "--guides",
            action="store",
            type="int",
            dest="guides",
            default=2,
            help="Number of guides",
        )

    def effect(self):
        """ Create the Guides.
        """
        # Check that the user has selected an object.
        if not self.options.ids:
            inkex.errormsg(_("Please select an object first"))
            exit()
        # Check the parent namespace.
        nv = self.document.xpath(
            '/svg:svg/sodipodi:namedview',
            namespaces=inkex.NSS
        )[0]
        # Store the user defined no. of 'guides' in 'guides'
        guides = self.options.guides
        # Now we will construct a query.
```

```
            # We want to know:
            #   'x': the position of the left uppermost corner;
            #   'width': the width of the object.
            # If these are unknown, their default value will be 0.
            q = {'x':0, 'width':0}
            # Query Inkscape for this information
            for query in q.keys():
                p = Popen(
                    'inkscape --query-%s --query-id=%s "%s"' % (
                        query,
                        self.options.ids[0],
                        self.args[-1],
                    ),
                    shell=True,
                    stdout=PIPE,
                    stderr=PIPE,
                )
                # Wait for the child process to finish
                p.wait()
                q[query] = p.stdout.read()
            # Get all the parameters we need to place the guides
            width = float(q['width'])
            x = float(q['x'])
            if guides > 1:
                step = float(width / (guides-1))
            else:
                step = 1
            # Create a guide for each step
            while (guides > 0):
                create_guide(str(x), '0', nv)
                x += step
                guides -= 1
c = GuideLineEffect()
c.affect()
```

See also

For more information, refer to the *Modifying an existing extension – Darker extended* recipe in this chapter.

Index

creating, from objects 85

H

I

Thank you for buying
Inkscape 0.48 Illustrator's Cookbook

About Packt Publishing

Packt, pronounced 'packed', published its first book "*Mastering phpMyAdmin for Effective MySQL Management*" in April 2004 and subsequently continued to specialize in publishing highly focused books on specific technologies and solutions.

Our books and publications share the experiences of your fellow IT professionals in adapting and customizing today's systems, applications, and frameworks. Our solution based books give you the knowledge and power to customize the software and technologies you're using to get the job done. Packt books are more specific and less general than the IT books you have seen in the past. Our unique business model allows us to bring you more focused information, giving you more of what you need to know, and less of what you don't.

Packt is a modern, yet unique publishing company, which focuses on producing quality, cutting-edge books for communities of developers, administrators, and newbies alike. For more information, please visit our website: www.packtpub.com.

About Packt Open Source

In 2010, Packt launched two new brands, Packt Open Source and Packt Enterprise, in order to continue its focus on specialization. This book is part of the Packt Open Source brand, home to books published on software built around Open Source licences, and offering information to anybody from advanced developers to budding web designers. The Open Source brand also runs Packt's Open Source Royalty Scheme, by which Packt gives a royalty to each Open Source project about whose software a book is sold.

Writing for Packt

We welcome all inquiries from people who are interested in authoring. Book proposals should be sent to author@packtpub.com. If your book idea is still at an early stage and you would like to discuss it first before writing a formal book proposal, contact us; one of our commissioning editors will get in touch with you.

We're not just looking for published authors; if you have strong technical skills but no writing experience, our experienced editors can help you develop a writing career, or simply get some additional reward for your expertise.

Inkscape 0.48 Essentials for Web Designers

ISBN: 978-1-849512-68-8   Paperback: 316 pages

Use the fascinating Inkscape graphics editor to create attractive layout designs, images, and icons for your website

1. The first book on the newly released Inkscape version 0.48, with an exclusive focus on web design

2. Comprehensive coverage of all aspects of Inkscape required for web design

3. Incorporate eye-catching designs, patterns, and other visual elements to spice up your web pages

Python 2.6 Graphics Cookbook

ISBN: 978-1-849513-84-5   Paperback: 260 pages

Over 100 great recipes for creating and animating graphics using Python

1. Create captivating graphics with ease and bring them to life using Python

2. Apply effects to your graphics using powerful Python methods

3. Develop vector as well as raster graphics and combine them to create wonders in the animation world

Please check **www.PacktPub.com** for information on our titles

Made in the USA
San Bernardino, CA
19 February 2013